the hip pocket guide to

NEW YORK CITY

TIM PAGE, editor

ASSOCIATE EDITOR
Vanessa Weeks

CONTRIBUTING EDITORS
M. George Stevenson
Josh Martin
Michael Fraser

ILLUSTRATIONS BY LEE BUCKLEY

HARPER COLOPHON BOOKS

Harper & Row, Publishers
New York, Cambridge, Philadelphia, San Francisco
London, Mexico City, São Paulo, Sydney

For my parents, Elizabeth Thaxton and Ellis Batten Page, and for Leonard Altman—three who never lost faith.

And for the memory of Dean Henry Cook, the gentle Reverend.

THE HIP POCKET GUIDE TO NEW YORK CITY. Copyright © 1982 by Tim Page. All rights reserved. Printed in the United States of America. No part of this book may be used or reproduced in any manner whatsoever without written permission except in the case of brief quotations embodied in critical articles and reviews. For information address Harper & Row, Publishers, Inc., 10 East 53rd Street, New York, N.Y. 10022. Published simultaneously in Canada by Fitzhenry & Whiteside Limited, Toronto.

FIRST EDITION

Designed by Ruth Bornschlegel

Library of Congress Cataloging in Publication Data
Main entry under title:
The Hip pocket guide to New York City.

  Includes index.
  (Harper colophon books)
  1. New York (N.Y.)—Description—1982—Guidebooks. I. Page, Tim.
F128.18.H56 1982   917.47'10443   81–48167
ISBN 0–06–090945–5 (pbk.)   AACR2

82 83 84 85 86 10 9 8 7 6 5 4 3 2 1

the hip pocket guide to

NEW
YORK
CITY

ABOUT THE EDITOR

Tim Page was born in 1954 and grew up in Storrs, Connecticut. He was a filmmaker in his youth, and is the subject of the documentary film *A Day with Timmy Page.* He moved to New York in 1975, at the height of the famous fiscal crisis, when ramparts of uncollected garbage lined all the Manhattan streets. He fell in love with the city anyway. Page originally intended to be a composer but ended up a writer, specializing in arts criticism, and has contributed to the *New York Times, Saturday Review, High Fidelity,* and the *Wall Street Journal,* among other publications. From 1980 until 1982, he was the classical music editor of the *Soho News.* Currently, Page hosts an afternoon show on WNYC-FM. He acknowledges a passion for poodles, a strong admiration for the works of Evelyn Waugh, a liking for bottled beer, a general sense of premonition about the state of the world, and an occasional urge to give the whole thing up and move to Newfoundland.

CONTRIBUTORS

CANDY AGREE is pursuing graduate studies at Columbia University.

CLAUDIA BLAINE watches a lot of television.

STEVE BLOOM was born in the Bronx and now lives in Brooklyn, where he worked on his first book, *Video Invaders.*

WILLIAM MICHAEL BROWN is a free-lance writer who came to Manhattan in the winter of 1979 with $30 in his pocket and lived to tell the tale.

JOHN BUCKLEY is a fiction writer and free-lance journalist primarily on the subject of music.

LAURA COTTINGHAM is a writer living in New York.

STANLEY CROUCH was born on December 14, 1945, and is expected to die sometime later.

LOIS DRAEGIN is not a dancer.

ENRIQUE FERNANDEZ writes, looks for an apartment, and always chooses from the Latin side of a "chinas y criollas" menu.

G. CHRISTOPHER FISH is an Upper West Side resident interested in motorcycles and movies, in that order.

DAVID FRASER, a prize-winning reporter and former magazine editor, loves to explore New York, despite having been mugged at the age of 12. He is the brother of Michael Fraser.

MICHAEL FRASER, who once turned the tables on a mugger, is the editor of the *Columbia Guide to New York,* published in 1981. He is the brother of David Fraser.

ELLEN FREILICH is a free-lance writer with a special interest in music and urban affairs.

MERLE GINSBERG writes about video, the downtown art scene, fashion, and where to go.

ERIC MARCUS, a native of Queens, divides his time between The Apple's Core (a midtown Manhattan architectural walking-tour service) and a developing career in architecture and urban design.

JOSH MARTIN lives in New York and he writes. You should be so lucky.

GERALD MARZORATI was the art editor of the *Soho News* and various arts publications.

MICHAEL MUSTO writes about music, film, and night life for the *Soho News, Us,* and the New York *Post,* and does a great Diana Ross impersonation as the lead singer of *The Must.*

PETER ORTNER, author of such minor classics as "A Zombie from Planet X" and "The Old Testament," lives in Australia where he is known as "Bruce Bereford."

ROCHELLE RATNER is a poet, critic, and editor of the *American Book Review.*

VITO RUSSO was born in East Harlem, where there are no gay bars, and is the author of *The Celluloid Closet: Homosexuality in the Movies.*

DIANE SALVATORE is a bereaved ex–*Soho News*er and a writer who aspires to fame and fortune, not necessarily in that order.

EDWARD SCHNEIDER is an editor, translator, and writer who was born in Manhattan and continues to live there.

ANDY SCHWARTZ was born in New York City in 1951 and grew up to be publisher and editor-in-chief of one of America's most adventurous rock 'n' roll magazines, *New York Rocker*.

DON SHEWEY has written regularly about theater and music for the *Soho News*, the *Village Voice*, *Rolling Stone*, and other publications.

GARY STERN was born in Manhattan, nurtured in the Bronx, raised in Queens, and is currently living in Brooklyn. He has been published in the *Daily News*, *Newsday*, and other periodicals.

M. GEORGE STEVENSON has "done a damned good job of wasting his life, even without the benefit of graduate school."

DOUG SUISMAN recently graduated from the Columbia Graduate School of Architecture.

AMY TAUBIN makes films and performances and was a film critic for the *Soho News*.

VANESSA WEEKS fancies herself a writer, used to be a musician, and never admits she moved to hip New York from L.A.

SANDY WELLS is an announcer on WFAS-AM in Westchester.

CONTENTS

INTRODUCTION

O.K. you're in New York. The Statue of Liberty, the Staten Island Ferry, and Times Square, right?

Wrong. The Statue of Liberty is a wonderful symbol, but rusting badly, and always attracting political activists from offbeat countries who chain themselves to Miss Liberty's coattails; the Staten Island Ferry is fun for half the trip out, but then you've got to wait for the long return to Manhattan, and Times Square is full of pimps, pushers, and other lowlife, and is currently a good place to be mugged, and an excellent argument for the neutron bomb.

We want to show you another New York—one that we think is much more interesting than the standard sights. And so we have put together the first *Hip Pocket Guide*.

What is the *Hip Pocket Guide?* We are exactly what we say we are. First and foremost, we are a guidebook, aimed at both the New Yorker and the tourist. Our book is for the person who has ridden the subway since he could crawl, as well as for the new arrival at Port Authority, who is carrying a suitcase in his hand and some dreams in his heart.

We are a guide to inexpensive living in Manhattan: cheap restaurants, hotels that don't cost an arm and a leg, and a lot of free places to visit around New York.

We are a guide to the New York underground. We know where the really interesting bars are, where the gay scene hangs out, and places to go where *nobody* will ever find you.

We are a survival manual; New York is hardly the most dangerous city in America, but common sense never hurt anyone. So we tell you what neighborhoods to stay out of, what times are best to use the subway, and the best attitude to affect on the street.

We are a sourcebook, too. We have lists of women's services, of emergency numbers, and of New York's alternative museums. We want our readers to know everything about this city, inside and out.

Some might say that we are a combination of *New York Unexpurgated, New York on $10 a Day, The Book of Lists,* and The Yellow Pages. That suits us fine.

Welcome to New York. It's the greatest city in the world, and this is one of the most interesting times ever to be here. You hold the key to the city in your hands.

TIM PAGE
New York City
1982

ACKNOWLEDGMENTS

The Hip Pocket Guide to New York is the result of many people's efforts, and I apologize in advance to those who are inadvertently left out of this general expression of gratitude.

Special thanks must go to the following: Peter Bejger, my editor at Harper & Row, who shared my vision of what the Guide could be and fought hard for it; Raymond Bongiovanni, my agent, who supported the project from the beginning and was invaluable in providing the moral support I needed to see it through; Josh Martin, M. George Stevenson, and Michael Fraser for their time and many good ideas; John Buckley and Lois Draegin for their immediate, speculative contributions; and Lee Buckley for her continuing input of gentle, thoughtful encouragement.

In addition, I must thank Josh Friedman, Carol Ash, Rob Manoff, and John Leese, former editors and publishers of the late, great *Soho News,* for their early and infectious enthusiasm.

Without the assistance of Vanessa Weeks, my associate editor, there would have been no *Hip Pocket Guide.* I will always be grateful for her kindness, patience, and unwavering devotion during a difficult time.

Finally, I am grateful to my writers, for contributing such fine work and for being so damned goodhearted.

TIM PAGE

> *For subway and bus information, call*
> **330-1234**

CONFRONTING PHYSICAL NEW YORK

I first came to New York, Manhattan specifically, in the mid-1970s in order to attend college. The plan was to go to school here and then return to Salt Lake City—the city of my birth and first eighteen years—and become a big success.

I stayed in New York.

I am not a big success; I live in what is considered a marginal neighborhood and make what is considered a very marginal salary. It's not a problem: I like it this way, and if occasionally I get caught up with nostalgia for my beloved hometown, it is simply because the beauties of the two cities are almost mutually exclusive and their manners of success have no relation. But I can get around New York without falling all over myself, and for the time being this is success enough. It's a *very* big town.

Getting to know the geography, the practical geography, of the Big Town is like a first-year anatomy class for a medical student; there is the entire human body to be mastered over a short period of time. For it to be done properly, it must be learned one artery, one portion at a time beginning with the exterior and gradually plumbing the system within, going into greater and greater detail until finally, the thing is familiar and the minor as well as the major aspects are so well known it is hard to remember not knowing them. From that point one can count on the snowball effect: One knows not only the physical existence of the workings but also how to function when certain of the workings fail or how to provide the best remedy for a queasy tourist. An R.D. (Resident Doctorate) and the calm that goes with it are a part of one's portfolio; without consultation, "Take the IRT Number One to Franklin Street, walk a block north and west to just past Hudson," issues forth in answer to, "Hey, pal, how do I get to the Cavern Club?"

New York's only a big town now.

It's also a very small town, from both a geographical standpoint and a social one, being one of the few parts of America with a well-developed European-style class system. But geography is my concern at the moment. Manhattan is small, about twelve miles long and two-and-a-half miles wide at its widest point. Those familiar with Norman Mailer's mayoral campaign of 1968 will remember his plan to make the city the 51st state and to make each neighborhood an incorporated town within the city-state. The argument is an excellent one—for example, I live in the Bloomingdale section of Morningside Heights, just east of the Manhattan Valley on a corner known locally as Little Cuba. If you live in the neighborhood, you know from the description which corner it is. Neighborhoods are like that, they can be very chummy, particularly the "bad" neighborhoods that are fairly well integrated. I would assert, from my own experiences and others, that if you are known on the block and are not real flashy, that the crime rate would be about the same as in a homogeneous small town. "Never live in a neighborhood that's too clean or too white," said a disgruntled former Eastsider after her second break-in in eight months. I concur with that verdict.

However, neighborhoods not meeting such criteria have their merits—as vacation spots, round trip $1.50. Really, Greenwich Village is a nice place to visit, but I wouldn't want to live there—and I feel the same way about most other neighborhoods I visit. But intrepid explorer that I am, I have made the rounds, from south to north. **Battery Park,** at the southern tip of the Island, is the large and pleasant gateway to the **Statue of Liberty** and the Staten Island Ferry (a must-ride at 5 A.M. or so) and deserted, except for commuters, after dark. To the east is **South St.,** home of the **Fulton Street Fish Market,** the New York *Post,* and the

South Street Seaport Museum. Just north, and also
deserted at night except for the rats and an occasional
late-working financier, is the **Wall St.** area, home of
both ancient and modern high-rises, the **Stock
Exchange,** and totally confusing streets and alleys. On
the west side of this maze is the **World Trade Center,**
where on a clear day, what you see from the top is
worth the cost of going up 107 flights to see it.

The north end of the World Trade Center also
delineates **Financial Downtown** from **Governmental
Downtown,** which is pretty much in the center of
things, midway between Independence Plaza on the
west and the **Brooklyn Bridge** on the east. **City Hall,**
the federal courts, and the departmental offices are all
located in one convenient lump. Serious housing begins
here, mainly on the east side of the island. At the north
end of the government buildings on the east side is the
southernmost neighborhood with any kind of
nonbusiness flavor—**Chinatown,** around Mott, Pell,
and Mulberry Sts. Restaurants, little shops, lots of
bustle and business conducted in Mandarin or
Cantonese, and a united but separate feel to the entire
area make it the first neighborhood on the itinerary
worthy of the name.

The north border of Chinatown is **Canal St.,** also the
north border of **Tribeca,** short for Triangle Below
Canal St., an area now being colonized as a residential
refuge from the burgeoning rents of the traditional
residential areas. It is also the home, on the west side,
of the best of the newer punk (or new wave, or
whatever; they were *punk* first) clubs in the warehouse
district north of Chambers Street. Above Canal St. on
the west side is **Soho** (South of Houston St., that's
House-ton St.), where most of the more progressive
galleries and boutiques are, and until about 1975–77,
when its trendiness caught up with it, an earlier rent
refuge. Soho is also known for its commercial buildings
with cast-iron façades, many of them landmarks of their
own genre. Despite a creeping respectability, it's still a
lovely place for a Sunday afternoon stroll.

Above Canal on the east side of the island is **Little
Italy.** Directly above Chinatown, it centers on Mulberry
St. and harbors Scorsese's *Mean Streets* as well as the
Festival of San Gennaro, an autumn event. East and
north of that is the **Lower East Side,** the "up from the

Jewish ghettos of the" Lower East Side, with the bargains on Orchard St., Ratner's restaurant, and a profusion of Central European dialects bumping up against the Italian- and Chinese-speaking areas. These parts of town tend to house older people who have been there all their lives, and the chance conversation struck up here will likely yield a sense of the New York of an earlier epoch, of Damon Runyon or Bernard Malamud.

Now, the Village—**Greenwich Village,** the first suburb, the most famous bohemia, and home of many subcultures. The West Village with its boutiques, piano bars, and leatherized waterfront, the more traditional "boho" area around New York University and Washington Square Park, and the **Bowery** and East Village, warehouse-and-loft-laden, home of the first punk clubs and little enclaves of ethnic variety all the way over to the East River. While the Village proper ends at 14 St. on the north, on the east side, around near Union Square, it retains a little of the character of the area, albeit with more large businesses thrown in, up to about 19 St. There it becomes terribly tony and, in the case of **Gramercy Park,** almost entirely residential and rich. Its west side counterpart, **Chelsea,** is now a very ethnic rent harbor slowly giving up its mercantile nature for a more residential one, but hit it at four in the morning and dodge the sides of beef with the other pedestrians as Sunday's roast is delivered on Wednesday morning.

At 23 St., the more thoroughly business part of the island begins to show itself more overtly. On the west side, the **Flower Market,** the **Fur District,** warehouses, and small factories are relieved by the various hotels, fancy-Dan restaurants, and other accouterments of midtown brazenly asserting themselves in upper Chelsea. More centrally located are the large insurance companies and certain publishing houses around Madison Sq. and the beginnings of Madison Ave. To the far east is the Bellevue Hospital Center, known for its Mental Health facility. But at 34 St., **Midtown** truly becomes a stereotypical reality. **Penn Station,** where commuters from New Jersey and Long Island unleash themselves upon the city, is located at 33 St. and Fashion (Seventh) Avenue, part of the complex that houses **Madison Square Garden.** The **Garment District,** with its carts and racks shuttling back and forth, also ties up a great deal of Seventh Avenue, so much so it changes its name. The high-rises begin in earnest, and the lunch foot traffic becomes almost theater of the absurd. On the east side it is really more of the same but with high-rent apartment buildings thrown in to make **Murray Hill** a somewhat more modern-looking Gramercy Park. The amenities of culture begin to be more prominent as well, with museums, libraries, and the like turning up alongside office buildings, including the **Empire State Building,** and department stores. Speaking of which, at **Herald Square,** Macy's, Gimbels, B. Altman, Lord and Taylor are all within a few blocks of that intersection of Broadway and Sixth Ave. (Avenue of the Americas).

Here, nearly everything centers on **Fifth Ave.,** the heart of midtown. The heart of the entire island, however, and the great dividing line, is **42 St.** Known mainly as a pornographer's Broadway, it is, east of Sixth Ave., a business and commuter byway with the lions of the New York Public Library and Bryant Park added for show. On the East River side is the **United Nations Plaza** and **Tudor City,** a small, wealthy residential neighborhood that regular folks enter only by mistake when looking for something else. The **Chrysler Building** at Lexington Avenue lends a little art deco class to the street with its spire, and **Grand Central Terminal,** the gateway to Westchester County and Connecticut, gushes forth with its commuters each morning and calls them back each evening.

Now Sin Palace, **Times Square** is another matter. The intersection of Broadway and Seventh Ave. is about eight blocks long and is the **Broadway** of Great White Way notoriety. At the south end, on 42 St., are the porno houses, the violent movies, the "10 Sexsational, Sextacular, Sexciting Love Acts on Stage" theaters, the stores with tawdry merchandise at inflated prices, and, more toward Duffy Square to the north, the legitimate movie and live theaters. The block between Broadway/ Seventh and Eighth Aves. is where the real concentration of "legit" theaters and the corresponding actors' and producers' nightclub and bar/restaurant hangouts are. At Eighth Ave., however, the businesses revert back to the sex-oriented nightmares of network documentaries.

The **Port Authority Bus Terminal** is at 42 St. and

Eighth Ave., and because of geographic circumstance, serious efforts are being made to tone down the shock upon leaving the terminal, particularly in the **Hell's Kitchen** area, formerly a very rough Irish neighborhood, now an incipiently trendy "artistic" community. Government-sponsored apartments and the Little Theater row on 42 St. between Ninth and Tenth Aves. do much to cosmeticize the area, as does Studio 54 to the north.

The Midtown East section is much different. It is New York at its most commercially presentable. **Rockefeller Center,** between Fifth and Sixth Aves., 48 to 52 Sts., is of an architectural whole, and its presence forces the areas around it to compete with gems such as **Radio City Music Hall,** the **RCA Building,** and the **Skating Rink.** Across Fifth Ave. is **Saks Fifth Avenue,** the department store, and **Saint Patrick's Cathedral.** Two blocks south is the **Diamond District,** two blocks north, the cluster of museums around the **Museum of Modern Art.** East, **Madison Ave.** of John Cheever story fame, and Park Ave., with the **Waldorf Astoria** and surrounding hotels, and the brownstone neighborhoods of **Turtle Bay** and **Beekman Place** make moneyed riffs on the Rock Center melody.

Moneyed **Fifth Ave.** starts at 49 St. and forges north to the **Plaza Hotel** at 58 St., passing Cartier, Gucci, Henri Bendel, Bergdorf Goodman, Van Cleef & Arpels, and Tiffany's along the way. At **57 St.,** however, it meets its chief competition as a merchant's Hall of Fame, along the East Side at any rate—Hammacher Schlemmer, Jag, Burberry, and just north on Lexington Ave., Alexander's and Bloomingdale's. All the way east are the restaurants and support shops for **Sutton Place,** as ritzy a neighborhood as you could want, a short walk from the corporate headquarters of much of the Fortune 500 located in huge steel and glass towers on Madison, Park, Lexington, and Third Aves. On the West side of 57 St., the performing arts venues around **Carnegie Hall,** located on the corner of Seventh Ave., and the art supply stores and galleries near the **Art Students League** prepare one for the West Side to follow.

Setting the tone for the East Side farther north is **Central Park South,** a collection of very well-heeled hotels and apartment buildings. CPS/59 St. is the

demarcation line for the end of the Midtown area;
everything north of this was conceived as a residential
neighborhood first, a suburb away from "the city" at
whatever time period the area was built up. **Central
Park,** the true geographical center of the island, was
planned for this very reason. Brought about through the
efforts of influential New Yorkers keen on pastorality,
the idea caught on well enough that by the mayoral
election of 1850, *both* candidates favored construction.
The land was acquired, a swamp in the boondocks
(remember, at this time Washington Square was *way*
uptown). A contest was held to determine the best
layout for the rather bold concept in urban planning.
The winners, Frederick Law Olmsted and Calvert Vaux,
did the concept one better by coming up with a
revolutionary and exemplary design that incorporated
underpasses for eventual crosstown traffic with
landscape planning that was responsive to the natural
lay of the land as well as demonstrating traditional
design along a European model. It was perhaps the most
far-reaching and important planning decision ever made
for the city, and the neighborhoods around it are largely
dependent on proximity to it for their tax base.

Ahem. The East Side. The **Upper East Side.** From
59 St. and Fifth Ave. to around 96 St. it is an area
characterized by its cleanness and whiteness. **Yorkville,**
or Germantown, is on the north end. The old mansions
that are now schools or museums (with, of course, the
exception of the **Metropolitan Museum of Art,** which
was conceived as part of the plan for Central Park) were
the country estates of the old wealthy. Many of the best
buildings are new. However, the brownstones and small
apartment buildings in the sixties, seventies, and
eighties are tremendously elegant and well done in the
blocks between Fifth Avenue and Park Avenue. Park
Avenue is nice. The restaurants, movie theaters, delis,
bars, and whatnot *all* are nice. So why the strident
tone? It's expensive. Pretentious. Inconvenient. Stuffy.

The **West Side** is different. The older of the two as
an urban area, the West Side is characterized by
diversity, a sense of commitment, and Chinese/Spanish
restaurants. Starting with Columbus Circle/59 St. on the
south, the West Side follows its Main Street,
Broadway, west to the **Lincoln Center** neighborhood,
informally known as the Dance Belt. With two world-

class ballet companies housed within fifty yards of one
another for most of the year and the Juilliard School
turning out the musicians to accompany them, the
performing arts orientation of the neighborhood is not
difficult to understand. Moreover, what makes the
neighborhood fascinating is the fact that it was artsy
before official culture moved everything there. The
rehearsal studios in the Broadway hotels were rehearsal
studios in the early part of the century. The Hotel des
Artistes at 67 St. and **Central Park West** is so named
because a lot of artists lived there. Rich artists, but
artists.

The Dance Belt doesn't get to the river because of the
railroad yards west of Eleventh Ave. and pretty much
ends as a neighborhood at 72 St. At that point, however,
Riverside Drive begins and with it Riverside Park.
Ten years ago, from 72 St. to about 86 St., a complete
and compact example of the best and worst of New
York's social diversity could be seen on the blocks
between the parks: Riverside and Central. From wealthy
and old Riverside, it was fairly middle-class to
Broadway, but from Broadway to Central Park West
were the junkie slums of Amsterdam and Columbus
Aves. Columbus also suffered the added supposed
stigma of being known for its gay population. Since
then, the gentrification and rejuvenation of Columbus
Ave., in particular, has given hope to the upwardly
mobile throughout the city who wish to have lots of chi-
chi little restaurants and East Side–type amenities in a
less rigid environment. The Fashionable-West-70s have
arrived. Some of the more notable nonarriviste features
of the area are the **Hayden Planetarium/American
Museum of Natural History** at 79 St. and the
Dakota, home of the late John Lennon and other
celebs, at 72 St. (as well as a major feature of
Rosemary's Baby), both on Central Park West. The
Dakota is so named because when it was built, in the
1880s, it was so far uptown that it was "thought" to be
in the Dakota Territory.

The territory between 86 and 96 Sts. from park to
park is marked by a sharp demarcation—west of
Broadway it is the beginning of the "old Reds" section
of the Upper West Side, an area filled with comfortably
set people of artistic or political bent who become
leftists (many associated with Columbia University).

Since the 1920s and 1930s it has been a very liberal, even radical, stronghold. East of Broadway it is similar to the quickly renewing West 70s but not so far along, despite being targeted for renewal. It is an experiment in renovation renewal and "sweat" equity, and the jury is still out on this one as far as trendiness is concerned. North of 96 St. is fairly similar west of Broadway but for the sharp rise onto the first slope of **Morningside Heights** known to the Dutch settlers as Bloemendael and later settlers as Bloomingdale. On the east side of Broadway are a number of interesting old buildings, a couple of low-income housing projects, and some junkie slums. It varies from block to block and avenue to avenue. Around 100 St., **Manhattan Avenue** begins, signaling the descent into the **Manhattan Valley,** one of the most dangerous neighborhoods in the entire city.

Broadway cuts off West End Avenue at 107 St., and from that point to 122 St. the area west of Morningside Drive north of **The Cathedral of Saint John the Divine** and Broadway south of 110 St. is dominated by New York's college on a hill, **Columbia University.** Though still lacking a comparable counterpart to J. Press or the Crimson Shop, the University Heights section of Morningside Heights is very Ivy League. Students, students everywhere, and where there are students there are greasy spoons, ice cream stores, and bookshops. Where there are professors there are nice apartment buildings and lower Claremont Ave. Where there are dead ex-presidents and Rockefellers there is **Grant's Tomb** and **Riverside Church.** Then there is **Harlem.**

The south end of West Harlem is **Hamilton Heights,** the site of a Revolutionary War Battle won by the Father of Our Country himself. The dividing line is **Manhattanville,** a hamlet located on what is now 125 St., where the Cotton Club now stands. **125 St.** is usually thought of as the Main Street of Harlem and is a nice walk during the late afternoon. But the most prominent feature of Hamilton Heights is **City College,** between Amsterdam and St. Nicholas Ave. from 130 to 140 Sts., in a neighborhood that housed the country estates of Alexander Hamilton and Anthony Bailey of Barnum and Bailey fame.

South Central Harlem, above Central Park North (110 St.) and below 116 St., is bad. Its west border,

Morningside Park is bad. Its east border, Fifth Ave., is worse. The buildings are former high-priced apartments that are now the junkiest junkie slums in town. Just north is Marcus Garvey Park, formerly Mount Morris Park. The section is still **Mount Morris,** originally a German Jewish settlement. **Spanish Harlem, or El Barrio,** from 96 to 125 Sts. is clustered with bodegas and projects alive with Puerto Rican, Cuban, Dominican, and other island Spanish dialects that bump up against Central Harlem only with reservations.

North of 125 St., largely toward the west, is wealthy Harlem, **Sugar Hill, Striver's Row,** and other beautiful blocks constructed for an earlier elite who never made it there. The north end of Seventh and Eighth Aves., in the 140s looking downtown at City College, and the row houses designed by some of the most noted architects of New York's Golden Age in the high 130s, are the equal of much of the more familiar East Side. The projects that run to Riverside Drive are also of excellent quality and design. As downtown rents increase, so does reverse white flight into previously black communities—how successful these self-styled "urban pioneers" will be is going to depend on their attitudes, and all deliberate speed will probably remain very deliberate.

Above 155 St. is **Washington Heights,** a neighborhood that, like mine, was once Irish and is now integrated into marginality but social calm. There are still good apartments to be had for reasonable prices. There are still museums, national institutes, professional societies, everything. Moving north, the **Columbia–Presbyterian Medical Center** is on the river side and a Historic District on the east, where may be viewed High Bridge, the oldest standing bridge from Manhattan across the Harlem River into the Bronx at 174 St. At 178 St. is **Port Authority at the George Washington Bridge,** a dingy bus station but a lovely bridge. The dividing line between Washington Heights and **Fort Tryon Park** is **Yeshiva University,** also marking the end of conveniently numbered streets in Manhattan, returning to the morass of names that mean nothing unless you live there. Fort Tryon Park, however, means the **Cloisters,** a beautiful jaunt into medieval culture, as calm and untroubled as the times

were violent. **Dyckman St.,** is the north end of Fort
Tryon and the south end of **Inwood,** named for Inwood
Hill Park, which, like Fort Tryon, is part of an old
estate. **Baker Field,** where the Columbia University
Lions have so rarely relished victory, is the extreme
north end of Manhattan.

Our study of the epidermis completed, let us delve
more deeply into New York. Finding where things are.
By now you know there is an **Uptown,** a **Downtown,**
an **East Side,** and a **West Side;** the head from the feet,
the torso from the arms. But where is the liver? (My
guess is E. 66 St.). There are directions to the liver if
you know how to read them. They're easy. The
directions to the feet and head are more difficult and
require memorization—too, you'll be a podiatrist before
you're a brain surgeon. Below 14 St., forget. The streets,
even the numbered ones, are so confusing a map is
necessary. Above 14 Street just remember that all
addresses on a numbered street are figured from **Fifth
Ave.,** run east and west (generally even—east, odd—
west, except the main streets, which run both ways),
and the building number, followed by a designation of
"East" or "West" will tell you how far from Fifth Ave.
the building is. The major exception is on the West Side
between 59 and 110 Sts., where the number will tell you
how far from Central Park it is. That determination is
easier going west—1–99, between Sixth and Fifth
avenues; 100–199, between Sixth and Seventh, etc., on
through to Twelfth Ave. Throw in the occasional
diagonal like Broadway or short street like Shubert
Alley and it still works if you know the avenues
correctly. Below 59 St., West Side, with alternate names
Fifth, Sixth (Avenue of the Americas to 59 St., Lenox
Ave. above 110 St.), Seventh (Fashion Avenue from 28
to 42 Sts., Adam Clayton Powell Blvd. above 110 St.),
Eighth (Central Park West from 59 to 110 Sts.,
Frederick Douglass Ave. above 110 St.), Ninth
(Columbus Ave. above 59 St., Morningside Drive above
110 St.), Tenth (Amsterdam Ave. above 59 St.),
Eleventh (West End Ave. between 59 and 107 Sts.,
Broadway from there to eternity), and Twelfth
(Riverside Drive above 72 St.). For extra credit,
Manhattan Ave. (between Central Park West and
Columbus Ave. above 100 St.) becomes St. Nicholas
Ave. above 125 St.

The East Side is always a problem—the avenues have names, and there are more little ones. The address numbers aren't always consistent. Forewarned, let's proceed with caution and generalities: 1–199—between Fifth and Third Aves., however many streets are in between; 200–299, between Third and Second; 300–399, between Second and First; 400–499, between First and York Ave. or Sutton Pl.; 600–beyond, east of East End Ave. Now the avenues going east. There are more but they tend to keep the same name: Fifth, Madison (above 23 Street), Park (Park Ave. So. below 33 St.), Lexington (Irving Pl. below Gramercy Park on 20 St.), Third, Second, First, York (Sutton Place from 57 to 59 Sts., Sutton Pl. So. from 54 to 57 Sts.) and East End. Quick shots: The higher the number of a street, the farther uptown (north) it is, the lower, the farther south (downtown). To figure addresses on the avenues, get a Manhattan telephone directory that has a complete and quite accurate system detailed in the front, before the listings, or get a *Hagstrom's 5 in 1* map, which lists street and avenue address numbers by block.

Now that we know where the liver is, what are the means we will use to get to it?

To make a bold suggestion right off the bat, walking is good for your heart, lungs, *and* liver, is inexpensive, and is quick during the day and any other congested time. Cars, buses, subways, and taxis may stall, but the feet have never failed.

Occasionally, however, the dogs do get tired and some other form of transportation is necessary. I happen to like the bus, one of the few modes of transportation that is able to surprise me with a route untraveled. This is largely because whoever is in charge of planning Manhattan bus routes is an arbitrary, capricious, sly old dog who thrives on throwing a route out of left field into the system, often to the exclusion of keeping up the functional routes. For example, there are two routes serving Riverside Dr. residents who work in midtown or who want to visit friends on the East Side. No other explanation offers itself except that the route planner was either a Riverside Dr. resident or a friend on the East Side. My favorite line is the Punk Clubs-in-the-East-Village-to-the-Upper-West-Side route, which takes me almost door to door and is, late at night, as quick as a taxi. For 75 cents. The buses are also useful in getting to know the city by making one familiar with which streets go uptown, which streets go downtown, and the important crosstown streets. List time, again, west to east, north to south. A bus that goes uptown on one one-way street will go downtown on the nearest parallel one-way street. Certain crosstowns also run on parallel blocks; most crosstown streets run both ways, most avenues do not: Riverside Dr., both ways; Broadway/ West End/Eleventh, both ways (Broadway below 59 St., downtown); Amsterdam/Tenth, uptown to 110 St., above 110 St., both ways; Columbus/Ninth, downtown; Eighth/Central Park West, uptown to 59 St., above 59 St., both ways; Sixth, uptown to 59 St.; Fifth, downtown; Madison, uptown; Park Ave. runs both ways but is too snotty to have buses; Lexington, downtown; Third, uptown; Second, downtown; First, uptown; York, both ways. The crosstown routes at 116, 96, 86, 79, 57, 42, 34, 23, 14, and Houston Sts. are pretty straightforward on the streets they service and may even have a few extra jogs into other territories as a perk. The crosstown routes at 59, 50, and 8 Sts. are also fairly simple; 59 runs on 58 and 60 Sts. in addition to the main crossing; 50 St. goes east and returns on 49 St.; similarly, 8 St. is the eastbound and uses 9 St. westbound. The 72 St. crosstown is hardly worthy of the name, tooling down Broadway to 57 St. between Fifth and Madison before getting up to 72 St. on the East Side. The last crosstown route, the Madison St./ Chambers St./Centre St./Vesey St./Park Row/Frankfort St./Grand St. line is as confused as downtown and probably not worth attempting.

The subway is certainly worth attempting, although, like the parks, it is best done by day. There are those who will champion even the graffiti as an emblem of the communal beauty of New York. I tend to look at the subway as the commuter beauty of the city—quick, well-planned, and, until recently, quite efficient. Two of the subway systems, the **IRT** (Interborough Rapid Transit) and the **BMT** (Brooklyn Manhattan Transit) were once private companies. The **IND** (Independent Line) has always been owned and run by the city. Each services at least three boroughs. The IRT is heavier in Manhattan and the Bronx, with a single line into Queens and three into a limited area of Brooklyn. The IND has a single line into the Bronx (but the most important, express service to Yankee Stadium) and is the most extensive carrier in Brooklyn and Queens. The BMT is the most spread-out of the three, particularly in Brooklyn, and serves business districts only in Manhattan.

Getting on the subway is easy; the station stops are generally located on the major arteries, most of them run all night (unlike the buses, a word of caution on that count), and for your 75 cents you can ride all day. All you'll see are other subway stations, but it can be done (and often is in winter by the bums and bag ladies). Also included in the fare are maps of the subway and bus systems, useful little items and suitable for framing. The problem with the newer subway maps (the old design was scrapped because it was difficult to tell exactly where the stations were geographically) is not telling where the stations are but where the junctions among the various lines occur and express and local stops coincide. Failure to understand where it is necessary to change trains can put you into a strikingly different neighborhood than the one intended. For example, failure to change from the IRT #2 or #3 Uptown Express at 96 St. to the Uptown #1 can leave you in Mount Morris instead of Sugar Hill. Check and double-check all routes if you are unfamiliar with the system. Ask the token booth attendants (entrance to the subway is by token only), that's part of their job. Read the signs (though many are confusing), keep low, stay in the light, and get in a car with other people in it. Of course, between the hours of 7:30 and 9:30 A.M. and 4 to 6 P.M. it is impossible not to get into a car with other people, often hundreds of other people, as these are the prime commuting hours. Not for the claustrophobic.

The other main form of transit in Manhattan is taxis. They are expensive ($1 for the first 1/9 mile, 10 cents for each 1/9 mile following and 10 cents for every 45 seconds not in motion, which the meter defines as under 8 miles an hour), they get stalled, the drivers are often rude, but they provide a necessary feeling of money-in-your-pocket, money-to-burn. If for this reason alone, they are worth having around. Don't count on getting one if it's raining.

Of all publically available transit, my current favorite is the JFK Express train to **Kennedy Airport.** From midtown it journeys into deepest Queens in less than 10 stops. At the end of the train ride it affords an excellent view of a portion of the Gateway National Recreation Area in Jamaica Bay that, in the summer, looks more like Jamaica, West Indies. From the last stop on the train, a bus takes you to Kennedy, where there are flights to nearly any place in the world, including the other two area airfields, **LaGuardia** and **Newark International** in north Queens and New Jersey, respectively. All are accessible, not only to one another but also by several forms of public transportation: Newark by bus from Port Authority in midtown (under $3), LaGuardia by the East Side Airlines Terminal on First Ave. and 39 St. (under $6). Both buses depart about three times an hour. Transport to Kennedy is also available from the East Side Terminal, and all can be reached by taxi for approximately $10 to 12 (La Guardia), $25 (Kennedy), or $35 (Newark). I prefer the train.

I like the Amtrak trains available at **Penn Station** and **Grand Central Terminal** for points elsewhere. I have also left the city via **Port Authority Bus Terminal.** I can't be in a port of entry or exit in this town without thinking about the entries and exits I have made in the past. In particular, I tend to dwell upon my first entry into the city, as a slightly nervous about-to-be college boy, overwhelmed by the vista, uptown to downtown, Manhattan Island, the United Airlines flight gave me on our third pass over LaGuardia. I had never been here before, had no idea how anything worked or moved or played on the weekends. But it had to be. From over two thousand miles away I knew what I wanted, and standing at the gate of the airport, I knew I could have it—because it was there to take.

Here is New York, physically.

You know what to do.

SAFETY
IN NEW YORK

"Lions and tigers and bears. Oh my!"
—from THE WIZARD OF OZ

Dorothy and her friends wouldn't stand a chance in
New York City. She would lose her virtue, the
Scarecrow would be torched, the Cowardly Lion would
be in a pawnshop, stuffed, and the Tin Man would be
stripped and sold for parts.

The Big Apple is no Emerald City, so a few tips on
how to avoid crime should make life easier.

Use common sense. A lot of people are victimized
because they do dumb things, like leaving keys in the
car, or counting cash on the street.

Safety on the Streets

Walk with confidence. Know where you are going and
how to get there. If you dart nervous glances over your
shoulder because you're afraid of getting mugged, you
may well be.

Don't be afraid to ask directions if you get lost.
Shopkeepers are generally helpful. At night, try to leave
yourself an escape route. Walk near the curb; if danger
threatens, step out into the street. Muggers, like
librarians, detest commotion.

If you are mugged, give 'em what they want. If they
want your left sock, let them have it. Try to be calm

and do what you are told. And don't run after them; instead, go to the police and give them a good description.

When it comes to attempted rape, we will not second-guess the experts on rape prevention: there are a number of good workshops and books available.

Your Car

The best advice is, don't keep a car here. However, if you are foolish enough to own a car in the city, as we are, there are ways to lessen the chances of unpleasant things happening to your wheels.

For those with short memories, wiring a bomb to the ignition is not recommended. But you can remove the plastic knobs on the inside door lock; tie the vent windows shut; buy an electronic alarm system; padlock the hood and lock the steering wheel.

Park in lighted areas near residences, with other cars fore and aft. Parking on the end of a block makes it easier to be taken advantage of. Of course, don't leave any suitcases or valuables visible in the car.

If you can afford it, put the car in a garage or parking lot.

Always, always roll up the window, take the keys, and lock the doors.

Your Apartment

Get heavy door locks with deadbolts. If you live on a lower floor or have a fire escape, install a metal grille outside the window. And if you really want to make your home your castle, invest in a Fox lock, with a metal pole that braces the door shut. This should stand up to anything short of a battering ram.

Call your local police station and ask for a free inspection of your home's safety.

If your building's entrance has a buzzer-intercom, always find out the identity of your visitors before you buzz them in. If there's no response, don't let them in.

For your personal safety, avoid elevators that harbor five guys sporting Sing Sing sweatshirts.

Safety on the Subways

While waiting, stand near the token booth. Step back from the edge of the platform as the train arrives.

Late at night, ride with friends or in the more populated cars. Riding in the same car as the conductor or motorman is a good idea. Don't flash your Hope Diamond on the express at 3 A.M.

If someone bothers you, calmly move toward a group of people, preferably not the guy's buddies. Your best bet, however, may be to become the mascot of the Guardian Angels, or Curtis Sliwa's main squeeze.

Weapons

It is usually illegal to carry concealed weapons, including mace, in New York City. Moreover, we believe that the sense of security achieved by weapons is false.

With a little common sense and caution, you won't need ruby slippers to feel safe in New York.

HOTELS

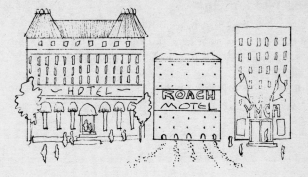

What Manhattan hotel you'll stay in when you're away from home is a very important decision, and with scores and scores of hotels to choose from, that decision isn't always easy or enjoyable.

So for your convenience, more than 40 hotels have been divided into groups according to their price range, listed from the least to most expensive as determined by the highest possible cost of a single.

Choose from the economy, moderate, moderate-to-expensive, or luxurious group. But wherever you stay, it's all a slice of Manhattan, so enjoy!

If saving money is your prime concern, this list of economy rooms is for you. Don't be shy about asking what your accommodations will be, especially on lower rents, where sometimes the sink is down the hall.

Vanderbilt YMCA, 224 E. 47 St., 755-2410
About the least expensive in the city, $16 will get you a single room for a night; $22 will get you a double.

Sloane House YMCA, 356 W. 34 St., 760-5860
Still a steal at $16 for a single, $24 for a double.

West Side Y, 5 W. 65 St., 787-4400
Singles are $18 a night and doubles (only available to women) are $23 per night.

Pickwick Arms Hotel, 230 E. 51 St., 355-0300
For $18, $22, or $30, you can stay in a single; for $40, a double.

Restricted Clientele

For Women Only

Martha Washington, 30 E. 30 St., 689-1900
Singles run from $20 to $30. Doubles from $32 to $42.

National YMCA, 135 E. 52 St., at Lexington Ave., 753-4700
Single rooms are $23; doubles, $44.

Eych-Troughton Memorial Residence, 145 E. 39 St., 490-5990
If you need to stay for a week, you can do it here for $75, two meals daily included.

For Single Women

Allerton House, 130 E. 57 St., 753-8841
For $28, you can stay in a single; for $60, a double.

For Working Women

Webster Apartments, 419 W. 34 St., 594-3950
Rooms aren't rented nightly here, but if you need to stay a few months, file an application and the prices will vary according to your salary.

For Students Only

International House of New York, 500 Riverside Dr. at 122 St., 678-5000
A single is $25, a double, $30. If you need to stay for a week, it's $70.

By Application Only

YM-YWHA, 1395 Lexington Ave. at 92 St., 427-6000
Extended stays only; a single or a double room ranges from $66 to $84 for a week's stay.

John and Mary Markle Memorial Residency, 123 W. 13 St., 242-2400
Some young businesswomen and senior citizens are allowed, but either way, the application must be filled out in person. It's $80 to $84 for a week with two meals a day.

For Active Military Persons Only

Soldiers', Sailors' and Airmen's Club Inc.
238 Lexington Ave., 638-4353
All rooms are semiprivate and cost $6. Retired military persons can stay for $1 more.

U.S.O., 1540 Broadway, 586-3340
For $25 through $29, a single can be had. For $36 through $44, a double.

This next group is moderately priced; you can still stay in the most expensive single room for under $75.

Hotel Carter, 250 W. 43 St. between 8 Ave. and Broadway, 944-6000
A single can be had for $30; a double for $40.

Hotel Diplomat, 108 W. 43 St. between 6 Ave. and Broadway, 921-5666
For $33 you can stay in a single. For $40, a double.

Chelsea Hotel, 222 W. 23 St., 243-3700
Singles are $27 to $35. Doubles $35 to $45.
You probably remember the Chelsea Hotel as the place ex–Sex Pistol Sid Vicious did in Nancy Spungen after shooting up with his mom. Or as the New York residence of Virgil Thomson, Thomas Wolfe, or Dylan Thomas. Or as the location of Andy Warhol's *Chelsea Girls*. Well, it was, or is, all those things, as well as being a very pretty and well-designed building known for the iron filigree balconies of the façade. Built in 1884 as one of the city's first co-ops, it became a hotel in 1905 and has hosted, in addition to those mentioned above, Sarah Bernhardt, Jackson Pollock, Mark Twain, Brendan Behan, O. Henry, and Tennessee Williams (all of whom are listed on plaques at the entrance), while remaining one of New York's most enduring artistic landmarks.

Hotel Olcott, 27 W. 72 St. off Central Park West, 877-4200
For $40 you can stay in a single room; for $45 in a double.

Hotel Seymour, 235 W. 46 St., 581-7000
Between $35 and $42 will get you a single room.
Between $45 and $52 will get you a double.

The Hotel George Washington, Lexington Ave. and 23 St., 475-1920
A single runs between $38 and $45; a double between $48 and $63.

Hotel Piccadilly, 227 W. 45 St., 246-6600
Stay in a single for $40 or $43, or a double for $49 or $52. A one-bedroom suite runs between $105 and $125.

Hotel Empire, Broadway and 63 St., 265-7400
For $45 you can get a single; $55 gets you a double.

Century-Paramount, 235 W. 46 St., 246-5500
Either $40, $45, or $50 will get you a single. Doubles are $56.

Hotel Taft, Seventh Ave. between 50 and 51 Sts., 247-4000
Singles rooms go for $45 or $50. Doubles are $50 or $60. And if you're looking for a one-bedroom suite, it's $110. Two-bedroom suites are $175.

Hotel Tudor, 304 E. 42 St. off Second Ave., 986-8800
Here a single is $50; a double is $56.

Travel Inn, 515 W. 42 St., 695-7171
For $50, stay in a single room, or for between $54 and $60, a double.

Prince George Hotel, 14 E. 28 St., 532-7800
A single room is $51 or $54. A double is $57 or $60. And if you're after a one-bedroom suite, it's $110. A two-bedroom suite is $160.

Barbizon Hotel for Women, Lexington Ave. and 63 St., 838-5700
Mostly for women, between $32 and $59 will get you a single room; between $41 and $64 a double.

Hotel Seville, Madison Ave. and 29 St., 532-4100
A single can be had for between $43 and $59. A double, for between $49 and $59.

Hotel Wales, 1295 Madison Ave. between 92 and 93 Sts., 876-6000
Both a single and a double cost between $28 and $60.

Hotel Wellington, Seventh Ave. and 55 St., 247-3900
Stay here for between $44 and $60, or in a double for between $54 and $60.

Howard Johnson's Motor Lodge, Eighth Ave. between 51 and 52 Sts., 581-4100

Stay in a single for between $55 and $65, or in a double for between $67 an $77.

Wyndham Hotel, 42 W. 58 St., 753-3500
Stay in a single for between $62 and $66, in a double for between $72 and $76.

Southgate Tower, Seventh Ave. and 31 St., 563-1800
Singles are $63, $65, or $68. Doubles are $73, $75, or $78. For $80 you can rent a one-bedroom suite; for $89, a two-bedroom suite. And on a Friday, Saturday, or Sunday, you can get a double room for $40 per night.

If you're looking for something that's just a cut above moderate, but where you can still stay in the best single for under $100, this group is for you:

Barbizon Plaza, 106 Central Park So. off 59 St., 247-7000
Single rooms are $74; doubles $84. But there's a special package for one night in a double with breakfast for $73.92.

Roger Smith, 501 Lexington Ave. at 47 St. 755-1400
Singles run from $59 to $77; doubles run from $71 to $88. A one-bedroom suite costs between $110 and $120; a two-bedroom, between $120 and $145. A free Continental breakfast is included on weekends for the price of the room.

Hotel Beverly, Lexington Ave. and 50 St. 753-2700
For $79, stay in a single; for $89, a double. A one-bedroom suite is $150, a two-bedroom suite, $225. Or try their Short and Sweet weekend for two nights at $99 per person and get a ticket to the New York Experience, breakfast, and free entry into the club.

Doral Inn, Lexington Ave. and 49 St. 755-1200
For $75 or $82, rent a single. For $87 or $94, rent a double. A one-bedroom suite is $150; a two-bedroom suite is $250. Or stay in a double any two nights for $139 and get breakfast, a food basket, wine, flowers, and chocolates.

Hotel Algonquin, 59 W. 44 St. 840-6800
Stay in a single room for between $76 and $82, or in a double for $83 or $85. Their one-bedroom suites are $152; two-bedroom suites are $240. For the Algonquin, the connection is always the literary one. Since the

1920s, when the famous "Round Table" lunches were
diligently reported in Franklin P. Adams's column, from
Sylvia Plath's fateful recollections of it in *The Bell Jar,*
to Jacqueline Bisset's affairs with younger men in *Rich
and Famous,* the Algonquin has been *the* literary
hangout of note. If they have any sense of loyalty and
you have any clairvoyant power, the ghosts of Dorothy
Parker, George S. Kaufman, and Alexander Woollcott
should make ectoplasmic their already felt historical
presence. Toast them at the Blue Bar or in one of the
plush chairs in the woody, charming lobby. Just don't
lose the coded card that is your room key. (Did I forget
to mention the Algonquin is a *progressive* literary
establishment?)

Windsor, 100 W. 58 St. 265-2100
For between $75 and $85, rent a single, or a double for
between $85 and $95. A one-bedroom suite ranges from
$140 and $150; a two-bedroom suite is $235. And if you
stay Friday and Saturday night, you pay $50 per night
for a double or single room.

New York Statler, 401 Seventh Ave. at 33 St.,
736-5000
Rent a single for $59, $68, $74, $78, $84, or $89. Doubles
are $74, $83, $89, $93, $99, and $104. Their one-
bedroom suites are between $150 and $175; their two-
bedroom suites are $225. Or try their package, the Two
Night City Fling, and stay any two weekend nights for
$52 per person, breakfast included.

Sheraton, Seventh Ave. and 56 St. 247-8000
A single is $72, $80, or $90. A double is $85, $95, or
$105. And if you want a one-bedroom suite, it's $145; a
two-bedroom suite is $305. For $57 per night, stay in a
double room on their package deal.

Loews Summit, Lexington Ave. and 51 St., 752-7000
Singles range from $75, $80, and $90. Doubles are $88,
$93, $98, or $103. The Summit Weekender is one night
with dinner and breakfast in a double for $140. For two
nights, it's $248.40, including theater tickets.

Loews Warwick, 65 W. 54 St. 247-2700
Stay in a single for between $85 and $95, or in a double
for between $100 and $110. A junior suite is $115; a one-
bedroom suite is $150, $175, or 250; a two-bedroom
suite is $230, $260, or $350. Or stay in a double one

night for $130 and get dinner and breakfast. If you want two nights and can arrive Thursday, Friday, or Saturday, pay $224 and get orchestra seats to a Broadway play as well as brunch.

The following are some of the most luxurious hotels in Manhattan. Most have special package deals, some of which are real money-savers, some of which are just fun.

Carlyle, Madison Ave. and 76 St. 744-1600
Here a single costs between $150 and $175; a double, between $160 and $185. A one-bedroom suite runs between $300 and $525; a two-bedroom runs from between $450 and $600.

Pierre, Fifth Ave. and 61 St., 940-8100
A single ranges from $150 to $190; a double, from $165 to $205. One-bedroom suites are $465 to $575, and two-bedroom suites are $605 to $800.

Plaza, Fifth Ave. and 59 St., 759-3000
Singles are $100, $112 to $160, $187, or for the deluxe, $215 or $230. Doubles are $125, $135, $140, or $160, or for the deluxe, $230 or $250. Suites are $455 or $475; deluxe suites are $575 to $640. Or for $360, stay in a double or single any two consecutive weekend nights and get champagne, breakfast, and dinner. For $600, you get the same package in a suite.

Surely the greatest architectural landmark among the hotels of New York, the Plaza was designed by Henry J. Hardenbergh who also did the Dakota. Edwardian elegance still reigns supreme in this most famous of all lodgings. Frank Lloyd Wright liked it so well he would stay nowhere else, a feeling no doubt helped by the proximity to the Palm Court (have dessert there, it's wonderful and worth the expense), the Edwardian Room Restaurant, and the great, solemn, yet oddly cheerful Oak Bar. Trader Vic's is in the basement—this is just a total pleasure palace (with Kubla Khan prices) but hell, jump in the fountain for the sheer joy of being in a place where such as this exists!

The Sherry Netherland, 781 Fifth Ave. at 59 St., 355-2800
There is no price difference between single and double rooms; they range from $115 to $175. The small suites range between $195 and $225; the large suites are $325.

Waldorf-Astoria, Park Ave. and 50 St., 355-3000

Singles are $70, $90, $110, $130, $150, $165, or $190.
Doubles are $105, $125, $145, $165, $185, $200, or $225.
A one-bedroom suite is between $235 and $360. A two-
bedroom is between $385 and $510. Their Rainbow
weekend is $244 to stay in a double Friday and
Saturday with breakfast, brunch, and tips included. The
Weekend at the Waldorf is a dollar more and includes
the same package, except dinner is the substituted meal.
The hotel with two names (because Mrs. William Astor
and her son, William Waldorf Astor, while feuding,
turned their homes, located where the Empire State
Building is now, into adjoining hotels) recently
celebrated its fiftieth anniversary at its current location.
Once very art deco, now rather pseudo-Edwardian, the
lobby, Peacock Alley (done in blue, of course), is still
one of the most elegant short walks in town. A pleasant
place to sit with your packages even if you're *not*
registered there. And as long as you look the part, ain't
nobody gonna say nothin'. Have yourself paged along
with the likes of kings, presidents, and celebrities, many
of whom refuse to stay anywhere else.

RESTAURANTS

Whether you want to catch a quick nosh before doing
the town, or want to "pig out" all night, New York
restaurants will hit the spot. Out of 32 pages in
Manhattan's Yellow Pages (and some don't even list
there) you're bound to find places to suit both your
wallet and cravings. Some people may disagree with our
list of favorites. After all, restaurants here are a more
popular topic of conversation than apartments, and
every New Yorker is a food critic. The editors chose the
following eateries because, for one reason or another, we
find ourselves returning to them. The price, food,
service, or ambience was memorable; in some cases, we'd
check off a box marked "All of the Above." Most of the
restaurants listed are reasonably priced, some quite
inexpensive. But we also wanted to suggest a few of the
finest dining establishments in the world . . . and those
don't come cheap.

Reservations are often mandatory. If you have your
heart (or taste buds) set on a particular place, call
ahead to see what the story is. As a rule, 15 to 20
percent gratuities are standard. Don't hesitate to adjust
the percentage in either direction for *exceptional*
service. At "Silver Service" restaurants, such as Lutèce,
remember there are captains, wine stewards, and the
coat checker to be tipped, too.

We've tried to include a cross section of cuisines in a
variety of neighborhoods. Assume that these restaurants
are in Manhattan and on street level unless otherwise
noted. Bon appétit.

The Abbey Tavern 354 Third Ave., at 26 St.,
532-1978
One of the better in a series of Irish bars *cum*
restaurants that proliferate throughout Manhattan.
Typical Irish fare—shepherd's pie, steak and kidney—as
well as good burgers, salads, surf 'n' turf. Bar open 12n–
4 A.M. 7 days a week; Lunch and Dinner 12n–2 A.M. Fri.,
Sat., till 1 A.M. Sun.–Thurs. No Bobby Sands jokes. All
major credit cards. Inexpensive.

Asti, 13 E. 12 St., 242-9868
The food at this place has never been the issue, which is
all for the best, since it is only mediocre. Asti is famous
as the home of the singing waiter, the musical cashier,
and when they team up to break into your favorite
Puccini aria, you may find the place amusing. Stick to
the simpler dishes, get drunk, and you can have a
unique and slightly wacky time at Asti. Not cheap, but
certainly less expensive than the Metropolitan Opera,
and you can chow down through "Casta Diva." Dinner
only, 5 P.M.–1 A.M. 7 days. All major credit cards.

Balkan Armenian, 129 E. 27th St., 689-7925
A good, moderately priced little restaurant, featuring
well-made Armenian food in comfortable surroundings.
The shish kebab is excellent, as are many of the chicken
dishes. Service is congenial and attentive; there are
some inexpensive and quite drinkable wines. Armenian
restaurants, by the way, are no rarity in New York, and
this is one of the best of them. Closed Sun. Lunch 12n–
2:30 P.M. Mon.–Fri. Dinner 4:30 P.M.–9 P.M. Mon.–
Thurs., 4:30–10 P.M. Fri., Sat. All major credit cards.

Bosphorus East, 121 Lexington Ave. at 28th St.,
679-8370
Mom's in the kitchen, Dad's at the bar, and daughter
sometimes waits tables. This is a real family place.
Don't say you don't like Turkish food until you've tried
Bosphorus. because many of the dishes have an almost
Parisian delicacy to them. We've been here thirty or
forty times and have never been disappointed. Try the
hot lamb broth with pungent garlic vinegar to start,
then swordfish or one of the many excellent lamb
dishes. Finest ingredients are chosen, everything cooked
to order, exotic turquoise atmosphere, and not very
expensive. We *love* Bosphorus East. Dinner only, 6 P.M.–
11:20 P.M. 7 days. All major credit cards.

Brasserie, 100 E. 53 St., 751-4840

If it's 5 A.M. and the evening is still young, you may want to consider a full dinner at the Brasserie. For many years this was New York's only quality restaurant open 24 hours a day, 365 days a year. We're past that dark age now, but the Brasserie is still worth a visit. Great omelettes, O.K. service, lousy atmosphere, but it still beats a coffee shop, and most after-hours clubs don't serve food. We've sobered up here many a time, and could put together a novel out of much of the conversation heard over late-night coffee. In midtown, no less! All major credit cards. Moderate.

Broome Street Bar and Restaurant, 363 W. Broadway, 925-2086

Good hamburgers in the heart of the Soho strip are offered by the Broome Street Bar. Actually, most of the food is all right, but nobody seems to order much but burgers. Lots of artists, musicians, and local color. A good bar, stocked with Rolling Rock Beer and top shelf gin. Broome Street is loud, vibrant, and a little frenetic—it always affects us like a strong cup of coffee. Good desserts. Cheap and popular. Open 12n–3 A.M. 7 days; kitchen closes at 12m. No credit cards.

Butler Hall Terrace, 400 W. 119 St., 666-9490

The Columbia University area is hardly a bastion of great food, although it is improving. The Terrace Restaurant—*way* uptown—was once one of the great undiscovered places in the city. Then the *Times* gave it a good review, and it doubled its prices and declined in quality. But it still offers good French *nouvelle cuisine* uptown, with great views of Harlem and the rest of the city. Located on the top floor of a Columbia graduate dorm, the Butler Terrace would be worth a visit simply for its wonderful Bananas Foster. Don't wander the area after dinner. Lunch 12n–3 P.M. Tue.–Fri. Dinner 6–10 P.M. Mon.–Thurs.; to 10:30 P.M. Fri., Sat. Closed Sun. All major credit cards.

B'way Bay, 2178 Broadway at 77th St., 362-5234

B'way Bay is associated in our minds with one word— lobster. Well, maybe *two* words—*cheap* lobster. Remarkable as it may seem, you can still get a good lobster dinner here for about $10. The other entrées we have tried have been something of a disappointment, and even the lobster is not *always* first-rate. But we

doubt you can get cheaper lobster this side of
Newfoundland. 11:30 A.M.–1 A.M. Mon.–Sat., 3:30 P.M.–
12m Sun. All major credit cards.

Café des Artistes, 1 W. 67th St., 877-3500
Now that you've visited the Algonquin, come and see
another spot where time seems to have stopped. The
wonderful nude murals on the wall of the café (painted
by Howard Chandler Christy many years ago) are only
the first delight. The food is first-rate, particularly the
fish courses, and the desserts are fine. A slight
condescension on the part of the staff is this
restaurant's only drawback. Harry Crosby shot himself
upstairs; many poets, artists, and writers have lived and
eaten here over the years. Moderately expensive, but
worth it. Lunch 12n–2:30 P.M. Mon.–Fri., Brunch 11
A.M.–3 P.M. Sat.–Sun. Dinner 5:30 P.M.–11 P.M. Mon.–
Sat., 5 P.M.–8 P.M. Sun. Jacket and tie requested.

The Captain's Table, 410 Sixth Ave. between 8 and
    9 Sts., 473-0670
Good-quality seafood at a reasonable price is why The
Captain is a long-time Village favorite. (There is
another branch uptown, but we have not been there and
cannot comment on it.) The atmosphere is geriatric—
flowered tablecloths, hanging plants—but the food is
consistently very good. We love their fried shrimp and
fish 'n' chips. The staff is attentive and pleasant. Closed
Mon. Lunch 12n–3 P.M., 12n–3:30 P.M. Sat., and dinner
4:30 P.M.–11 P.M. Tues.–Fri., 5 P.M.–12m Sat., 12n–10
P.M. Sun. Lunch and dinner prices are the same, so a
better bargain at dinner. AE, MasterCard, Visa, DC.

Cellar in the Sky, 1 World Trade Center, 938-1111
The oenophiles' dream-come-true. The haute cuisine
here on the 107 floor is superb (if not the view, which
doesn't exist) but the spotlight here is on the fine wines
accompanying each of the seven courses. But it's more
than just a wine-tasting: full bottles are opened at each
table. The one seating per night (7:30 P.M.) is held in an
active wine cellar—cool and cozy. At press time, charge
per person is around $55. *Reservations a must.* Closed
Sunday. All major credit cards. Coat and tie and *no*
denim.

Charlie & Kelly, 259 W. 4 St., 675-5059
An eccentric little spot on a charming block in the West
Village, Charlie & Kelly specializes in traditional dishes

made, well, droll—garnished with fennel, or lime or
something else a touch uncommon. Good desserts. A
good place to take a date—straight or gay. The place
abounds with couples of all inclinations; the lights are
low and *very* romantic. Dinner 5 P.M.–11 P.M. Sun.–
Thurs., 6 P.M.–12m Fri., Sat. All major credit cards.
Moderate.

Chez Vous, 78 Carmine St., 242-2676
A different and worthwhile restaurant, Chez Vous
advertises itself as the "Italian Restaurant with the
French Name." It is moderately priced, features photos
of unknown celebrities (all gratefully inscribed),
displays wine bottles everywhere, and serves some damn
good food. A Chicken Florentine we had here one night
was excellent, and was followed by a grand Key lime pie
for dessert. Service is attentive, and there is a touch of
old Greenwich Village to Chez Vous we find irresistible.
Lunch 12n–2:30 P.M. Mon.–Fri. Dinner 5 P.M.–10:30 P.M.
7 days. MasterCard, Visa, DC.

The Coach House, 110 Waverly Pl., 777-0303
The Coach House represents the all-but-forgotten
patrician side of Greenwich Village—*Washington
Square* and Edith Wharton novels. Well, Washington
Square isn't what it used to be, and neither is the Coach
House. It is now terribly expensive, but its simple dishes
are marvelous—particularly a memorable rack of lamb.
But we also tried a strange concoction that can only be
described as veal with ketchup (you can imagine). The
black bean soup is justly famous. Jackets are required—
uncommon in the Village. Bring lots of money and
reserve in advance. Dinner only 5 P.M.–10:30 P.M. Closed
Mon. All major credit cards.

Coq au Vin, 939 Eighth Ave., between 55 and 56 Sts.,
541-8273
Coq au Vin is a good place to know about in midtown.
Although the food is never truly great, it is a decent
sampling of provincial French peasant fare for a very
reasonable price. Lunch is a particular bargain; you can
get soup, salad, entrée, and dessert for about $7.50. The
coq au vin itself is good (as one might expect), as are
some of the simpler dishes, and the service is motherly
and speedy. Perfect for a quick meal before a Carnegie
Hall concert. Lunch 12n–3 P.M. Mon.–Fri. Dinner 5
P.M.–10 P.M. Mon.–Thurs., 5 P.M.–11 P.M. Fri., Sat.
Closed Sun. All major credit cards.

Dardanelles, 86 University Pl., 242-8990
Dardanelles may well be the best Armenian restaurant
in New York City. It is a long-established Village
favorite and seems incapable of presenting a bad meal—
from the splendid shish kebab through the delicate and
perfectly spiced filet of sole. We especially like the
lemon-chicken soup, which unfortunately is not always
available. For the quality of the food presented,
Dardanelles is a real bargain and has an inexpensive
lunch that is highly recommended. Lunch 12n–2:30 P.M.
Mon.–Fri. Dinner 4:30 P.M.–9:30 P.M. Mon.–Thurs., 4:30
P.M.–10:30 P.M. Fri., Sat. Closed Sun. MasterCard, Visa,
CB, AE.

Dobson's, 341 Columbus Ave., at 76 St., 362-0100
Located in the heart of the "Fashionable West 70s,"
Dobson's is a casual and friendly spot to have brunch.
The more ambitious dishes served at lunch and dinner
are only average, but we recommend their desserts,
especially the lemon or lime pies. Dobson's has a rather
large seating capacity, but at peak brunch hours, there's
sometimes a short wait. Lunch, Brunch, and Dinner
11:30 A.M.–12:30 A.M. Sun.–Thurs., 11:30 A.M.–1:30 A.M.
Fri., Sat. AE, MasterCard, Visa only. Moderate.

Elaine's, 1703 Second Ave., at 88 St., 534-8103
A place to see and be seen—or to see and be ignored.
Actually, we have always been treated very well at
Elaine's, but the rumor persists that if you are not a
star (in film, publishing, soaps, or any other celebrity-
generating field), you will be shut out here. It's worth a
visit, though. We like the mainly Italian fare, and the
atmosphere has an undeniable glamor. (We like to star-
gaze, too.) Lunch and dinner 12n–3 A.M. Mon.–Fri., 6
P.M.–2 A.M. Sat., Sun. Reservations necessary after 9 P.M.
AE. Be cool.

El Faro, 823 Greenwich St., 929-8210
A remarkably good little Spanish restaurant in an
obscure corner of westernmost Greenwich Village.
Lunch (11–3 Mon.–Fri.) is quite inexpensive and a real
bargain at around $5. Dinner (served to 12m) is more
expensive. We love the shrimp ajillo (shrimp with
garlic), and the arroz con pollo (chicken with rice) is
also first rate. El Faro has been here forever—a Village
landmark. No credit cards.

El Parador, 325 E. 34 St., 679-6812

You are greeted by the friendliest host in Manhattan, behaving like a long-lost brother. This sets the tone for the place, one of the best Mexican restaurants in New York and a fine way to spend an evening. The tacos, tamales, and enchiladas are wonderful, as are the more ambitious shrimp dishes. Biting, perfect homemade lemonade is available at the bar, and the bean dip is spicy enough to ruin your breath for the evening, if not the week. It's wonderful. Have a sampling of Mexican beer—it's merely great. Dinner only 5 P.M.–11 P.M. Closed Sun. No credit cards.

Empire Diner, 210 Tenth Ave., between 22 and 23 Sts., 243-2736
This is a very chic place, made from an actual dining car, all art deco and seductive slink. The food is only fair, and sometimes worse than that. But the Empire is open 24 hours, has a definite theatrical atmosphere, and can be really interesting about 4 A.M. in the proper shattered condition. Good desserts. No credit cards of any kind.

Food, 127 Prince St., at Wooster St.
This spacious and pleasant Soho cafeteria-style restaurant has a cheerfulness about it on even the bleakest days, perhaps because of the enthusiastic staff, delicious food, and heavy traffic. Food is a crossroads of sorts for downtown residents and visitors alike. The menu contains a hearty and wholesome choice of soups, sandwiches, salads, hot dishes, and desserts, priced in the $5 to $10 range. The bill could mount up, but one can eat frugally by just having bread and a steaming bowl of soup. The avocado and brie on French bread sandwich and poppy seed cake with sour cream–lemon frosting, are only a couple of examples of the tasty selections available. The crowd can run thick, especially evenings and weekends, but it all sorts itself out gradually as people settle down to eat well in pleasant surroundings. Hours: 12n–10 P.M. Mon.–Wed., 12n–11 P.M. Thurs.–Sat., 11:30 A.M.–4:30 P.M. Sun.

The French Shack, 65 W. 55 St., 246-5126
The French Shack is one of the most reliable restaurants in New York. It is only moderately expensive and always delivers first-quality food, generally in *huge* portions. The seafood pancake appetizer—a crêpe stuffed with shrimp, mussels, and

scallops—is only $3, and can be a small meal in itself.
The duck is excellent, as are the desserts. We have
never had a bad meal here, and always leave feeling
content and satiated. A must in midtown. Lunch and
Dinner 12n–10 P.M. Mon.–Fri. Dinner only 5 P.M.–11 P.M.
Sat., 4:30 P.M.–10:30 P.M. Sun. All major credit cards.

Gage and Tollner, 374 Fulton St., Brooklyn,
875-5181

You need to cross the Brooklyn Bridge to visit Gage and
Tollner, but the trip is worth it. Over 100 years old and
lit by gaslight, Gage and Tollner features a huge menu
concentrating on steak and seafood and has a grace and
hospitality rarely found in New York. Try the lobster
bisque—a meal in itself. Lunch and Dinner 11:30 A.M.–9
P.M. Mon.–Fri. Dinner only 4 P.M.–10:30 P.M. Sat.
Sunday brunch 12n–3 P.M., Sunday dinner 3 P.M.–9 P.M.
All major credit cards.

Gargiulo's, 2911 W. 15 St., Coney Island, Brooklyn,
266-9096

We love Gargiulo's. This massive Coney Island
restaurant is a long subway ride from Manhattan, but it
serves great Italian food for very little money. Every
course we've had here has been first-rate. Try the garlic
bread, the chicken soup, and the zabaglione dessert.
Just first-rate. Everything. Lunch and Dinner 12n–11
P.M. 7 days. All major credit cards.

The Ginger Man, 51 W. 64 St., 724-7272

A good spot for a bite before a Lincoln Center concert,
and worth a visit even if you happen to hate music,
ballet, theater, and everything else across the street. We
have had nice duck here, and the steak preparations are
usually excellent, too. Prices are a little high for the
basically unpretentious food, but there is an undeniable
charm to the Ginger Man. On the fifteenth anniversary
of its opening, the Ginger Man charged opening-day
prices for one evening. The place was packed with
customers eating $3.25 duck and drinking 35-cent draft
Heinekens. Watch the ads for the twentieth anniversary
celebration. Lunch and Dinner 11 A.M.–12m, 7 days. All
major credit cards.

Granados, 125 MacDougal St., 673-5576

This is our favorite Spanish restaurant in New York,
and one of the best places in the city. Granados serves
peasant food, so don't expect haute. Simply feast on

good, solid unpretentious food in mammoth servings.
We love the arroz con pollo (chicken with rice), and
friends have raved about the octopus. Homemade
sangria. Prices are moderate. Granados makes its own
salad dressing—spicy and delightful. In the heart of
Greenwich Village. Dinner only 4 P.M.–1 A.M. Tues.–
Thurs. Brunch and Dinner 2 P.M.–2 A.M. Fri., Sat., 2
P.M.–12m Sun. Closed Mon. All major credit cards.
Moderate.

Grand Ticino, 228 Thompson St., 777-5922
Although the food at Grand Ticino is really only okay,
we find ourselves eating there quite a lot. For one thing,
it's located only a block or two south of Washington Sq.,
right in the heart of Greenwich Village. The food is
quite inexpensive and always decent. The chicken
dishes are often excellent; the veal as well. The pastas
are poor—so avoid them. Grand Ticino is located in the
basement of an old apartment house and is loaded with
Greenwich Village charm. Lunch and Dinner 12n–3 P.M.,
5 P.M.–10:30 P.M. Mon.–Sat. Closed Sunday. No credit
cards.

Harvey's Chelsea Restaurant, 108 W. 18 St.,
243-5644
Although Harvey's has been around forever, it is,
paradoxically, the big favorite with residents of the *new*
Chelsea. It is basically a burger joint with some good
beer on tap, friendly service, and lots of people, but it is
well worth knowing about. Try it if you're in the mood
for a simple, unpretentious meal and one drink or ten.
Lunch and Dinner Sun.–Thurs. 12n–12m, Fri., Sat. 12n–
1 A.M. No credit cards, but will take checks with proper
ID.

Hisae's Place, 35 Cooper Sq., 228-6886; 174 Eighth
Ave. at 19 St., 691-3559; 45 E. 58 St., 753-6555; 12 W.
72 St., 787-5656
The full name for these restaurants is Hisae, The Place
for Fish, and they offer a "not-for-carnivores" menu.
The fish dishes are always reliable, and the selection of
vegetarian fare is wide. We found a few of the veggie
dishes a little bland, but then we have a carnivore's
palate. Dinner at all locations but 58 St.: 5 P.M.–12m
Mon.–Thurs., 5 P.M.–1 A.M. Fri., Sat., 4 P.M.–11 P.M. Sun.
58th St. location: Lunch and Dinner 12n–11 P.M. Mon.–
Fri., Dinner only 5 P.M.–12m Sat. and Sun.

Entertainment at all locations. All major credit cards. Moderate.

Hunan Balcony, 2596 Broadway, at 98 St., 865-0400
One of the best of the many Chinese restaurants located on the Upper West Side. But head uptown—good Hunan food (from Central China—spicy, yet delicate at the same time). We love the crispy shrimp here. Relatively inexpensive, and a real oasis in this area.

Indian Oven, 285 Columbus Av., between 73 and 74 Sts., 362-7567
Located right in the hub of the Columbus Ave. gentrification scene—a very trendy area with lots of designer jeans and roller skates—Indian Oven is, happily, a reliable and reasonable place, with wonderful breads and soups. The tandoori chicken is a real bargain, and always excellent. Indian Oven is friendly and priced right, so what more can you want? Lunch 12–3 P.M. Tues.–Sat. Dinner 5 P.M.–11 P.M. Tues.–Thurs., 5 P.M.–12m Fri., Sat., 3 P.M.–11 P.M. Sun. Closed Mon. AE, MasterCard, Visa, DC.

Joanna's, 18 E. 18 St., 675-7900
Its magnificent wooden exterior and full-length windows, draped in Victorian lace, are an odd sight on this heavily industrial block. But as with many *au courant* eateries, Joanna's is located in an area currently off the beaten path. The decor is charming and the food is good, although quite expensive. The help is competent but condescending. Call for reservations. Private parking available. Lunch and Dinner 11 A.M.–1 A.M., 7 days. Limited menu 3 P.M.–6 P.M.. *Dress well.* AE only.

John's Pizzeria, 278 Bleecker St., 242-9529
Probably the best pizza on the East Coast, and we hate to publicize it further. Back in our Village bohemian days, we used to stroll into John's and get seated at any hour. No more! The word is out. John's makes splendid pies (no slices) with any ingredients the customer may want. We prefer the classic unadorned pie—pure and perfect. Expect somewhat surly service (at least until they get to know you). In the heart of the Village. Take a Bleecker Street stroll after dinner. A bargain, but the wait outside on winter evenings can be freezing. 11 A.M.–11 P.M., 7 days. No credit of any kind. (It's a pizza joint.)

Katz's Delicatessen, 205 E. Houston St., 254-2246
One of the more casual kosher delicatessens—you're
given a ticket as you enter and they punch it out as you
select what you want, old-time cafeteria style. Katz's is
inexpensive and a good place to refuel during a day of
bargain-hunting on the Lower East Side. 7 A.M.–11:30
P.M. Sun.–Thurs., 7 A.M.–1 A.M. Fri., Sat. Closed on
Jewish holidays. No credit cards.

Kiev, 117 Second Ave., at 7 St., 674-4040
Kiev is one of the best bargains in New York City, yet a
very chic spot at the same time. For only a couple of
dollars we've stuffed ourselves here on homemade
soups, *challah* bread, kasha, and the fabulous apple
pancakes. The cast of characters that make up the
clientele—Kiev is in the heart of the East Village—is
entertainment in itself. The place is open 24 hours a
day, 7 days a week. No credit cards.

La Bonne Soupe, 48 W. 55 St., 586-7650; 987 Third
   Ave., between 58 and 59 Sts., 759-2500
There are two Bonne Soupes, and we emphatically
prefer the one on 55th Street. For some reason, it
always seems to turn out better versions of the same
dishes. As one might imagine, there are fine *soupes*
here—particularly the French onion, layered with a ton
of rich cheese. There are also some good glorified
hamburgers—the one sautéed in wine and shallots is
usually first-rate. Quite inexpensive, especially for
midtown, and service is quick and passably attentive.
58th St., Lunch and Dinner 11:30 A.M.–12m Mon.–Sat.,
11:30 A.M.–11 P.M. Sun. AE only. 3rd Ave.: Lunch and
Dinner 11:30 A.M.–1 A.M. 7 days. MasterCard and Visa
only.

La Chaumière, 310 W. 4 St., 741-3379
A delightful little French spot in the West Village. With
real Village charm and a romantic ambience, La
Chaumière also manages to serve some very good food.
We have had excellent duck here and good onion soup.
Prices are moderate, service helpful. Dinner only, 6
P.M.–12m Mon.–Sat., 5 P.M.–11 P.M. Sun. All major credit
cards.

Landmark Tavern, 626 Eleventh Ave., at 46 St.,
   757-8595
All three rooms are charmingly Olde New York—this
one really *is* a landmark! American and Irish fare are

featured—great soups, huge salads, but stay clear of the deep-fried things. We would recommend Sunday brunch; make reservations unless you don't mind a wait. The drinks aren't generous, but the griddlecakes, omelettes, and Irish soda bread more than make up for this. Lunch and Dinner 12n–12m Sun.–Thurs., 12n–2 A.M. Fri., Sat. Kitchen closes 4:30 P.M.–5 P.M. daily. No credit cards.

Lüchow's, 1533 Broadway, at 51 St.
Although it has moved from the magnificent 102-year-old building on 14 St. that it had occupied for 100 years, Lüchow's continues to serve well-prepared German food. It is a very touristy place, and the food is somewhat expensive, very heavy, almost Wagnerian, but the goose is good, and the apple pancakes splendid. Other specialties are the Sauerbraten mit Kartoffel Kloss (beef and dumplings), Gespickter Hasenruken (rabbit in sour cream with red cabbage), and Schnitzel à la Lüchow. Call for reservations. Lunch 12n–5 P.M., Dinner 5 P.M.–11 P.M., 7 days. All major credit cards.

Peter Luger, 178 Broadway, Brooklyn, 387-7400
There are more reasons than one to cross the river into Brooklyn, and Peter Luger is a first-line member of this list. It's an old steak house, with strong turn-of-the-century feel, located on the main street of Brooklyn's down (but not out) Williamsburg section. The steaks are great, as are the lobster dishes, and the potato preparations better still. Cheesecake for dessert. Lunch and Dinner 11:30 A.M.–9:45 P.M. Mon.–Thurs., 11:30 A.M.–10:45 P.M. Fri., 11:30 A.M.–11:15 P.M. Sat., 1 P.M.–9:45 P.M. Sun. No credit cards, but a house charge account is available.

Luna, 112 Mulberry St., 226-8657
An unfriendly, crowded, uncomfortable little Southern Italian restaurant, with little charm and less style. Yet Luna packs them in, and we eat there often. Why? We're not sure, but the cheap prices must have something to do with it. And the food is good, if simple. Lotsa garlic, lotsa noise. There is a sort of reverse mystique about Luna—one expects noise and rude service, and one is never disappointed. It adds to the strange appeal. The portions are large; the check will be small and you *will* enjoy it. Lunch and Dinner 12n–

12:30 A.M. Sun.–Thurs., 12n–1:30 A.M. Fri., Sat. No
credit cards.

Lundy's, Ocean Ave. and Edmund St., Sheepshead
Bay, Brooklyn, 332-3879. Temporarily closed;
Reopens summer 1982
This is a cavernous old family-run restaurant serving
excellent seafood out in the wilds of distant Brooklyn.
Located in the solidly middle-class Sheepshead Bay
district, Lundy's is a great spot to visit for an early
summer dinner—take a walk along the Brooklyn
boardwalk once you've stuffed yourself with fresh fish.
Prices are very reasonable, and Sheepshead Bay is easily
reached by subway. See a part of New York many don't
know exists.

Lutèce, 249 E. 50 St., 752-2225
Lutèce is generally considered to be the best restaurant
in North America. It serves superb French cuisine at
high prices and is usually solidly booked up a full
month in advance. (Hint: Sometimes you can make an
early reservation, and they will serve you if you promise
to vacate your seat by standard New York dinner
hour—i.e., approximately 8 P.M.) *Everything* is first
rate—it is silly even to discuss the particulars. Service is
very graceful and—important—not intimidating. Lutèce
wants you to *like* them; no elitist games are played here.
Prepare to spend at least $150 for dinner for two,
including wine and tip. Your money is well spent; go
hungry for a week or two if you have to. It's worth it.
Lunch 12n–2 P.M. Tues.–Fri. Dinner 6 P.M.–10 P.M.
Mon.–Sat. Closed Sun. Coat and tie. AE, CB, DC only.

Mme. Romaine de Lyon, 32 E. 61 St., 758-2422
A perfect restaurant in its strange way. Mme. Romaine
de Lyon serves nothing but omelettes—over 500
varieties! They are all inevitably first-rate, from the
classic plain omelette through a snazzy deluxe model
made with truffles. The price will depend on the
omelette you select—generally around $6 per. Open
luncheon hours—about 10:30 A.M. till about 3 in the
afternoon. Call first. The decor is charming, the service
hospitable and helpful. Dress. Bring cash.

Marchi's, 251 E. 31 St., 679-2494
Marchi's occupies the ground floors of three
brownstones on this lovely Murray Hill block. It's
perfect for people who don't like to make decisions;

there are none to be made. The Marchi family has been serving the same dinner every night (except Sundays) for over 50 years. Don't eat too much too soon, there is always more to come. The prix fixe (approximately $18) may seem expensive, but you get a five-course meal for it, antipasto and salads, melt in the mouth lasagna, beef, chicken, fish, a mountain of desserts and a bottomless cup of expresso. The only extra charges are for drinks. Dinner only 5 P.M.–10 P.M. Mon.–Fri., 5 P.M.–11 P.M. Sat. Closed Sunday. Jackets required, AE only.

Maxwell's Plum, 64 St. and First Ave., 628-2100
Maxwell's is, of course, *the* quintessential singles bar— as secure in its sterling position as Studio 54 is as the king of discos. It's a friendly, frantic, happy place, serving good food at all sorts of prices. Maxwell's Plum is one of the few places in town that one can get a good hamburger dinner for only about $5, as well as a full-course Continental meal for about $25, as well as everything in between. Good desserts, fabulous decor, singles action a little more subdued these days, but still a fair bet for the man or woman on the make. Lunch and Dinner 12n–12:20 A.M. Mon–Thurs., 12n–1:20 A.M. Fri., Sat. Sunday Brunch 11 A.M.–4:30 P.M., Dinner 4:30 P.M.–12m. All major credit cards.

Mon Paris, 111 E. 29 St., 683-4255
We think this is one of the best French restaurants in Manhattan. It's *not* cheap but is a bargain (approximately $20 for a complete dinner), considering the quality of the food you will be served—excellent French food at half the price of the *really* expensive places. Everything we have sampled here has been good. Two secrets: a splendid lobster bisque, and the best Grand Marnier soufflé you ever tasted, are *not* listed on the menu; the latter should be ordered at the same time as your meal. Fancy, but friendly—not stuffy about dress codes. Lunch 12–2:45 Mon.–Fri. Dinner 5 P.M.–10:30 P.M. Mon.–Sat. Closed Sun. AE, MasterCard, Visa.

Mortimer's, 1057 Lexington Ave., at 75 St., 861-2481
Another place to see and be seen—the jet set's spot for lunch or pre-disco dinner. The Continental food is all right but a tad overpriced. An excellent place, however, for after-dinner drinks—the pianist, who plays 11:30 P.M.–2:30 A.M. Tues.–Sat., can do twenty minutes of "A Train," and the drinks are not horrendously overpriced.

The social scene predominates, which is why it is better
for drinks; you never forget that you're on the East
Side. Worth it if Bianca Jagger and that crowd are your
fancy or you have a great affection for the East Side.
Lunch 12n–3:30 P.M. Mon.–Fri. Dinner 6 P.M.–12m 7
days. Brunch 12:15–4:30 Sat., Sun. Late Supper 12m–2
A.M. Tues.–Sat. All major credit cards.

Museum Café, 366 Columbus Ave., at 77 St.,
799-0150
A pleasant, relatively inexpensive restaurant on the
Columbus Avenue renaissance strip. Good burgers, fish
dishes, and some nice desserts are served. Very hip, in
the heavy-duty materialistic way of this area: watch the
world skate by listening to a Walkman as you nibble
your quiche. Service is good-natured if a little
inattentive. Lots of singles action—gay and straight. A
good place to be young and upwardly mobile. Lunch
and Dinner 11:30 A.M.–2 A.M. Sun.–Thurs., 11:30–3 A.M.
Fri., Sat. AE, MasterCard, Visa only.

Nirvana on Rooftop, 30 Central Park So., 752-0270
The best feature of this Indian-Pakistani restaurant is
the panoramic view from 15 floors above Central Park—
Fifth Ave., Central Park West, and beyond. It's
particularly romantic if your reservations coincide with
the sunset. The large menu offers traditional Indian
fare, but much of it is only average, excepting the
curries and some splendid appetizers (we love the onion
fritter). The various breads served are reason enough to
ignore even a serious culinary miscue. Prices are
moderate, they accept all major credit cards, and they
will accept a personal check with proper ID. Don't
forget to request a window table. Lunch and Dinner
12n–1 A.M. 7 days.

Nodeldini's Park East, 1311 Madison Ave., between
92 and 93 Sts., 369-5677

The Butterfish Hole, 1394 Third Ave., at 79 St.,
879-0991

The Cock-Eyed Clams, 1678 Third Ave., at 94 St.,
831-4121

Hobeau's, 963 First Ave., at 53 St., 421-2888

Four restaurants that share the same menu, same locale
(Upper East Side), and as far as we can tell, the same
chef. Nodeldini's, like the rest, serves good seafood at

absurdly reasonable prices. The simple stuff's the best, a grand swordfish preparation the standout, and the whole thing can be had (this is dinner, with salad *and* drinks), for around $10. This far up and this far east, there ain't much in terms of good eating spots in general, so the chain is a welcome addition. All locations Lunch, Brunch, and Dinner 11:30 A.M.–12m 7 days. No credit cards.

Odessa Restaurant, Inc., 117 Ave. A, between 7 & 8 Sts., 473-8916
This unassuming Ukrainian coffee shop on the far reaches of the East Village has become very popular. And with good reason. Where else can you get soup, main course (with *two* vegetables), dessert, and coffee for about $5? Granted, many may dismiss the fare as pure greasy spoon and others may feel squeamish traveling this far east (it is, after all, on the fringe of "alphabet city"—a neighborhood still too raw for some tender sensibilities), but those in the know will appreciate the delicious soups, pirogi (boiled or fried, with meat, cheese, or potato filling), and other Slavic dishes. This place can get steamy and hectic, with a crowd at the door waiting for tables, but the hassles are minor, especially as your budget can only benefit. Beer and wine are served. Open every day except Mon. 7 A.M.–11 P.M.

The Odeon, 145 Broadway, 233-0507
Certainly the classiest and best addition in the colonization of the Tribeca neighborhood. The decor is modern sterile, relieved by a charming old wooden bar. Nouvelle cuisine, finely prepared, and casual but attentive service make up for any chill in the atmosphere. Semipricey, and reservations are required. Lunch 12n–3 P.M. Mon.–Fri. Dinner 7 P.M.–12:30 A.M. Mon.–Sat., 7:30 P.M.–12:30 A.M. Sun. Brunch 12n–3:30 P.M. Sat.–Sun. Late Supper 1 A.M.–2:30 A.M. 7 days. AE, MasterCard, Visa.

Oh-Ho-So, 395 West Broadway, 966-6110
Soho's answer to the Chinese restaurant; fittingly, unlike any other in New York. The decor is all wooden, elegance à la California. The Cantonese cuisine we've had has been mild but tasty. Try the "angry drunken chicken" (sounds like a parody but tastes delicious) or the delicate lobster dishes, live from the tank. Prices are

higher than those at most Chinese spots but moderate
by Soho standards. Lunch and Dinner 12n–1 A.M. 7
days. AE only.

O'Neal's Baloon, 48 W. 63 St., 399-2353
O'Neal's serves a nice, inexpensive meal, so is a welcome
sight to those looking to eat in the Lincoln Center area
without spending a fortune. It's basically a hamburger
joint, with a few additional dishes available, such as fish
and chips or their famous chili. O'Neal's is often very
crowded until 8 P.M. (curtain time at Lincoln Center
across the street); after that one can do some leisurely
dining. Lunch and Dinner 11:30 A.M.–circa 12m
depending on the Lincoln Center schedule. 7 days. All
major credit cards.

One Fifth, 1 Fifth Ave., at 8 St., 260-3434
Another in the slew of fancy places where the
atmosphere and the time-honored sport of people-
watching take priority over intimate dining. One Fifth is
a popular hangout. Make reservations for weekend
dining. Service is somewhat snooty, but passable. We
like the atmosphere better than the food, which aspires
to more than it can deliver. Stick with the simpler
dishes. Lunch 12n–3 P.M. Mon.–Fri. Dinner 6 P.M.–12m
Sun.–Thurs., 6 P.M.–1:30 A.M. Sat. Jazz in Bar area 9:30
P.M.–2 A.M. 7 days. All major credit cards.

103 Second Avenue, at 6 St., 533-0769
Open 24 hours a day, seven days a week, this sleekly
decorated yet comfortable and casual bar and restaurant
attracts an interesting downtown clientele. A good place
to go for drinks before or after the clubs, 103 attracts a
slightly more upscale crowd than at Kiev, just up the
block. The menu is eclectic, ranging from eggs and
burgers to soup, salads, and specialty-of-the-day
entrées. The specials, which include salad, are generally
under $10, and sandwich and burger plates go for
around $5 or less. The quality, while almost always
good, has been known to be uneven, but the portions
are large and the desserts uniformly excellent. 103 is a
good place to go when one wants an alternative to the
usual heavy ethnic fare in the East Village. An excellent
place to hang out. No credit cards.

162 Spring Street, 401 W. Broadway, 431-7637
This has been a flourishing Soho restaurant since there
was a Soho, maybe even a little before. Back before the

artists invaded, when Spring was a grimy old factory street, this spot opened—a restaurant that everyone refers to as the "Spring Street Bar" or sometimes just "Spring Street." It's still one the the best restaurants in Soho, and the roast chicken is justly famous. Good desserts. Very trendy place; it has weathered Soho's shift from denim to punk to whatever the hell it's about now. Lots of artists, writers, *Soho News* staffers used to hang out here: your waiter may well be an aspiring rock star. Lunch and Dinner 12n–2 A.M. 7 days. AE, MasterCard, Visa only.

Oyster Bar and Restaurant, Grand Central Terminal Lower Level, 490-6650
The Oyster Bar is a magnificent structure, deep in the bowels of Grand Central Station. There has been a restaurant here since 1906, and, predictably, this is a huge, cavernous place with lots of hustle and bustle. Prices are a bit high for the quality of the food, which is only fair, but the simpler preparations are usually well made, and the lobsters are quality. The chowders are good, and one can order clams and oysters by the piece at the counter. Service is machine-like; you are *processed* rather than served: the Oyster Bar has an amazing turnover. Loud, rushed, hectic; a perfect introduction to New York. Come here after a train ride! Lunch and Dinner 11 A.M.–10 P.M. Mon.–Fri. Closed Sat., Sun. All major credit cards.

P. J. Clarke's, 915 Third Ave., at 55 St., 759-1650
Clarke's is the quintessential Irish/sports/political/ singles bar on the East Side—at the bar, look for your favorite football, baseball, or City Hall star bending an elbow; in the back room, look for them hashing out a book deal or borough policy over the very standard bar fare. Great burgers, good steaks, nice side dishes, and nearly every beer is on draft as well as by the bottle. Raucous, yes; glitzy, yes; overly expensive, not really—a great nonintimate place to talk intimately and look important. Dress the part. 11 A.M.–4 A.M. 7 days. No credit cards.

The Palm, 837 Second Ave., between 44 and 45 Sts. 687-2953; **Palm Too,** 840 Second Ave., 697-5198
The Palm offers the best steaks in Manhattan and—for a price—a magnificent, boat-like, 5-pound lobster that is one of New York's most decadent pleasures. But

there is more. This is a real city landmark, in the same spot for over 50 years (there is now a Palm Too to catch the spilloff from the original restaurant, right across the street). No reservations, no menu. The waiter recites what is available the day of your visit. Prices, especially for lobster, are high. Cartoons by many artists make up an offbeat mural on the walls. Fast-paced, loud, exciting. We love the onion rings. The Palm Too has the same food but somewhat less magic. A New York classic. Lunch and Dinner 12n–10:45 P.M. Mon.–Fri., 12n–11 P.M. Sat. Closed Sunday. All major credit cards.

Parioli Romanissimo, 1466 First Ave., at 76 St., 288-2391

Parioli Romanissimo is simply one of the best restaurants in America. It serves Northern Italian food at high prices in a charming and romantic atmosphere. You *must* make your reservations in advance, and gentlemen are required to wear coats and ties. The service is first-rate. Everything we have had here has been wonderful, but the veal dishes are particularly fine. Call ahead and request that the management reserve you a slice of their phenomenal chocolate cake. This is an expensive restaurant but one in which the patron never feels let down; you *do* get what you pay for. Their extensive wine list ranges from $20 to $4,000 a bottle. Dinner only 6 P.M.–11 P.M. Tues.–Sat. Closed Sun., Mon. AE, DC only.

Patsy's, 236 W. 56 St., 247-3491

Patsy's is a conservative, quality Southern Italian restaurant near Carnegie Hall. The decor has a remarkable fifties air to it—old clocks, etched glass, and so on. The pastas are terrific, perfectly done, and well seasoned. Since this is Southern Italian food, there is an emphasis on garlic, which suits us just fine. Prices are moderately high—this is midtown, after all—and men must wear coat and tie. However, Patsy's is not stuffy, and we've always found it a very friendly establishment. Recommended. Lunch and Dinner 12n–10:45 P.M. Sun., Tues.–Thurs., 12n–11:45 P.M. Fri., Sat. All major credit cards.

Phoenix Garden, 46–48 Bowery Arcade, 233-6017

One way to gauge the quality of a Chinese restaurant in Chinatown is to determine how many of the patrons live in the neighborhood. If the clientele is generally

Oriental, you have probably hit upon a good spot.
Phoenix Garden is a restaurant that some tourists know
about, but it seems to do most of its business with the
locals. Try the pepper and salty shrimp—not for those
on a low-sodium diet, but delicious. We love the hot and
sour soup. There may be some difficulty getting your
waiter to understand you. BYOB. 11:30 A.M.–10:30 P.M.
Tues.–Sun. Closed Mon. No credit cards. Inexpensive.

Piro's, 1302 Madison Ave., between 92 and 93 Sts.,
534-3016
This place is terribly eccentric, and those who like
Piro's love it, while others . . . We've always had good
meals here, once you get past the quirks of the house.
Each person at the table must order the same entrée,
making Piro's an unlikely spot for large groups.
However, almost every entrée we have had here has
been excellent, particularly the lemon chicken and the
shrimp provençale. Dinners are served with a wonderful
buttered pasta and a ricotta cheese turnover. Prices are
moderately high. The chef is a character and will often
come and introduce himself in the middle of your meal.
Try Piro's; if you like it, you may love it. Lunch 11:30
A.M.–2:30 P.M. Dinner 5:30 P.M.–11 P.M. 7 days. Jacket
and tie, AE only.

Poletti's, 2315 Broadway, at 84 st., 580-1200
The Upper West Side is still an area where really good
restaurants are hard to find, but Poletti's is a strong
addition. We have never been disappointed with the
food here, and at times have been quite excited by it.
Start with homemade spaghetti or fettuccine—you can
see the pasta being made through a glass window—and
continue with one of the excellent shrimp, chicken, or
veal dishes. Prices are a bit higher than your typical
West Side restaurant, but then it's a much better place
to eat. Dinner only 5 P.M.–11 P.M. 7 days. All major
credit cards.

Prince Street Bar, 125 Prince St., 228-8130
Located in the heart of Soho, the Prince Street Bar
serves okay hamburgers, good salads, and excellent
desserts, to name only three elements of a large and
ambitious menu. It's a very happening place, with lots
of young people discussing their writing, artwork, and
theatrical ambitions. Prices are quite inexpensive, and
an after-dinner walk through bustling Soho can put the

cap on a very enjoyable evening. Try the Indonesian
dishes for a change. Lunch and Dinner 12n–1 A.M. Sun.–
Thurs., 12n–2:30 A.M. Fri., Sat. No credit cards.

Ray's Pizza, 465 Sixth Ave., at 11 St., 243-2253
There are those who swear by Ray's Pizza—which now
has branches in several locations throughout the New
York area. Alas, we find it greasy and terribly overrated.
There is bread galore, cheese by the pound, and a
strange sort of pizza-sweat which oozes out with every
bite. It depends on what kind you like, which pizza
philosophy you subscribe to. We hold with the Johnists,
the Rayists be damned. In any event, it's a cheap lunch,
but you may be standing on line for quite a while.
Pizzas made by pie or slice. 11 A.M.–2 A.M. 7 days a
week. No credit of any kind.

The River Café, 1 Water St., Brooklyn, 522-5200
The food at the River Café is only so-so, but what the
hell. It's in such a spectacular location—at the foot of
the Brooklyn Bridge, with all Manhattan stretching out
in front of you—and is such a happy, pleasant place to
spend an evening that we have found ourselves taking
the short subway trip out to Brooklyn many times to
visit. Almost everything you order will be all right; little
will be much better. Stick with the standard stuff.
Maybe you'll just want a quick drink, but this view,
along with the irrepressible *joie de vivre,* is hard to
resist. Lunch 12n–2:30 P.M. Mon.–Sat. Dinner 7 P.M.–
11 P.M. 7 days. Sunday brunch 12n–3 P.M. AE, DC, CB
only.

Rocco, 181 Thompson St., 677-0590
Rocco is a decent, unpretentious Italian restaurant
located in the heart of the South Village. The food is
generally very good, and some of the chicken and veal
preparations quite a bit more than that. This is your
fabled candles-in-the-chianti-bottle, darkened, friendly,
inexpensive Village restaurant, celebrated in song and
story. Well worth a visit. Lunch and Dinner 12n–11:30
P.M. Mon.–Fri., 12n–12:30 A.M. Sat., 1 P.M.–11:30 P.M.
Sun. All major credit cards.

Ruelles, 321 Columbus Ave., at 75 St., 799-5100
One of *the* places for *the* West Side beautiful people.
The decor is a cross between antique and modern chic.
They serve dinner, drinks, and weekend brunch; don't
be surprised if the hostess chooses not to seat you for

drinks at some hours. The Continental menu is diverse, salads, seafood, and daily specials, but it all seems a little overpriced. Lunch and Dinner 11 A.M.–12m Sun–Thurs, 11 A.M.–1 A.M. Fri., Sat. All major credit cards.

The Russian Tea Room, 150 W. 57th St., 265-0947
The Russian Tea Room has gotten quite expensive of late, but it is still a very special place, and well worth the money. Long a hangout for people involved in the arts (Carnegie Hall is right next door, and West 57th St. contains a ghetto of music managers of all stripes), the Tea Room serves good, authentic old Russian food in a setting of Czarist splendor. Good brunches, many types of imported caviar, private-label vodka, and a festive air that never dissipates. Try the karski shashlik and borscht. Jackets required at dinner. Lunch and Dinner 11:30 A.M.–12:30 A.M. 7 days. All major credit cards.

Sardi's, 234 W. 44 St., 221-8440
The walls are covered with celebrity caricatures, and Broadway's stars are bound to have their pre- and post-theater meals at this famous spot. We give the food a solid B despite the sometimes excellent steaks. Prices are fairly high, but you never know who you'll be rubbing elbows with. Different menus are used for light suppers and complete dinners. Specials every day; the food is a melange of French/Continental/Italian/American, but the glitter is indefinable. Lunch, Dinner, and Supper 12n–12:30 A.M. 7 days. All major credit cards.

Scarola's, 1608 E. 19 St., Brooklyn, 645-7100
This family-run Southern Italian restaurant is well worth the subway ride to Brooklyn. Prices are reasonable, and the food is always quality. Call ahead for special productions of operas, directed and performed on a makeshift stage by Michael Scarola, Jr.—often surprisingly good, and always entertaining. The service is more than hospitable, and the food excellent—especially if you love garlic. Brooklyn is a world unto itself, and an after-dinner walk through this safe, heavily Italian neighborhood is a pleasure. Lunch and Dinner 12n–10:30 P.M. Sun., Tues.–Thurs., 12n–11:30 P.M. Fri., 12n–1 A.M. Sat. Closed Mon. Visa only.

Seeda Thai Restaurant, 204 W. 50 St., 586-4513
Within a few blocks of what is aptly a "seedy" neighborhood, there are several fine Thai

establishments. The cuisine is becoming very popular, and if you have never tried Thai food, Seeda is a good place to start. Most of the food is very spicy, but mild offerings are interesting and tasty. The dishes may look and sound similar to other Oriental cuisines, but Thai food has a special, indefinable kick all its own. Seeda is cheap, but don't loiter in the neighborhood after dinner. Life can be cheap. Lunch and Dinner 12n–10:30 P.M. Mon.–Fri. Dinner only 5 P.M.–10:30 P.M. Sat., Sun. All major credit cards.

Sloppy Louie's, 92 South St., 952-9657
Sloppy Louie's is a bustling seafood restaurant in the midst of the Fulton Fish Market neighborhood. It is open only on weekdays and closes at 8 P.M. Quite inexpensive (for a seafood restaurant), Sloppy Louie's has a pleasant ramshackle charm and is located in a seemingly crumbling old building. The simpler preparations (broiled or fried fish) are recommended over the more pretentious dishes. And the bouillabaisse! The fish is always fresh, and Sloppy Louie's is always loud, raucous, and fun. Everyone eats at communal picnic tables, so it may not be the best place for a quiet romantic dinner. No credit cards.

Soho Charcuterie, 195 Spring St., 226-3545; 3 E. 57 St., 832-1246
This spot (and its uptown branch) is divided into an actual charcuterie (a retail gourmet delicatessen) and the restaurant. The basis for the menu is what might be called "cuisine obscure," featuring rare specialties for the well-trained palate. The menu undergoes drastic changes every few months, but the pâtés remain terrific. The Soho Charcuterie was a pioneer in nouvelle cuisine and is very expensive. Reservations for lunch and dinner are required. Lunch 12n–3 P.M. Tues.–Sat. Dinner 6 P.M.–11 P.M. Tues.–Thurs., 6 P.M.–11:30 P.M. Fri., Sat. Sunday Brunch 11 A.M.–4:30 P.M. No dinner Sun. Closed Mon. AE, MasterCard, Visa, DC.

Spring Garden, 340 E. 86 St., 535-5009
This may be the best undiscovered Chinese restaurant in New York. Located on the Upper East Side, Spring Garden is a tiny place, owned and operated by a tight-knit family. Only fourteen people can sit and eat at a time, but Spring Garden also runs a take-out service. Good, spicy Szechuan fare is offered, and we

particularly like the diced chicken with dried red
pepper and hot and sour soup. This very reasonable
place is a real bargain on ritzy Uptown East. You don't
have to go to Chinatown to get good Chinese food.
Spring Garden is proof. Lunch and Dinner 12n–10:30
P.M. 7 days. No credit cards.

Tavern-on-the-Green, Central Park West and 67
St., 873-3200
It's almost worth the rather high prices to see the
multimillion-dollar decor. Some dishes we've had here
have been excellent, but others have been seriously
disappointing, so we'd have to say the food quality and
the service at Tavern is somewhat inconsistent. Which
is odd, because it is run by the same people who run
Maxwell's Plum. The atmosphere is lavish, almost
superhuman, and it may not be the best place for an
intimate dinner. The wine list is superb. The decor,
with its rococo splendor, is the main knockout. Lunch
12n–3:45 P.M. Mon.–Fri. Dinner 5:30 P.M.–12m, 7 days.
Brunch 10 A.M.–3:30 P.M. Sat., Sun. All major credit
cards.

Trattoria da Alfredo, 90 Bank St., 929-4400
Trattoria da Alfredo serves some of the best Italian food
in New York. It's a BYOB place (but a liquor store is
right next door), and very small; reservations are
required and best made a week in advance. When you
call, reserve a portion of *dacquoise* for dessert; if you
like rich mocha butter cream, you won't regret it. Prices
are quite moderate considering the quality of the food.
Lunch 12n–2 P.M. Mon., Wed.–Sat. Dinner 6 P.M.–10:30
P.M. Mon., Wed.–Sat., 5 P.M.–9:30 P.M. Sun. Closed Tues.
No credit cards.

Ukrainian Restaurant, 140 Second Ave., between 8
and 9 Sts., 533-6765
This features one of the best examples of the cuisine
found in the Eastern European neighborhood. The old
building, no sign out front to indicate a restaurant, is
the Ukrainian National Home. The atmosphere is okay
and the service is coffee shop style. Much of the food
may be too exotic for the unaccustomed palate, but old
standards exist, too—blintzes, borscht, kasha. Quite
inexpensive. Reservations required on weekends. Lunch
and Dinner 12n–11 P.M. Sun.–Thurs., 12n–12m Fri., Sat.
No credit cards.

1, 2, 3 (Café Un, Deux, Trois), 123 W. 44 St.,
354-4148
A good restaurant, specializing in pleasantly eccentric
Continental food, in a lousy neighborhood, which is all
the more reason for applauding its arrival. Until very
recently, theater-area restaurants were either old New
York standbys or cheap coffee places. This place is
streamlined, chic, hot. Prices are somewhat high, but
the food is decent stuff, the chicken dishes especially.
We recommend Un, Deux, Trois, particularly for pre-
theater dining. Call for reservations; a great many
people have adopted this place, for a great many good
reasons. Lunch 12n–3:30 P.M. Mon.–Sat. Dinner 5 P.M.–1
A.M. 7 days. Sunday Brunch 12:15 P.M.–4 P.M. AE,
MasterCard, Visa, DC.

V & T Pizzeria, 1024 Amsterdam Ave., between 110
and 111 Sts., 663-1708
This is a popular spot for Columbia University students
and serves very filling pizza, thick-crusted, coated with
cheese, and possessed of a fairly astonishing mass
density. Good if you're in the area and feel like pizza.
The rest of the entrées are less appetizing, and the
pasta is downright poor. But the pizza just might be the
best above 96th Street. Lunch and Dinner 11:30 A.M.–1
A.M. Tues.–Sun. Closed Mon. No credit of any kind.

Villa Pensa, 198 Grand St., 226-8830
Villa Pensa is an excellent, down-to-earth restaurant in
Little Italy. Everything is recommended, from the
hearty veal dishes to the fine chicken preparations.
Daily specials which, like the rest of the menu, are very
reasonable, especially at lunch. Service is never
unsmiling. Lunch and Dinner 12n–11 P.M. 6 days. Closed
Wed. All major credit cards.

Windows on the World, 1 World Trade Center,
938-1111
Windows is divided into two sections, the main
restaurant and the hor d'oeuverie/bar. The restaurant
serves fine Continental cuisine, à la carte or prix fixe,
and the view from the 107 floor makes the considerable
expense worth it. In the restaurant, you face north, and
the whole of Manhattan sparkles at your feet. At the
bar, look out over New York Harbor and Brooklyn.
Recite Whitman's "Crossing Brooklyn Ferry." Realize
your position in the Universe. Have another drink. All

this for a small cover charge; the view is *that* awesome.
Weekdays lunch is a private club. Dinner seatings
nightly (reservations, jacket and tie and no denim a
must) at 5 P.M., 5:30, 6, 6:30, 7, 8:30, 9:30, and 10 P.M.
Mon.–Sat. Buffet and Brunch seatings every half hour
from 12n–2:30 P.M. Sat., and from 12n–7 P.M. Sun. All
major credit cards.

   Ye Waverly Inn, 16 Bank St., 929-4377
The Waverly Inn serves good, if a little bland, American
food in a self-consciously Colonial context. It is located
in one of Greenwich Village's lovely old townhouses, and
there is something of another era to the Waverly.
Simple dishes are best—fried chicken, cobbler
desserts—and a bad meal is hard to come by. Full
dinners are still not very expensive, and the Inn is a
bargain by today's standards. A good place to take the
folks or out-of-towners who want the Olde Village
atmosphere but nothing *too* real. Lunch 11:45 A.M.–2
P.M., Mon.–Sat. Dinner 5:15 P.M.–10 P.M. Sun.–Thurs.,
5:15 P.M.–11 P.M. Fri., Sat. All major credit cards.

COFFEEHOUSES

There's something about the dark, smoky atmosphere of the coffeehouse that invites deep, probing conversations. In a coffeehouse, people read Sartre, write letters and poems, and discuss existentialism and Bergman films, as well as lighter subjects such as whether the Yankees will win the pennant this year. Most of all, the coffeehouse functions as a respite for the hurrying New Yorker to stop, lounge, and relax over a cup of cappuccino.

The Village has long been the mecca for coffeehouses. In the 1950s the original Café Figaro and Café Rienzi were the prime meeting places for beats like Allen Ginsberg, Jack Kerouac, Gregory Corso, and entourage. To this day MacDougal St. is to coffeehouses what 47th St. is to diamonds.

Caffè Reggio, 119 MacDougal, 475-9557, open for fifty-five years, epitomizes the dim atmosphere of a coffeehouse. Ersatz Renaissance paintings fill the walls, but years of cigarette smoke have made the portraits indecipherable. Now the patron has nowhere to stare except at his companions or within himself. Reggio serves as a haven for NYU students on a break, old Italian men who crave espresso, and lovers of the Paul Mazursky film *Next Stop, Greenwich Village,* which filmed several scenes there.

Anyone with European flair will journey to **Café Dante,** 79-81 MacDougal St. past Bleecker, 982-5275. Italian, German, and French émigrés are lured here by word-of-mouth, and come to revive their nationalistic

feelings. Cappuccino is strong and tangy, just the way
Europeans like it.

The new version of **Le Figaro Café,** at the crossroads
of MacDougal/Bleecker, 677-1100, is a throwback
to the heyday of the beatnik age. This two-tiered
establishment always draws a lively, chattering crowd,
with many tourists, show-goers, and people-gazers.

Other possibilities in the Village include **Café Sha
Sha,** 510 Hudson St., 242-3021, known for its private
outdoor garden; **Café Feenjon,** 117 MacDougal St.,
254-3630, where backgammon and chess are played; and
Bruno's Bakery on 506 LaGuardia Place, 982-5854,
which offers a view of a nearby Picasso sculpture.

Little Italy specializes in two kinds of coffeehouses:
Café Roma, 385 Broome St., 226-8413, representing the
old style, unpretentious, marble-floored coffeehouse,
and **Caffé Primavera,** 50 Spring St., 226-8421,
conveying the sleek, modernistic look with its large
plate glass windows, hanging plants, and nifty lighting
fixtures.

In Soho, the **Cupping Room Café,** 359 West
Broadway, near Broome, 925-2898, long frequented by
cappuccino lovers, has now added a liquor license and a
bar, so it's debatable whether the Cupping Room can be
considered a coffeehouse anymore. **Café Borgia II,** 161
Prince St., 677-1850, has a homey feel to it, and **Caffé
de Medici,** 475 West Broadway, off Houston St.,
982-7445, is a favorite haunt of gallery-goers.

Eastside, westside, uptown, downtown, coffeehouses
are everywhere. On the Upper West Side, **Café La
Fortuna,** 69 W. 71 St., 724-5846, is reminiscent of a
Florentine coffeehouse because of the piped-in opera
music, a favorite of the owners.

In the Gramercy Park environs, **La Continentale,** 30
St. and Second Ave., 685-7628, near several medical
complexes, is filled with hospital workers, and offers a
panoramic view of the Second Ave. passing scene.

On the Upper East Side, **Café Galleria,** First Ave.
and 76 St., 737-6238, which doubled its size by taking
over an adjacent store, creates an arty environment with
photographs of dancers and musicians on the wall.

In the ever-moving, frenetically paced, constant
energetic flow of Manhattan, the coffehouse says slow
down, enjoy, sit awhile, sip some cappuccino, relax, for
life is short.

DIM SUM

Dim sum, or Chinese lunch, usually consists of steamed or fried tidbits, accompanied by tea. Some of the items appear on other Chinese restaurant menus as appetizers, but in limited variety. Dim sum has no menu. It works something like a cafeteria, but in reverse. The server wheels a cart past each table, offering one or two specialties, and you may take as much as you'd like, or just wait to see what's on the next cart. The server will describe each dish and refill teapots. Since you select one dish at a time, and may choose to skip a few rounds, it is a leisurely meal—and a refreshing alternative to "brunch" foods. When you feel that you've had enough, the check is figured according to the number of plates left on your table.

Popular dim sum dishes include a variety of steamed and fried dumplings (filled with pork, shrimp, or vegetables), lotus leaves stuffed with fried rice (not unlike Greek dolmas), fried stuffed green peppers, steamed egg custard, and *much* more.

The restaurants listed here only offer this meal at lunch (and breakfast) times, most of them closing by 3:00 P.M. A few places also have separate dining rooms where standard Chinese cuisines, ordered from menus, are served. Anything named tea "parlor" or "house" is exclusively for dim sum.

Cam Fung, 20 Elizabeth St., 964-5256

Chun Cha Fu, 2450 Broadway, at 90 St., 362-2200
Serves dim sum on weekends only.

Foo Kai Tea Parlor, 68 Mott St., 226-6572

Hee Seung Fung (H.S.F.) Teahouse, 46 Bowery, 374-1319

Offers a somewhat limited selection and can get extremely crowded, but the dumplings are very good.

H.S.F., 578 Second Ave., near 32 St., 689-6969

Hong Gung, 30 Pell St., 571-0545

Kuan Sing Dumpling House, 9 Pell St., 349-0503

Does not have carts but features a Mandarin version of dim sum, ordered from a menu.

Nom Wah Tea Parlor, 13 Doyers St., 962-8650

Number One, 202 Canal St., 227-1080

The last two in this list are regarded by some as being the best dim sum restaurants in New York City.

EAT IT RAW
NEW YORK'S SUSHI OBSESSION

Sushi, Japanese for, basically, raw fish, seems to have evolved into the New York eating phenomena of the last year. Of course, for style-conscious New Yorkers, every year it's something else. There was the year of quiche, the year of spinach salad, the year of vegetable pastas. And supply in New York always meets demand, often exceeding it. Japanese restaurants are popping up in every neighborhood, east and west, quicker than you can say "Nikon." (And a lot quicker than you can learn how to use one.)

It was inevitable that sushi have its day. It's the best combination of both worlds—healthy and delicious. Yes, it does take some getting used to; after all, it is *raw,* and is often wrapped in slender slices of nori (seaweed) and dotted with sprightly Japanese mustard. A friend of mine seriously questions my voracious appetite for sushi: "The stuff looks like toys," she contends.

All these obstacles aside, sushi is pure protein, except for the ball of rice each piece is set on, which enhances its flavor and texture. Once the fish is dipped into soy flavored with some more of the green mustard, there are so many levels of taste exploding in your mouth you forget all about the raw and fish part of it.

Going out for sushi is a totally ambient experience, all the more reason it appeals to New Yorkers. The lighting in most Japanese restaurants is softened by rice paper, the music an Eastern tinkling of notes. The waiters and waitresses are often Japanese and highly polite. A couple of warm sakes enhance the environment and the taste buds.

One doesn't have to be a fish expert to enjoy the actual meal, but minimal acquaintance with the terminology is helpful. Tekkamaki (a bit of tuna rolled in rice and seaweed) and kappamaki (cucumber done up in the same fashion) are part of the sushi tray, as are usually a sushi of shrimp, one of tuna, squid, snapper, salmon, roe, crab leg, and a mysterious "sushi omelet" that's a lot like, you guessed it, an omelet on rice (and surprisingly yummy). In most Japanese restaurants, there's a regular sushi and a deluxe—the difference being price and selection. You're more likely to get the roe (caviar) and the crab leg on the deluxe order, which is also often accompanied by soup (clear or miso) and a small green salad.

Or, if you can forgo table service, sit at the sushi bar, where all the hard-core sushi fanatics can be found. There, you can order your sushis individually, making sure you get your favorites.

The following is a highly annotated list of fine Japanese restaurants where you can guarantee the sushi is fresh (of prime importance):

Starting in the Village, there's **Shima** (12 Waverly Pl., 674-1553), a charming place with some tables on platforms where you can sit Japanese style (shoes off, on mats, legs curled under the table). The prices here are pretty reasonable, and, if you like, you can forgo the rest of the sushi and have entire orders of tekkamaki or keppamaki. There's also a good special deal—a sushi dinner, with select fish, plus tempura appetizers, salad, and soup, for about $8 or $9. Often crowded.

Japonica, 90 University Pl., 243-7752, favored by a lot of downtown theatrical types, is also one of the area's most expensive Japanese restaurants. Sushi, without any of the accouterments, starts at about $9. With salad, soup, sake, you can't get away with less than $15 to $18 a person. However, it's also reported to be one of the best Japanese restaurants in the area. Certainly, the lovely haikus on the menus make it seem very special. Often *very* crowded.

New Tokyo, very nearby (100 University Pl., 924-6500) is larger than Japonica, airier, a bit less expensive, but for some reason not as popular. (It's newer.) If you can't get into Japonica, don't give up and go for pizza—come here. Or come here first.

Shoei, 28 W. 8 St., 228-6688, right in the heart of 8 St. (great shopping), is upstairs—you'll know you're there when you see the fake tempura in the glass case at street level. Don't let that put you off: Shoei has respectable (nonfake) sushi and is probably the best for the money ($6–$7 total) anywhere in the city.

Over in the East Village, **Mie** (196 Second Ave., at 12 St., 674-7060) is everybody's favorite, perhaps for the prices (moderate) or the food, which is always really good. There's always a wait. All the people in here, customers and staff, look as if they do something interesting on the side—and they probably do.

Uptown, on the West Side, **Sushiko,** 251 W. 55 St., 245-9315, has been packed ever since Mimi Sheraton, the *New York Times'* picayune food critic, praised it to the point of gushing, but it was probably crowded before that: It's near all the theaters and is one of the best restaurants in the city. Expensive, and worth it.

Take-Zushi, 101 W. 45 St., 391-1045, located near the Peppermint Lounge, the Savoy, and the theater district, is a brightly lit and popular sushi place, also good for lunch, as it is near Rockefeller Center.

Where can you go if you suddenly have a mad craving for sushi in the middle of the night? They don't carry it in your local all-nighter deli, and most Japanese restaurants close at the modest hour of 11 or 12. The Hotel Woodward, 210 W. 55 St., 586-0160, sports **Chin-Ya,** open until about 4 A.M., where supposedly all the musicians, night-owl celebs and dope-dealers go for their sushi fix. The restaurant itself looks a bit tacky and fluorescent, with cracked vinyl-covered chairs (if there were such a thing as "Japan Town," this would be the prototype), but the sushi is good although not terribly cheap (whadya want at that hour?), and the conversation is always a kick.

The best way to end a sushi meal, or, I should say, the only way (since most of these restaurants offer very few American desserts), is with green tea ice cream—unsweet, cool, and different; and yokan, a red bean cake, naturally sweet, with the consistency of jello and the taste of frozen yogurt.

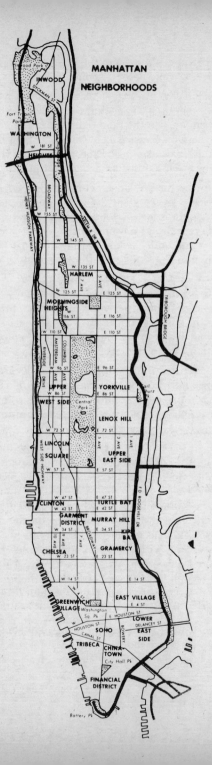

MANHATTAN

NEIGHBORHOODS

THE NEIGHBORHOODS

Downtown Life

I know a lot of people who are terrified of going above 14 St. And for just reasons. So comfortable are they in their downtown neighborhood's idiosyncrasies that the discovery of a steel cold bustling international metropolis at the other end of a subway ride might be permanently alienating.

Downtown is where uptowners go to look at art, performance, funky clothes, old movies, old bookstores, cafés, and weirdos. Downtown is where downtowners live because they wouldn't live without those things, and because they want the advantages of city life without the "cityness"—skyscrapers, views of skyscrapers, and the anonymity that high-rise blocks always tend to produce.

I've lived downtown, in the Village, for all my time in New York, and I'm absolutely vehement about it. Downtown and uptown folk in this city are nearly as polarized as New York and L.A. I walk to work every day, I gloat. My friends are all within an interesting walk's distance. And I've got six distinct different communities, almost like six different towns, all within relatively near reach. Of course, it's still city life— there's still trash, sirens, honking horns—but it seems more intimate than uptown life.

The West Village, possibly the most well known of these "towns," starts at 14 St. and is bordered to the east by Fifth Ave., to the south by Houston St. The

East Village is its funkier twin sister, who lives on the other side of Fifth Ave., also bordered on the south by Houston. Below Houston is Soho (hence its name— "South" of "Houston"), extending down to Canal St. Below Canal, you come on to Tribeca, the "Triangle Below Canal," which extends west to the Hudson River and is such a new neighborhood that I'm not quite sure what its other parameters are. To the east, from Prince St. on down to Wall, are the inimitable Little Italy and Chinatown.

The West Village is where I call home. I moved there in 1975 because I thought I couldn't move anywhere in the States that could look and feel more like Europe. It's got brownstones, cobblestone streets, old cafés, street singers, flea markets, fruit stands, and tree-lined blocks that attracted poets and artists *en masse* in the fifties. Some of the bars and coffeehouses were frequented by beats, and still have that aura around them, though *now* they don't attract much but tourists and students.

In the early sixties, the West Village became the fashionable home of eccentricity. Many of the stores were filled with Warhol-like soup cans, and long twisted-neck coke bottles. The smells of pot and incense wafted by on warm spring nights. Head shops were rampant. People drifted in on weekends to watch the hippies and weirdos, who sold the incense on the street and performed on junk guitars. Later in the sixties the head shops gave way to expensive mod boutiques, like Paraphernalia, and 8 St. (famous for shopping) became like Carnaby Street West. A strong gay community grew up to the extreme west, mostly because many of the gays were artists and designers, and because sexual eccentricities were more at home here.

Although fashions came and went, the aura of the literati and poets never left the Village. It was supposed to be a refuge for them, and it still probably has the best bookstores in the city and more poetry readings than anywhere else. When the West Village turned to music for refuge, it was to the folkies and troubadours of the Bob Dylan type. Folk City, 130 W. 3 St., 254-8449, which spawned all this, still gives podium to folksingers and poets.

By the early seventies the West Village was such a paradise for students, artists, and idiosyncratics that it

also became very attractive to the bourgeois. So
attractive that rents went sky high, the students were
forced to leave, the artists went South to Soho, and the
Village went commercial—the way, I suppose, of all
great neighborhoods started by artists.

Which takes us up to the present. The West Village is
highly commercial, in some ways more so than even the
Upper East Side. Eighth Street has more shoe stores
per square inch than any other street in the world.
There are still young people roaming about, mostly
NYU students, but the majority of them are the young
professionals who can afford its rents, restaurants, and
delis. The gay community thrives on, particularly
around Christopher St., but it's mostly a well-dressed,
working, gay community. On weekends, the whole area
is packed with unsuspecting tourists looking for what
hasn't lived here in years—imagination. But it's still
charming to look at, if you come from somewhere else.

The East Village really always had a lot more
character, mainly because it had a lot more characters,
funkier and poorer than their West Village
counterparts. Originally the home of the city's Polish
and Ukrainian populations, it became more "attractive"
as it caught more and more of the West Village spill.
Many of the hippies who poured into the city in the
early sixties came here because they couldn't afford to
live anywhere else.

Moreover, it was a flourishing drug capital, and the
play *Hair* was written from and about its streets. The
Fillmore East, where the Grateful Dead and other
bastions of hippiedom played, drew kids from all
corners of the earth, and a lot of them just stayed. The
rents for the tenement rooms were cheap, the
restaurants were small, dark, and cheap, and it didn't
matter that it was tough, ethnic, and basically kind of
dangerous. It was *cool*. (This is the spirit that spawned
punk, ten years later, out of the same grimy
neighborhood.)

Used to be, it was cool to live only as far east as
Second Ave. After that, the street gangs and crime were
too intimidating. Later, it stretched down to First Ave.,
where the fruit and vegetable stands stay open all night.
Now, there are students, actors, artists, and musicians,
punks and nonpunks, living all the way over to what
was formerly no-man's-land: Avenues A, B, and C (D is

still the outer limits). It's no longer cheap to live here, but it isn't impossibly expensive.

There are tons of stores here now, the famous Saint Marks Place housing everything from punk chic to retro chic to cheap chic. There are more restaurants. Some even of the West Village variety, and even that price range. And there is more than a leftover taste of punk defiance, which came out of local bands playing clubs like CBGB's and Max's in the late seventies. Punk was founded by English rebellious youth, but you would never have known that in the East Village. All forms of black Spandex costume and pastel hair colorings, chains, and safety pins found their way onto the street. Although the core of violence has disappeared from this look, you can still see leather-clad couples roaming the streets on the way to the all-night greasy spoon. The East Village isn't cheap any more, and it isn't really dangerous, although it might like to think so. But it's still cool.

Soho is a community whose time had come by the early seventies. The artists who'd come to live in the West Village to be surrounded by their peers found that their peers could no longer afford to live there. And neither could they. They needed space, to paint and sculpt and build, so they moved below Houston ("house-ton") St., into cast-iron factory buildings that became available for residence through zoning law changes.

They took down walls, put up walls, or learned to live in one gigantic nondivided space, with home-installed plumbing, and very large windows. A community was born. Soon there were some galleries to show the work in, some restaurants, a few boutiques. Nothing fancy. Just neighborhood.

Ten years later . . . Soho is now probably the artiest, most fashionable neighborhood in the world. Lofts are for luxury living. There are gourmet restaurants. There is a thriving gallery scene. The clothes stores are chic, offbeat, and pricey. Once again, the artists outwitted themselves by creating a neighborhood so attractive it forced them out. The community is still young, chock-full of artists and alternative spaces (where video, performance, film, and dance are shown), but these are the artists and spaces who are survivors, and are now an establishment (even if a young one) in their own right.

One thing led to the other, which led to the relatively new community of Tribeca. It used to be nowhere's-ville: an amorphous business area that paved the way to Wall St. Benefiting from the Soho spill, it's now *the* burgeoning neighborhood for artists, musicians, and conceptualists. The loft spaces are more rugged, and the restaurants less chi-chi, though not all. Places like the Odeon (see RESTAURANTS), a chic and expensive hangout for the successful of the art world represent the more affluent aspect of Tribeca.

Another thing about Tribeca is that its particular zoning allows for rock clubs, whereas Soho's doesn't. So there is a relatively thriving night life down here, accompanied by the old neighborhood bars—Puffy's, Prescott's, Mickey's. At any hour between midnight and 8 A.M., you can run into people, dressed in black, coming from a party or a club. They're probably on their way to the Market Diner, a real live truck stop open 24 hours. The Mudd Club, a bit past its punky heyday, still plays host to artists and scenemakers and local bands.

I should put in another word about Tribeca's restaurants. The oldest of them (about five years old), the Bread Shop (157 Duane St., 964-0524) and Riverrun (176 Franklin St., 966-3894), are good standards with attractive interiors that draw in the neighborhood crowd. Some of the newer ones, Capsouto Freres (451 Washington St., 966-4900) and Washington Street Café (433 Washington St., 925-5119), 211 (Franklin St. and West Broadway, 925-7202), and the Commissary are airy and chic, with special gourmet food, and attract young "sophisticated moderns" from all over the city.

In another couple of years, Tribeca could be the place to be. Who knows, it might begin to attract doctors and lawyers, and the artists would again be forced to move—to Hoboken?

Black Manhattan

Black Manhattan, which usually means Harlem, isn't what it used to be but it is far from down and out. Like many communities, it has suffered extensive urban blight. Still, there is much to do among the ruins and many places that are quite fine and fancy. The most famous street is, of course, 125 St., up and down which there is an incredible blare of contrasting styles and a range of vernacular accents that give the talk in crowds a great complexity. One hears an orchestra of speech as the people from the Islands, the Northeast, and the South swap tales, experiences, and dreams. It is easy to understand why the community was so long considered the capital of black America, and one can feel in the air the presence of history, for this was once the place where so many great minds and talents met, talked, and performed, where political visions often as moving as they were mad got shouted from street corner podiums, where musical revolutionaries like Louis Armstrong, Duke Ellington, and Charlie Parker lived and changed American art. And though Harlem is now a sleeping giant on the verge of great political power, it still possesses great vibrance and contains places where one can eat, do research, get guided tours, or just hang out.

The Baby Grand, at 319 W. 125 St. (864-8880), is near St. Nicholas. It's an old-fashioned black bar with a bit of elegance and a large back room with a stage on which jazz can now be heard on the weekends. **Your Bakery #2,** at 301 W. 125 St. (666-7340), is one of the better things left over from Elijah Muhammad's empire. Regardless of what one thought of the Black Muslims' politics, the quality of their baked goods was always beyond dispute, the specialty a delicious thing called a bean pie. **Sylvia's,** one of the very finest restaurants uptown, is located between 126 and 127 Sts. on Lenox Ave. (534-9414) and is open from 7:30 in the morning to 10:00 at night. Everything they have is good, from breakfast to dinner. A few blocks up on Lenox Ave. at 135 St. is the **Schomburg Center for Research in Black Culture** (862-4000). It is a fantastic collection of manuscripts memorabilia, papers, and materials on African and African-American culture. (By African-Americans, I mean people of African descent in the Western Hemisphere.) It offers a fine lecture series and tours of Harlem that focus on places of historical significance and the range of superior architecture within its borders. These can be arranged by calling the center and speaking to Lucy Eldridge. **Joe Thomas's Blue Book** (710 St. Nicholas, near 145 St., 694-9465) is a good bar with a fine atmosphere, and it offers music from Thursday through Sunday. It is much liked by musicians like Stanley Turrentine, George Benson, Irene

Reid, and Etta Jones, any one or all of whom might be heard jamming with the house band on a swinging night. Three restaurants I haven't been to but which were recommended by Thomas were **Wilson's Bakery and Restaurant** at 158 St. and Amsterdam Ave., **Three-Eyed Shrimp** at 118 St. and Amsterdam Ave., and **Copeland's** at 145 St. and Broadway. Adam Clayton Powell Blvd. (Seventh Ave.) has four hot corners at the intersection of 138 St., where there is good food and good music, plenty of variety in the buoyant characters one often encounters, and fair prices. On one corner is the **Red Rooster,** a bar and restaurant that offers music Thursday through Sunday (283-9252), with chitlins and champagne, an offering of particular interest on Wednesdays. Next to the Red Rooster is the **New Jock's,** a boisterous and joyful bar that was once the hangout of Adam Clayton Powell himself. Across the street is **Kenny's Lounge** (283-8005), a bar that offers music on Friday and Saturday nights by groups like Jack MacDuff and a jam session on Sunday evening. **Lickety Split,** catty corner from the Red Rooster, is a bar that is always dressed up like it's in the middle of a New Year's party. There are balloons and streamers hanging from the ceiling and the bands it hires are getting better and better.

And finally, if you happen to want to run around in Lower Manhattan and would like to get some down home cuisine, there's **Jack's Nest** at 310 Third Ave. (260-7110), near 23 St., or, in the West Village, there is the **Pink Teacup,** a few doors west of Seventh Ave. at 310 Bleecker (243-8117).

Latin New York

Not too long ago, when I lived in Pennsylvania, I came to New York on a work trip and stayed at a midtown hotel for a few days. When it came time to pay up, I had to wait in line while a guest unsuccesfully tried to argue his difference of opinion about the bill. This unfortunate blond, midwestern businessman was having a hell of a time arguing his case with the South American front desk clerk; the latter, whose English was correct but rudimentary, seemed unable (or was he?) to follow the guest's complicated reasonings, which had to do with seasonal rates, weekend versus weekday rates, single-double rates, special package deals, and so on.

The guest looked desolately around him for some help, but from whom? The entire hotel staff was Spanish-speaking, as were all the guests except for a handful of Asians. I felt the same urge to assist I had often felt when encountering lost Americans in Spanish-speaking countries or vice versa (more of a temptation to show off bilingualism than a true Samaritan spirit), but I remained aloof. A sense of having stepped into some kind of mutation of history—what else could I call this scene in which an American was a foreigner in his own country?—prevented me from interfering. New York, I realized, had become a Latin American city.

A *Panamerican* city. There's the large Puerto Rican community, by size alone the most important factor in New York's Latin life; Cubans and Dominicans, Carribean neighbors with identities of their own; and Colombians, whose culture bridges the very different Caribbean and Andean cultures. Plus, of course, there are Mexicans, Panamanians, Argentineans, Chileans, everything. But in order to identify many of New York's Latin Americans, it might make sense to realize that they are here for the same reasons as folk from Milan, Montana, or Tokyo: It's the trying ground for both the restless and the dispossessed.

This means that New York enjoys both a popular Latin American culture as rich as, and in some ways *richer* than, any Latin American city and a cultural life, in the more elitist sense of the word, that spans across national frontiers. You might not see a Fernando Botero exhibit at a 57 St. gallery, meet Manuel Puig at a reading from his latest novel at the Center for Inter-American Relations, hear Eddie Palmieri set a salsa club on fire, and make it to the opening of a Vanguardist Newyorican play in the same week. But, then again, you might.

Some of Latin New York is that part of the Latin American glamor intelligentsia that happens to be in New York at the time, rather than, say, Paris (or to look at it from a different perspective, that part of New York's glamor intelligentsia that happens to be Latin American). If your experience with Latin American culture includes celebrity watching, you already know what the players look like. In that case, seeing a famous

cinematographer at the movies or surprising a famous
novelist at lunch at a Cuban-Chinese restaurant holds a
thrill of its own. Otherwise, you can go to the openings,
readings, or other official functions in which it's always
possible, indeed desirable, to meet the famous person.
The best place to find out who's where at any given
time is the **Center for Inter-American Relations,** 689
Park Ave., 249-8950, which houses a fine gallery and
sponsors a series of readings by important Latin
American authors.

The last few years have seen a minor boom in the
New York Latin stage, with a number of established
houses offering full seasons of professional theater,
much of it in English. **The Spanish Theater**
Repertory Co., 138 E. 27 St., 889-2850 specializes in
the classics: 17th-century Spanish drama, Lorca, major
Latin American playwrights, *zarzuela* (Spanish
operetta). By contrast, **Intar,** 420 W. 42 St., 695-6134, is
boldly experimental. And the **Puerto Rican Traveling**
Theater, run by its founder, actress Miriam Colón,
presents a mix of the Latin American repertoire and
works by new writers at its new house at 304 W. 47 St.,
354-1293.

If you're museum-hopping along 5th Avenue you
should keep walking uptown to **El Museo del Barrio,**
1230 Fifth Ave., 831-7272, for exhibits of Latin
American art. And if you're doing the Soho gallery
scene, **Cayman Gallery,** 381 W. Broadway, 966-6699,
offers more of the same. For dance performances call
the **Puerto Rican Dance Theater,** 215 W. 76 St., 724-
1195, and the **Ballet Hispanico of New York,** 167 W.
89 St., 362-6710, for their schedules.

Of course, to many, Latin New York means New York
Latin music, salsa. Salsa is Cuban in origin—a
reworking of old Cuban dance music of the forties and
fifties—but it's the New York Puerto Rican musicians
that have given it its current shape. Most major salsa
acts work in New York; all of them wind up here
sometime in the course of the year. **Victor's Café** at
236 W. 52nd St., 586-7714, and **Asia Numero Uno,** 920
Eighth Ave., 246-9151, are favorite eateries of the Latin
music industry. But the best place to see Latin
musicians, obviously, is at a salsa club, like the famous
Corso, 205 E. 86 St., 534-4964 or the funkier **Casino**
14, 60 E. 14 St., 475-9270.

If you're heavily into the music (or would like to be), two places are a must: **The Village Gate** at Bleecker and Thompson Sts., 475-5120, where two top salsa bands and a guest jazz musician keep a mixed crowd of Latins and Anglos at the edge of ecstasy every Monday night. And **Soundscape,** 500 W. 52 St., 581-5893, for Latin jazz jams on Tuesday and Wednesday nights, often with the participation of recently arrived Cuban musicians, who have made Soundscape their home.

There are Latin music concerts throughout the year from performances in alternative spaces to big shows at Madison Square Garden. Pick up a copy of *Latin New York* at the newsstands for information.

Although there are big salsa concerts all year round, there is one monster merengue concert at Radio City Music Hall that should not be missed if you're lucky to be in the city for the day of Dominican independence, February 28. It's a patriotic feast, so the songs chosen for the concert are often nationalistic. (They're still a bit pissed off about the marines and all that.) All the top merengue bands from the Dominican Republic are there to play some of the world's most infectious music.

Of course, the world's most infectious music is Brazilian samba. Experience carnival in Rio by flying there for Mardi Gras or, if you're in New York around the end of February, go to the carnival sponsored by the **Brazilian Promotion Center,** 37 W. 46 St., 719-4025. It's a mad maelstrom of nonstop dancing at the Waldorf-Astoria, and guests daring enough to wear nothing but a *tanga* (string bikini) can leave their clothes at the coat check.

If all that sambaing has whetted your appetite for rice and beans, lunch (or dine) the next day at **Cabana Carioca,** 123 W. 45 St., 581-8088. Run by Portuguese, it's a favorite of New York's Brazilian community. Most generous portions (of any kind of food) in town, and their rice and beans are without parallel.

The most evident Latin food in Manhattan is Cuban, particularly at the ever-present Cuban-Chinese restaurants. The Chinese ran modest restaurants in Cuba that served traditional Caribbean dishes to a down-home clientele not given to experimenting with things foreign. As part of the Cuban migration, these restaurateurs found themselves in a city that loved

Chinese food and that had a large Hispano-Caribbean population that ate nothing but creole food, thus comidas chinas y criollas. Asia Numero Uno, mentioned above, is a big comfortable place with good fare of this kind.

Actually, the creole cuisines of Cuba, Puerto Rico, and the Dominican Republic are best sampled in private homes, so if you have Latin friends, get yourself invited to dinner. Second best is eating out. For Cuban food, try the above; for Puerto Rican, **Ponce de Leon,** 171 E. 116 St., 348-5580, in the heart of the barrio, enjoys a good reputation; and for Dominican, those in the know swear by **El Deportivo,** 168 St. and Amsterdam Ave., 781-4234.

Two cosmopolitan favorites are the above-mentioned Victor's Café (I prefer the Latin showbiz glitter of the 52 St. locale to the Upper West Side bourgeois respectability of the Columbus Ave. one) and **Sabor,** 20 Cornelia St., 243-9579, a chic little New York restaurant that serves food of Caribbean extraction and delicious drinks.

Oh yes, almost anywhere in New York, you're never too far from some kind of authentic Latin café (most of the humble eateries are such) where you can enjoy a cup of ... *café;* black or with steamed milk, it's espresso and cappuccino without the coffeehouse hype and at the price of an honest cup of java. Go in and have a cup while you ponder your next move in Latin New York.

Manhattan Districts

Beyond neighborhoods, Manhattan is divided into very specific districts. Every neighborhood has a name, and some of these areas center around a cultural or industrial theme. New York has representatives of every nationality; some live in highly integrated sections of town, others in very closed communities. Manufacturers of some products distribute and retail—almost exclusively—within a few blocks. General location doesn't seem to influence competition for these industries; it provides comparison shopping within walking distance for the consumer. Here's a list of some of New York's well-defined neighborhoods:

Books

Bookstores are in all neighborhoods, but there are two districts in particular that have the greatest concentration, because many printers operate nearby: Fifth Ave. between 13 and 21 Sts., and 4th Ave. (Park Avenue, south of Union Square) and its vicinity between 10 and 14 Sts. Establishments here offer the widest selection of rare or out-of-print books, and the lowest prices in the city.

Canal St.

Canal Street between Lafayette St. and Hudson is a bargain hunter's dream (or nightmare) come true. Much of what's for sale is junk—but useful junk. Bins on the street and seedy stores offer merchandise for next to nothing. Items you might find on Canal St. are: hardware (not just old hammers but old nails, too), paint supplies, housewares, discounted cleaning supplies, combs, handkerchiefs, blue jeans, old appliances, picture frames, and bits and pieces of almost anything. It's best not to go with specific items in mind, because you never know what you'll find. One person's junk is another's treasure.

Chinatown

Soooo many Chinese restaurants . . . you wouldn't believe it! Gift stores sell imports, from cheap trinkets to *cloisonné* and jade; the prices can be quite reasonable, since some of the finer wares sell uptown for twice Chinatown's prices. Markets offer the ingredients for any Chinese dish—herbs, noodles, fresh produce, seafood, even roast ducks with the head and feet (considered the ultimate delicacy) still attached. Be conscientious while shopping, for both price and quality. Wander New York's only blocks with bilingual street signs. Chinatown's boundaries are Canal Street, Centre Street, East Broadway, and Worth Street, with a few places spilling over beyond those streets. (Chinese holidays: see "Annual New York," page 219.)

City Hall Area

This area offers some discount shopping on Chambers

St. and Church St., but Municipal New York is worth a self-conducted walking tour, because it is the most important architecturally and historically. On such a walk you might want to include City Hall itself, which dates from 1811 and is located at Broadway and Murray St.; the Municipal Building (1913), Centre St., straddling Chambers St.; Criminal Court (1872), 52 Chambers St.; The Potter Building (1883), Park Row and Beekman St.; Park Row Building (1899), 15 Park Row; Woolworth Building (1913), 233 Broadway between Barclay St. and Park Place; St. Peter's Church (1840), at 22 Barclay St.; County Courthouse (1927), 60 Centre St., which is across the street from the U.S. Courts (1936). One highlight is St. Paul's Chapel (1766), bounded by Broadway, Church, Vesey, and Fulton. It's the only pre-Revolutionary War church still standing in New York.

Jewelry

Diamonds and other fine jewelry can be found in the Diamond District, 47 St. between Fifth and Sixth Aves. Retail jewelers line both sides of this street, including an arcade connecting with 48 St. in the middle of the block. Upstairs from these shops, nearly every floor of the buildings houses private diamond and gem brokers—usually seen by appointment. The southwest corner of 47 St. is the International Jewelers' Exchange, the best place to shop if you know what you're looking for and can recognize quality. The Exchange has independently rented booths, many carrying the same merchandise—comparison shopping under one roof— and you may be quoted different prices. Precious metals are usually sold by weight multiplied by current market value. If you're serious about buying or selling, check the newspaper's financial page for current commodities prices.

East Village

New York has a neighborhood for just about every ethnic group, and the Eastern Europeans are no exception. E. 7 St, between Second and Third Aves., as well as a surrounding portion of Second Ave., is almost exclusively Ukrainian. Several places on E. 7 feature

Ukrainian gifts, books, and crafts. At 203 Second Ave.
there's the Ukrainian Museum (228-0110), which
presents folk art. Ukrainian Gift Store: 145 Second Ave.
(254-0888); Ukrainian Restaurant, 140 Second Ave.
(533-6765) and more . . . The East Village neighborhood
is an interesting cultural mix. St. Marks Place is
dominated by the rock 'n' roll scene—*the* place for wild
and vintage clothing. East 6 St., between First and
Second Aves., has at least ten Indian restaurants, next-
door to each other, on the south side of the block. It's a
surprising find; prices are comparatively inexpensive.
One place we tried, Mitali, 334 E. 6 St. (533-2508),
rivals any of the uptown Indian restaurants. (See also
"Downtown Life, page 61.)

Financial District/Wall Street

Unless you need to see your broker, the best reason to
see this part of town is for its history and architecture.
The New York Stock Exchange, obviously a major
attraction, holds guided tours for visitors (for
information call 623-5167). The building itself, at 8
Broad St., was constructed in 1903. Federal Hall (1842)
marks the site where George Washington took his oath
of office, 28 Wall St. Citibank, formerly the Merchant's
Exchange, 55 Wall St., was also built in 1842. Since
1699, a Trinity Church has been located at Broadway
and Wall St. The original burned down in 1776, and the
one standing today was completed in 1846. The
graveyard still has tombstones dating from the 1700s. A
more modern building downtown is the Chase
Manhattan Plaza (1961) at Pine and William Sts. The
rectory of Our Lady of the Rosary (1793–1806), 7 State
St., between Pearl and Whitehall, was originally a
private home. The 26 Broadway building (1924) faces
the Custom House (1907) at Bowling Green. The 77
Water St. building (1970) has perhaps the most amusing
lobby in the city. We'll let you discover it for yourself.

The Flower District

Sixth Ave. between 26 and 30 Sts.—and on those streets
between Sixth and Seventh Aves. This is the wholesale
and retail center for all manner of houseplants, trees,
cut flowers, and artificial foliage (plastic, dried, and

fabric). These stores also sell the clay, vases, planters, bulbs, seeds, soil, lighting, and all accessories for plant care and arrangement.

The Fulton Fish Market

Where Fulton St. meets the East River, the source for all seafood in the city. Their retail store is at 18 Fulton St. (952-9658). Featuring maritime art and artifacts, the South Street Seaport Museum, at 16 Fulton St. (766-9020), is open daily from 11 to 5. There are guided tours of historic ships, and indoor shops selling sea-related books, gifts, and model ships. As you might imagine, the seafood restaurants in the area are good (see listings for Sweet's and Sloppy Louie's in the restaurant section). Fishing supplies can be purchased at Fulton Supply Co., 199 Front St. (267-4642).

Furniture

The retail and wholesale furniture district is bounded by Madison and Lexington Aves., 26 to 35 Sts. Prices *should* be lower than at department stores, but at least you're guaranteed the largest selection here. Besides stores offering individual lines of brass, plastic, rattan, or wood merchandise, there are a few co-ops carrying different lines—not unlike the Jeweler's Exchange. A few of these places are The Exchange, Lexington Ave. between 32 and 33 Sts.; National Furniture Showrooms, 115 E. 29 St.; and New York Furniture Center, 41 E. 31 St.

The Garment District

Primarily wholesale distributors and showrooms. It's located between Sixth and Seventh Aves. in the 30s; very few places sell retail. The district where fur garments are manufactured, wholesaled, *and* retailed is on Seventh Ave. between 27 and 30 Sts. There are close to a hundred furriers in these few blocks, and it's the least expensive place for buying fur.

Little India

Centers on Lexington Ave., between 26 and 30 Sts.

Several spice emporiums are the best in the city to buy curry ingredients and anything else needed to prepare Indian food. Import giftshops offer records, brassware, and jewelry. There are a couple of "fast-food" Indian places (not really recommended) and some very good restaurants in this area. Beautiful saris are sold at some stores, and you're likely to see the neighborhood women dressed in them.

Little Italy

Divided into two sections; one is in the vicinity of Sullivan and Thompson Sts., from West 4 to Spring St. This section has several good Italian restaurants. The larger area called Little Italy is bordered by Houston, Canal, Baxter, and Elizabeth Sts. Here you'll find stores selling the finest Italian cheeses, fresh pasta—any Italian food. Some merchants sell Italian recordings, imported trinkets, and religious articles. Shock your friends with a Mussolini T-Shirt. Pastry shops are terrific. The restaurants—delicate Northern and hearty Southern Italian cuisines—range from very inexpensive to quite costly (see "Restaurants," page 27). One note of caution: The immediate neighborhood is extremely safe, but don't get overly curious at some door marked "Private Club."

Lower East Side

Generally bordered by Houston, Bowery, the East River, and Manhattan Bridge. We recommend staying within a rectangle formed by Houston, Bowery, Essex, and Canal Sts. This is the old Jewish immigrant section of New York. Orchard St., is the best spot for bargain hunting. The entire spectrum of clothing (designer fashion to the dime-store variety), leather goods, textiles, sporting goods, and *kitsch* are for sale—nearly every building houses a discount retailer. Some merchants can be bartered with, others are very firm on their prices. It's worth the time and effort if you're looking for great values. Several good kosher delicatessens and dairy restaurants in the area—nearly every place is open on Sundays, all are closed Saturday.

Madison Avenue

Madison between 57 and 86 Sts., represents two
districts: the uptown galleries (and best auction houses)
and the exclusive designer boutiques. When Madison
Ave. is called the advertising capital of the country, the
area referred to centers on East 42 St.

Museum Row

Several museums are located elsewhere in the city, but
Fifth Ave. between 103 St. (Museum of the City of New
York, 534-1672) and 70 St. (The Frick Collection, 1 East
70th, 288-0700) includes the most—Metropolitan (5th
Ave. at 82nd, 535-7710), Guggenheim (5th Ave. & 89,
860-1313), Cooper-Hewitt (2 E. 91 St., 860-6898), to
name a few.

Musical Equipment

Popular instruments, amps, sheet music, and repairs are
available at a number of stores—the majority of which
are on West 48 St., between Sixth and Seventh Aves.
Classical instrument, music, and repair shops are
primarily found on 56 and 57 Sts. between Sixth and
Seventh Aves.

Photographic Supplies

The district specializing in cameras, film, developing
equipment, and so on, is an area bounded by Broadway
and Seventh Ave., from 30 to 35 Sts.

Pornography

Broadway, Seventh and Eighth Ave., from 42 to 50 Sts.,
including 42 St. between Sixth and Eighth Aves. This is
certainly *not* the safest neighborhood in town, but if
you must, you must. Although many "All-Male Revues"
are interspersed, the emphasis here is on heterosexual
peep shows, adult bookstores, porn movie theaters, and
what's billed as "live sex acts on stage." The peep show
quarters run out too quickly and the shows never live
up to the provocative posters outside. Some of the

topless and go-go bars aren't sleazy at all, but these places usually require admission, cover charge, and a minimum. You'll be drink-hustled at any of these places. Ladies-of-the-evening and drug dealers (in this neighborhood odds are you'll pay for oregano or sugar) can be found on the sidewalks. Since the area surrounds the theater district, it's easy to see how some Broadway-going tourists start rumors about Big Bad New York. Be careful.

Restaurant Row

Named simply because of the number of restaurants on the block. Located on W. 46 St. between Eighth and Ninth Aves., these restaurants range from relatively inexpensive to very expensive and are a short walk to Broadway theaters.

Theater District

This refers to the Broadway theaters; they're on 43 through 53 Sts., between Broadway and Eighth Ave. These magnificent old buildings house America's most popular plays and musicals. Consult newspaper listings for what's playing where. Black Mondays; Saturday and Wednesday matinees are standard. Tickets available at individual box offices, or stand in line at TKTS, Broadway and 47 St. (354-5800) and try for half-price admission. Keep in mind that the restaurants on these immediate blocks *play* to the tourist. (See also "The Performing Arts," page 122.)

Yorkville

The German section of New York is located roughly from 82 to 88 Sts., Lexington to First Aves., with 86 St. being the area's main street. Bremen House, 220 E. 86 St. imports cookware, gourmet foods, giftware, cosmetics, books, and records from Germany. There are German coffeehouses, bakeries, and restaurants. Try Café Geiger, 206 E. 86 St. (734-4428); Bavarian Inn, 232 E. 86 St. (650-1056); or Shaffers, 1202 Lexington Ave. (650-9492). Many of the neighborhood merchants speak German; the newsstands on 86 St. sell German-language newspapers and magazines.

SHOPPING

Bookstores

Perhaps because of the publishing houses, the theater, the fact that New York is the cultural center of the world, no matter what the reason, New York has the most complete and best-stocked bookstores of any city in America and some of the best commercial finds this side of a suburban garage sale. The following are the most notable bookstores in Manhattan and the reasons for their fame—or notoriety:

B. Dalton Booksellers, 666 Fifth Ave., 247-1740 The flagship store of the nationwide chain, the Fifth Avenue Daltons is *big,* with three floors and sections on nearly everything you could want to find. The lower level is also notable for its remainders. Other Manhattan locations for Daltons are at Lexington and 42 (in the Hyatt Hotel) and 6 Ave. and 8 St. in Greenwich Village.

Barnes and Noble Bookstores, headquarters at 105 Fifth Ave., 255-8100 This is a major bookstore with branches all over town and new ones cropping up all the time. Barnes and Noble bought out the late, lamented Marboro Books locations but do not, despite being "the largest bookselling complex in the world" do as well in stocking remainders or books of less than general interest. You won't, however, ever pay full price for anything. This is particularly nice when purchasing their justly famous discount bestsellers. If it's reasonably popular used textbooks or general reading at the main location, or popular books and remainders at any of the other locations (Rockefeller Center, Penn Plaza, Penn Station, 57 St. and Seventh Ave., Times Square, or 59 St. and Third Ave.), and you don't mind a little looking about, what you want is probably *somewhere*.

Books and Co., 939 Madison Ave., 737-1450
If you want a current bestseller, or a current trendy book with the author's signature in it, this is the place to go. Specializing in "quality" books of fiction and nonfiction, there isn't a more chi-chi bookstore in town. Smaller range of titles but good sales help—*if* you're not looking for Mickey Spillane.

Brentano's, 586 Fifth Ave., 757-8600
Three floors of delight, including rare books and very complete selections of any subject they choose to stock. The basement has the best paperback selection in town, recently expanded to include even more of the best.

Coliseum Books, 771 Broadway, 757-8382
Columbus Circle's best spot to waste an hour or two. Good remainder stock, excellent paperback selection, and tremendously well organized floor arrangement. Academic books take up the basement of this always interesting store.

Doubleday Bookshops, headquarters at 673 Fifth Ave., 953-4805
Though the "main" store's two floors are nice, the 57 St. location (724 Fifth Ave., 397-0550)—recently remodeled to include four floors of books (very well stocked with an excellent selection of nearly anything in print), records, maps, and deluxe editions (second floor)—is the preferred browse. Good all-round store, and the chain is no slouch, either. Other locations at 777 Third Ave., Citicorp Center, and 80 Broad St.

Gotham Book Mart, 41 W. 47 St., 757-0367
What Books and Co. wants to be; a very literary bookstore, good new, used, remainder, and small-press selection. Notable for stocking complete-works sets and extensive biography choices for even the most recent authors. Also a first-edition and rare-book section.

Harper & Row Bookstore, 10 E. 53 St., 593-7065
Across from Rand McNally's map store, located in the

Harper & Row building, it is a cinch to find Harper & Row titles, of whatever vintage, in this store. Selections of other publishing houses Harper & Row distributes are included as well. Best for books of current interest.

McGraw-Hill Bookstore, 1221 Ave. of the Americas, 997-4100
Specializing in professional and business-oriented works, it is still a good all-round bookstore and at its best with obscure technical and professional journals and texts.

Marloff Paperback Corner, 10 Sheridan Square, 924-5864
Paperbacks and periodicals are this store's strong points, although remainders and other clothbound books can be found. A good browsing spot, particularly in the sci-fi and mystery sections.

Naseralishah Bookshop, 240 W. 72 St., 873-0670
Good general literary and arts bookstore notable for its paperback racks, it also doubles as a specialty shop for titles on Eastern thought and the occult.

National Bookstore, 15 Astor Pl. and 725 Broadway, 475-4946
The Astor Pl. location of this New York University area tandem is the more scholarly, while the Broadway half is devoted to paperbacks, but both have that good old academia orientation that enables one to find the standard works on any subject without too much trouble. Lots of university press and small-press offerings.

New Morning, 169 Spring St., 966-2993
Perhaps the most self-consciously hip store in the city, New Morning is a paperback haven for the chronicles of life that led to Soho, the location of the shop. A must for hip historians of the modern age and those addicted to periodicals and comics about how we live now.

New Yorker Bookshop, 250 W. 89 St., 799-2050
Another great browse on the Upper West Side, the New Yorker lets you climb the stairway to paradise in the form of a 20 percent discount on all hardcovers over $5. Good paperback, political, arts, and literature stock and the most progressive children's book section in town.

Rizzoli International Bookstore, 712 Fifth Ave., 397-3700
A large, beautiful store justly renowned for its art and

foreign language selection. Emphasis is on European works and Western culture in general. A more pleasant and classier bookstore cannot be found anywhere.

St. Marks Bookshop, 13 St. Marks Pl., 260-7853
Straight to you from the East Village, the alternative bookstore granddaddy. Almost nothing of general interest but plenty of every alternative to it. Small presses, Eastern thought, drugs, occult topics, and alternative arts. For the Marxist mystic acidhead homosexual who does conceptual art/dance/theater/video/music. Or anybody that wants to find out more about that person.

Scribner Bookstore, 597 Fifth Ave., 486-4070
Books of all publishers and a fine general-interest and current-release store with good sales help who know what is and isn't there. Good all-round selection and a woody, genteel browse at midday.

Walden Bookstore, 57 Broadway, 269-1139
This New York flagship of the national chain has a very well-stocked business section.

Specialty Mentions

Astor Place Magazine and Bookshop, 80 E. 11 St., 260-2650
Can't live without that old issue of *Esquire* you remember changing your life in the 1940s? This is a good place to look—back issue mags of all kinds, some going as far back as the 1800s.

Back Issues, 960 Eighth Ave., 757-3959
More 20th century than Astor Pl., specializing in the popular periodicals of general interest.

The Ballet Shop, 1887 Broadway, 581-7990
Everything in print and much of the out-of-print stuff about dance, opera, and the music that accompanies them. Some rare books.

Cinemabilia, 10 W. 13 St., 989-8519
Screenplays, movie stills, posters; it has what you want in terms of both serious and frivolous movie mania.

Cityana, 16 E. 53 St., 752-2079
What Cinemabilia is to movies, Cityana is to New York City. Prints, *New Yorker* covers, and books about the Big Apple; sort of New York Hip through the ages.

Drama Bookshop, 150 W. 52 St., fifth floor, 582-1037

If you have a passion for theater in the form of playscripts, technical manuals, or acting texts, the Drama Bookshop can supply those as well as books on all other aspects of performing arts. Make sure to remember that it's not on ground level.

Eeyore's Books for Children, 2252 Broadway, 362-0634

A bookstore for children's books and books about children for adults. Specialists in child development staff the store.

Flying Saucer News, 359 W. 45 St., 582-6380

Self-explanatory. Also general occult books and self-help.

Jaap Reitman, 167 Spring St., 966-7044

Art in all its varieties is chronicled then stocked at Reitman's. Good for the more technical aspects of art, photography, etc., as well as art history.

Metropolitan Bookstore, 38 E. 23 St., 254-8609

Art literature at a 20 percent discount, remainders, and out-of-print books, including complete sets of important critical and instructive works of the past. Also a nice general section.

Oceanic Primitive Arts, 88 E. 10 St., 982-8060

Bookstore and gallery of primitive art and the accompanying anthropological works that explain it, including the out-of-print and rare volumes on this subject.

Old Friends, 202 E. 31 St., 532-8234

Disneyana, Walt and Mickey and Donald, Goofy, just anything and everything about our old friends from the Disney Studios. Why? Because you like them.

Joseph Patelson Music House, 160 W. 56 St., 582-5840

Music scores, music criticism, biographies of important composers and musicians, all at a 15 percent discount, make Patelson's, located in back of Carnegie Hall, *the* headquarters for serious musicians and amateurs in the know.

Quinion Books, 541 Hudson St., 989-6130

Run by someone in love with cooking and theater, Quinion stocks every major British and American playscript and cookbooks from all over the world. Related subjects (acting, wine, history, and biography) are also carried. For the actor who dreams of playing James Beard.

The Science Fiction Shop, 56 Eighth Ave., 741-0270 Nothing but sci-fi fantasy and works related to or about it. New, used, and remaindered titles as well as posters and records.

Village Comic Art Shop, 319 Sixth Ave., 255-8868 New, backlist, rare, collectible, tradable comic books and daily and Sunday strips. Also posters and art.

Weiser's Bookstore, 740 Broadway, 777-6363 Take a philosophical approach to the selling of occult and metaphysical books and you have Weiser's, one of the largest specialty bookshops of its kind. Very complete selection of most areas of occult interest, and rare books.

West Side Comix, 107 W. 86 St., 724-0432
East Side Comix, 302 E. 82 St., 535-7443 Current, back-issue, out-of-print, and rare comics, and books relating to comics, are all in stock. Underground comics, too, for the more perverse lover of line drawings. Virtually everything related to the field is available at these sister stores.

Political Bookstores

Djuna Books, 154 W. 10 St., 242-3642 Very political store dealing with feminism in all its varieties. Heavy on small-press books, periodicals, and nonsexist children's literature.

Laissez-Faire Books, 206 Mercer St., 674-8154 For the anarchist in all of us, a bookstore centering on why everybody should be left alone to trade in a free market. Anti-authoritarian books on most subjects.

Liberation Bookstore, 421 Lenox Ave., 281-4615 Slightly less overtly political than its name, the Liberation Bookstore offers the most complete selection of Afro-American and African works in the city. Has recently expanded its list to include Caribbean and other Third World topics. Range includes all general interest works of this nature as well as political ones. Particularly strong in the fine and performing arts, history, and juvenile works. Periodicals and small-press titles are also well covered.

Oscar Wilde Memorial Bookshop, 15 Christopher St., 255-8097

The most complete selection of titles relating to homosexuality, its history, importance as a cultural phenomenon, and current life-styles as now exists. Works of a serious nature only, concerning both male and female homosexuality, as well as the related periodicals and out-of-print works.

Universal Distributors, 54 W. 13 St., 243-4317

Marxist philosophy in all its variations, including translations of Marxist works from all over the world, and as a Marxist bookstore this is it. Does not adhere to a specific party line. Also strong on Maoist literature, periodicals, and out-of-print works.

Womanbooks, 201 W. 92 St., 873-4121

To feminists what Universal Distributors is to Marxists. Complete and very up-to-date selection, with the emphasis on total availability of works rather than the current political line. Reading room and periodicals, rental library, and lists of similar stores also available.

Used Book Dealers

Argosy Bookstore, 116 E. 59 St., 753-4455

Six floors of the antiquated, gently used, and rare of nearly every subject. The quaint entrance, which harbors the clearance books (under $3), is indicative of what is inside—lots of beautiful, old books and maps (a section unto itself), well arranged and competitively priced.

Dolphin Bookshop, 2743 Broadway, 866-8454

Good-quality used books, in particular academic and critical works set in a small, bookish storefront that could be nothing other than what it is. Best "Books About Books" section in the city.

Fourth Avenue Bookstore, 138 Fourth Ave., 254-1822

The archetypal Fourth Avenue used bookstore, of which there are many, the best two listed here. This is the crossroads of the used-book world, and the shops here, Fourth Avenue Bookstore and Manny's, are the best-organized and most complete there are. The most serendipitous browses of anyone's life can be had on Fourth Ave., and Fourth Avenue Bookstore is the best place to start.

Greenwich Books, Ltd., 127 Greenwich Ave., 242-3095
A specialist in the Beat Generation, Greenwich is the center of the 20th-century art and culture used-book circuit. Certain of the sales help can tell stories of their days with Jack and Neal, or at least reasonable enough facsimiles to keep you entertained and sell you on an autographed copy.

Jolly Roger, 190 Columbus Ave., 877-1836
Narrow in its range of selections, what Jolly Roger stocks, they stock well: art, literature, music, and the accompanying criticism.

Manny's Book and Records, 114 Fourth Ave., 336-7829
Art, Americana, and fiction are the forte of this excellently and popularly stocked store. Check out their out-of-print records as well.

N.R.S. (No Real Specialty) Bookstore, 1181 Amsterdam Ave., 666-3060
Stacks and stacks of old books, magazines, and records, N.R.S., near Columbia University, is a terrific browse if you've got all day—otherwise, you'll find yourself late for a great many appointments, as sifting through all the wonderful stuff is all too engrossing. Liberal arts and scholarly works could be said to be a sort of emphasis, but it's all too general and too interesting to categorize.

Paperback Exchange, 1388 Second Ave., 861-8890; 269 Columbus Ave., no phone; 270 Third Ave., no phone; 2145 Broadway, 595-2283
An interesting example of coop-ism applied to books: at the rate of 25 percent of the cover price of a paperback, you can trade used paperbacks in for other used paperbacks, which cost 50 percent of the cover price. Or you can cough up the cash and have done with it that way. In any event, it's not a bad way to pick up some new mass-market goodies. Some excellent titles show up, at a very marginal price. And it's a good place to get rid of some of your bookshelf clutter.

Pomander Bookshop, 252 W. 95 St., 866-1777
Liberal arts, nothing technical—a poet's used bookstore
with lots of rare and first-edition volumes. Scholarly
works of today and yesterday.

The Strand Bookstore, 828 Broadway, 473-1452
The biggest damned bookstore in the world, specializing
in hardcover classics, remainders, reviewer's copies, and
some trade paperbacks. If it's anywhere, this is the
place to start looking, because they probably have it. An
immense physical layout and helpful staff make it easily
the most fruitful, if not most intimate, place to seek
that used version of whatever. Everything is at least
half off, and at the stands outside they are even less.
Bookhunter's paradise.

Sylvan Bookshop, 827 Broadway, 473-2243
A nice general-interest store specializing in history,
music, and environmental subjects. Ancient paperbacks
at prewar prices. A very decent place to while away a
Saturday afternoon.

A Guide to Hip Clothes

Looking "hip" in New York has about as many
variations as *being* hip does. "Hip is in the eye of the
beholder," one might say. In Manhattan, the first
priority is dressing to suit the occasion. If that fails, and
you get caught in your T-shirt at an expensive upper
East Side restaurant, you can carry it off with *attitude.*

Actually, dressing hip in New York is really more
about attitude than anything else. And the attitudes
suit the different neighborhoods. On the East Side,
you're likely to see a lot of designer and expensive
clothes worn casually. On the West Side, you're likely to
see less expensive though trendier clothes, worn more
self-consciously. In the West Village, you get a lot of
casual clothes worn interestingly. In Soho, you see a lot
of black clothes, a lot of T-shirts and sweatshirts, a lot
of flat shoes and interesting haircuts, worn *very*
interestingly. In the East Village, you'll get the same,
but somewhat *less* interestingly.

Hip, all in all, means dressing to express some
personal vernacular, often related to one's profession
and/or major interests. "What is hip?" an old song asks

in its refrain, but it doesn't get an answer. I wish I could tell you the hippest clothes shops in New York, but I can't—it's too personal. However, I would say "hipper clothes" are more likely to be found in the boutiques than in the department stores, more often in the East Village antique clothes haunts than in swank Madison Avenue designer's row.

The following is a tour through some of Manhattan's hipper emporiums, which, luckily, are also often cheaper (though not always) than more mainstream outlets. A lot of the outfits that turn up at the gallery openings, Tribeca restaurants, after-hours clubs, the Film Forum, and loft parties are going to have been strung together out of these racks.

Capezio, 177 MacDougal St., in the West Village, used to outfit dancers. Now it outfits everyone, with a wide range of downtown designers, and the most downtown of the uptown ones—Willi Smith, Norman Kamali, Betsey Johnson, etc. Their clothes range from middle expensive to just below expensive, but they are usually of high quality and fashion, with enough of a funky edge to be "hip." Lots of great belts, jewelry, handbags, and downstairs, a whole floor of the famous Capezio shoes, mixed in with other brands. The sales help tend to be rather snotty and impatient; ignore them and browse. Great bargains at sale times, which are around mid-season.

Patricia Field, 10 E. 8 St., in the heart of the Village, was once an expensive shop with tailored and unusual clothes for women. Then, in the late seventies, it was one of the first bastions of "punk" chic. Now it's the best of both worlds, since Pat Field combines young whimsical taste with a great high-fashion sense, and a cultivation of new downtown designers. You'll see things here you won't see anywhere else, but most of them aren't outrageous, just . . . *interesting.* Always great sweaters and pants. Her dressy items are perfect for weekends and clubbing, and the more offbeat night scene. Prices range from very reasonable to expensive, but there are often great sales.

Betsey Johnson, 130 Thompson St., in Soho, one of the few real design innovators to be accepted by the Seventh Ave. elite, now has her own shop in Soho, painted bright pink. Inside, there are continuous videos of her past fashion "events" (they're more than just shows), and wide display of the current season's collection. Her things tend to be stretchy (Lycra) or flouncy (cotton petticoat) or puffy (giant sleeved lace-up corduroy jackets). There's always a large touch of whimsy in these things, which are reasonable to expensive, but they do last and suit just about every occasion, and again, her sales are great.

The Merchant of Venice, Prince St. between West Broadway and Thompson, is a skinny little boutique that sells a lot of Italian imports, mostly tight jeans, colored and pastel sweatshirts, and leather and vinyl jackets. They also carry independently made earrings, pins, and bracelets. The things here tend to be reasonably priced and don't look like anything you've ever seen anywhere else—because you haven't.

Canal Jeans, 504 Broadway, a bit east of Soho, is a warehouse full of mostly very inexpensive clothes like army/navy items—sweatshirts, jeans, T-shirts of every possible design, bomber jackets, slickers, shoes and boots, and a great supply of antique and used clothes— sweaters, suit jackets, tweed coats, wool skirts, cotton skirts, etc.—at fabulous buys. I once bought three antique cocktail dresses (they specialize in these) for $5 in here. Most of the real artists in Soho dress out of this place, because they can't afford to dress out of anywhere else.

Unique, 718 Broadway, in Noho (north of Soho), is an even larger warehouse, carrying much the same merchandise as Canal Jeans, only a lot more of it, with perhaps some trendier items—hats, belts, handbags. They specialize in those wide-lapel tuxedo jackets, and their antique-clothes department is immense and beautifully organized—tons of frilly party dresses, jackets, coats, sweaters, great leather jackets, all in about a $10 to $50 range. Go, and be hip.

Soho Zat, on West Broadway, near Canal, is mostly a magazine/newspaper store, with every conceivable U.S. and foreign art/fashion/music/film/video/poetry/fiction publication. They also sell antique clothes—leather jackets, coats, skirts, suit jackets, and often some new items out of Britain, which tend to be more expensive than the former items, which are real cheap.

Trash 'n' Vaudeville, 4 Saint Marks Pl., in the East Village, is two-leveled. Upstairs are the new items, mostly by local designers, many of which are one-of-a-kind. Downstairs, there are used things, great sweaters, and great shoes. These clothes are *very* hip—maybe *too* hip—and are really becoming to the East Village lifestyle. But with a little imagination, you could find great bargains here. Prices are mostly reasonable, with the occasional overpriced or underpriced item.

Saint Marks Place, between Second and Third Ave., is a wonderful and idiosyncratic place to shop. A lot of the stores on this block have been here forever (since the sixties); some opened with the punk revolution of the mid-seventies. They sell all sorts of things—used clothes, new miniskirts, boots, antique shoes, kimonos, scarves—and you could find just about anything here, in various conditions.

World's End, on Prince St., near Sullivan, is the shop of innovative English whirlwind Vivienne Westwood. Hers were the premier designs of the New Romantic movement in London, and she designs all her own fabrics, which are bright cotton prints, often matched together in the same outfit with varying prints and patterns. These clothes are super-hip, moderately expensive.

Major Department Stores

All major New York department stores have been established for at least 50 years. These retailing institutions are elegant examples of the cross between traditional, old New York, and the most current new York styles. And they're great if you're in the market to buy, enjoying browsing, want a snack, or just need to kill some time.

Alexander's (593-0880), located on Lexington Avenue at 58 St., stocks almost as wide a variety as its across-the-street neighbor, Bloomingdale's, but caters to the more budget-minded. If you can recognize quality, and have the time to look for it, Alexander's is a good place to compare before buying elsewhere.

B. Altman & Co. (689-7000), a 1906 building at Fifth Ave. and 34 St., still has its crystal chandeliers, grand white columns, and wooden floors: traditional old New York. The complete department-store merchandise also features Rare Books and Autographs: a fine selection of first editions, signed volumes, rare documents, and autographs—ranging from a $20 contemporary example to an authentic John Hancock.

Barney's (929-9000), 111 Seventh Ave. at 17 St., contains an encyclopedic selection of men's and boys' fashions, as well as a recently opened women's shop. You'll find entire floors devoted to American, English, and European tailored clothes as well as a special sizes department for the extra tall, short, wide, or thin. An essential stop—not only for the vast selection but also for the many gorgeous salesclerks.

Henri Bendel (247-1100), at 10 W. 57 St. (near Fifth), is primarily known for the more exotic designer tastes. The ground floor, a series of alcoves, comprises several mini-departments: stationery, crafts, gadgets, hats, scarves, gourmet foods, hostess items—everything on a small scale. Bendel is a good place to buy "thank you" gifts. The selection is neither large nor wide, but all merchandise is of a high caliber and just a little out-of-the-ordinary.

Bergdorf Goodman (753-7300) is at Fifth Ave. and 58 St. *Haute hauterie* for men, women, and children. Van Cleef and Arpels jewel boutique for a diamond tiara, Delman shoes, a full-length sable, and a gown from one of the designer salons . . . get the picture? Pasta and Cheese Café on the fifth floor.

Bloomingdale's (355-5900), Lexington Ave. and 59 St., offers a vast, diverse array of almost anything you could name. The focus is on the latest trends and fine quality. Bloomie's is known for its dramatic flair. Chic clothes, chic housewares, chic food, and *surprises* in some departments. This is where to buy for the "people who have everything."

Bonwit Teller (593-3333) on 57 St., just east of Fifth, is the only one of the old establishments to be housed in modern quarters (Trump Tower). The original building was replaced in 1980 by an ultra-modern maze of mirrors. It carries exclusively women's finery: cosmetics, jewelry, leather, and the gamut of high fashion. Tiffany and Co. is next door, on the corner.

Brooks Brothers (682-8800), now located on Madison Ave. at 44 St., was founded downtown in 1818. Abraham Lincoln wore a Brooks Brothers suit the night he was shot in Ford's Theater. The goods (here men's departments outnumber women's) are conservative, classic, business-like apparel. Clothes that will last and never go out of style are best bought here. There is *nothing* in the trendy department. Lifetime tailoring service is provided with your purchase.

Gimbel Brothers (564-3300) is at Broadway and 33 St., with a branch (Gimbels East: 348-2300) at Lexington Ave. at 86 St. Macy's and Gimbel's competitive relationship is famous. Gimbels comes close to duplicating much of Macy's stock. Special sales make the difference.

Lord & Taylor (391-3344), Fifth Ave. at 38 St., is another bastion of upper-crust New York society. Fine clothing and traditional furnishings in abundance, sometimes sale racks offer terrific values. The Soup Bar is a great spot to take a break from shopping, to enjoy homemade Scotch broth and apple pie.

Macy's (971-6000) Herald Sq., Broadway and 34 St., is truly the world's largest department store. Under one roof, Macy's serves any buying need. Besides the widest selection of fashion, housewares, furniture, electronics, Macy's has a pet shop, a pharmacy, a fish market, a butcher, a fresh produce market, an espresso bar, a health food bar, a *real* bar (a P. J. Clarke's, no less), and entire boutiques devoted to everything imaginable.

Saks Fifth Avenue (753-4000), last but not least, is located at the corner of 49 St., right across the street from Rockefeller Center and St. Patrick's Cathedral. The decor *defines* old-world elegance. Featured at Saks are the finest in couture, shoes, jewelry, bridal gifts, and other formal services. The employees aren't any snootier here, and sale prices can be quite competitive.

Fine Fleas
for Nearly Nothing

"Finding a bargain isn't as easy as it looks," says Gillian Rattner (not her real name), who's spent years haunting the city's thrift shops, sidewalk flea markets, and bargain-bin avenues both on her own and as a professional trend-spotter for out-of-town fashion designers. "You've got to bring some real talent to the job, or you'll wind up paying double for third-rate stuff you don't really want or need."

First you've got to know what you want. "If you've just got to have a kitschy rayon kimono from the fifties, don't spend hours poring over bins full of handbags—no matter how beautiful and cheap they are. You're not only wasting time, but sooner or later it'll sour you on the whole game."

Then be bold. "Some of the best places look like opium dens from the outside. Don't be afraid—most are reasonably clean and friendly inside. And if you just can't hold your nose and try on a dirty shirt for the fit, forget it: You belong in Lord & Taylor."

Bring some imagination and style, too. "The laboratory glassware on Canal Street does fine for planters and terrariums, and some of it will even look good on your table. That dirty formal shirt will look even better once it's cleaned and pressed. And I've still got a tweed skirt that must have been twenty years old when I found it—and it's tailored far better than anything I could buy new."

Last, be an explorer. "Places disappear all the time, and new ones come along. Staying on top of the best takes a lot of word-of-mouth, a little stamina, and a really good pair of walking shoes."

If you feel you're ready, here's a selection of current hot spots and some old favorites:

Columbus Avenue in the Seventies—For antique clothes and a taste of what can be discovered elsewhere. "Some of what you see in these shops came from dingy storefronts downtown that are heaped to the ceiling with mounds of old clothes. They just pick through the piles, clean up the best things, and sell them uptown at triple the price. If you can afford it, it's fine to have somebody else doing the work for you—but you're no bargain hunter.

Orchard Street from East Houston to Canal— Solidly lined with dozens of shops selling "dirt cheap" yard goods, handbags, shoes, luggage, hats, coats, men's and women's fashions. "I've picked up designer clothes there at thirty percent off—same season, same quality as the stuff in the department store windows uptown." Don't forget to poke through the side streets just off Orchard: "They're gold mines most people just pass by."

Saint Marks Place between Second and Third Avenues—"If you want to punk out, this is the place to do it—and the prices for that stuff are fine." Secondhand furs and less-bizarre clothes are also present.

First Ave. from 3 to 12 St.—More secondhand clothes of superior quality, and discount shops that handle everything from socks to soap. Side streets contain a few of those "dingy storefronts" mentioned earlier.

Bowery from East Houston to East 4 St.—An old standby for restaurant-trade pots, pans, cutlery, and dinnerware. "The place to stock your new kitchen. You may not find real bargains, but it's always cheaper, and quality goods."

Bowery from Great Jones St. to Kenmare St.—More kitchen stuff (with a heavy Chinese accent), and cheap lighting goods from raw sockets to crystal chandeliers.

Fulton St. from Broadway to South St.—A little bit of everything, both new and used. Some of the nearby surplus stores have a reputation for beating even Orchard St. prices.

Chambers St. from Broadway to West Broadway—Fulton St. north, with an emphasis on tape players, stereos, radios, and the like.

Canal St. from Sixth Ave. to Lafayette St.—The old reliable for casual clothes, hardware, housewares, and art supplies, with an admixture of antiques, a flea market or two, and name-brand appliances. Worth the trip even if you don't find anything, and Chinatown, Little Italy, and Soho are all a short walk away.

14 St. from Park to Sixth Ave.—Another classic: Discount City for more years than anyone likes to remember, and offers bargains in housewares, Kleenex, detergents, etc. "A lot of the other stuff is schlocky, but I still come down for the housewares," says one habitué.

Free Lance Flea Markets—"They're all over,

usually near the other bargain places to catch the same
traffic." Most of the stuff is apartment-sale junksville,
but there are often great items at very distressed prices.
Since it's illegal to flog your personal property on the
sidewalk without a license, they come and go—but as
the new Depression takes hold, you'll probably see more
coming and fewer going. At this writing, two of the
biggest are located near Cooper Square, at the
intersection of Third and Fourth Ave., and in a parking
lot near the corner of Broome St. and West Broadway.

Peddler Clusters—The busiest sidewalk entrances
of the major department stores are usually jammed with
peddlers throughout the week. Many are licensed and
honest, but for those who aren't, consumer fraud is the
name of the game. "If you want to buy a $25 'Cartier'
watch for $5 with works made in Outer Mongolia, be my
guest."

Block Fairs—A summer tradition among the city's
neighborhood organizations, and the only kind of legal
street flea market. They usually last only a day, fall
mostly in late spring and summer, and offer the best
bargains when they're small, one or two-block affairs.
Hard to catch, but worth it—notices of upcoming events
usually get posted on local bulletin boards, in
community newspapers, and sometimes the major
dailies.

Food

Most people in New York have their own favorite
sources for most kinds of food and drink, so if you are a
native you will probably find I have missed the shops
you swear by and recommended highly, even deified,
the shops you hate. Too bad. I have gone through the
same thing myself many times. You get over it.
Sometimes you find out something new, but more often
than not your opinions remain unchanged (which, of
course, is why more than one of any kind of store can
survive in business).

If you are a visitor, you will be taking things more on
faith, so if the occasion for which you are shopping is an
important one, such as a dinner party for a Crowned
Head of State, taste before you buy to make sure what I

like is what you and your Crowned Head like.

This listing will be by product, with the shop names set out in boldface type. An address and telephone number directory will follow in an alphabetical list. Best not to get into hours of opening here, as these change all too often. Phone before you go.

Appetizing

Let us first of all get our parts of speech right. *Appetizing,* as used in New York shopping circles, is a noun: an appetizing store is not a store that whets the appetite (although it usually is that too) but rather a store that sells appetizing. By appetizing we mean the whole gamut of smoked fish, various fresh cheeses, and so forth: in short, the makings of a Sunday brunch (the word brunch pre-dates the introduction of eggs bénédict to the saloon menu; it used to mean bagels and lox and cream cheese and maybe just another little slice of sturgeon, please—and no Bloody Marys). For the purposes of this guide, we shall include certain nontraditional appetizing, such as caviar, and will go so far as to mention a pickle merchant or two. A lot of people, when asked to name their favorite *traditional* appetizing store, would say **Russ and Daughters** or **Murray the Sturgeon King,** but I say nuts to them. While admitting that their stuff is excellent, I retain my love for **Saperstein's,** whose owner is so enthusiastic and whose cat is so contented. Ask if the sable is good, the delightful man will show you in mime what your guests' reaction to it will be. If you like your whitefish schmaltzy (not that many people do nowadays, which is great for we smart people who like it plenty schmaltzy), you'll get it schmaltzy. He also sells an excellent line of canned sardines. Now, if you want gilt-edged appetizing (Scotch smoked salmon, Russian caviar, and other upwardly mobile food), I suggest **Zabar's.** In fact, you can buy *all* your appetizing there if you don't insist on an appetizing-only store. I have never had bad appetizing from Zabar's; Zabar's appetizing is world-class. It is also not as expensive as people think. Their caviar is very good. Better is the caviar from the **Petrossian** outlet in Bloomingdale's, but it is EXTREMELY costly. If you have a Bloomingdale's charge account, however, use it to buy some on the installment plan. Another good source for caviar (Russian and American, the latter very nice) is **Iron Gate.** Good old **Macy's** is fine for all this stuff, too, and **Caviarteria** sells decent caviar as well, including what would be called seconds in the rag trade: the bruised eggs from the bottom of the container. To go with all this fish you need cheese (cream cheese and farmer cheese and, if you like, pot cheese). It's good at Zabar's and it's real good at **Ben's.** Pickles, new, half-sour, sour; pickled tomatoes, melon rind, and mixtures; sauerkraut (all out of the barrel) should come from **Hollander's** or **Guss's,** if you want to do it right, or from any of the other places we've mentioned (apart from the ones on the East Side north of Houston St.) if you don't feel the need to discuss the pickles you buy. Bagels, incidentally, are all lousy nowadays. You used to hurt your jaw chewing a bagel. No more. So buy them anywhere they are freshly made.

Bread

For Italian bread, **Zito's.** For Jewish, Middle European, and Russian breads, **Orwasher's.** For French bread, go soak your head. It's not *that* bad, actually. **David's Cookies** bread is amazing: wonderful flutes of crisp-crusted, pully, chewy bread. **Au Bon Pain** bread is crusty and light (makes wonderful toast). "Swiss Peasant Bread" from any number of places, including **Eclair,** is also a first-rate bread. But none of it is really like French bread. Rumor has it that a while ago Macy's was negotiating to bring Poilâne bread in from Paris. That fell through. We'll live without it—just.

Butter

Land o' Lakes is fine by me. The pasteurized Normandy butters you can get are not that much better, and the quality control is fallible. Now sometimes at **E. A. T.** or **Dean and DeLuca** you can get more exotic French butters from Charente or Echiré; that already is another story, although don't go expecting what you get on the spot in France. If you want salted butter, I don't know what to tell you; go to Idaho, or buy a wooden spoon and some salt and mix it in yourself.

Charcuterie

I do not think that there is any *really* first-rate French-style charcuterie to be had in New York, except at a few of the best restaurants. **SoHo Charcuterie** is better than most, and decent pâtés and things are sold at **Les Trois Petits Cochons,** which also sells their products to many other outlets: call them and ask for the name of the one nearest to you. Check **Dean and DeLuca, Zabar's, Bloomingdale's** (which often has some very interesting sausages), and **Macy's. E. A. T.** and **Dumas,** as well as some of the others I've listed, sometimes have fresh-ish *foie gras,* but in my book it's all overcooked. For Germanic sausages and pâté-like confections, **Schaller and Weber** is my favorite, although there is a uniformity to their seasonings that gets to you after a while, and **Kurowycky** has lovely Polish and Ukrainian products, including a rice- or kasha-based version of haggis. (It may be my imagination, incidentally, but I'd swear that the pâtés from **Trois Petits Cochons** were better when the store first opened some years ago.) For general and Italianate sausages, try a good butcher (see MEAT).

Cheese

Boy, have things changed on the New York cheese scene! A few years ago you could get chalky (or overripe) pasteurized brie, some crumbly Roquefort, and a few mediocre domestic cheeses; now, if you shop around, you can find raw-milk cheeses from France, a good selection of English cheese in decent condition, lots of excellent cheeses from various parts of the United States, and goat cheese after goat cheese after goat cheese. I believe that the first cheesemonger to start bringing in unpasteurized French cheeses was Eli Zabar of **E. A. T.** Now you can find a selection of them at **Macy's, Bloomingdale's, Fairway, Dean and DeLuca,** and scattered other stores. In all these places state of ripeness and quality can vary: They are none of them specialists in cheese, after all, and even if they were there are no guarantees with temperamental bacteria at work. Bloomingdale's has started to carry British cheeses from Paxton & Whitfield, one of London's fanciest and best cheese stores, so if you want

some really old farmhouse cheddar or some Lancashire,
that's where to head. Especially when buying fragile
soft, fatty cheese (some of the French *triple crèmes* get
up to 75 percent fat), try to taste before you commit
yourself; most shops will oblige, except where a cheese is
sold only whole, although don't be so crass as to hold
things up in Bloomingdale's little deli department at 5
P.M. when there are twenty-five people waiting to be
served by a staff of three or four. **Zabar's** has a lot of
cheese too, some of it very, very good; **Murray's** is
variable, but worth checking for good buys. The best
stravecchio Parmesan I've had recently came from
Todaro's, and they are good for cheese in general as
well. For fresh Italianate cheeses (ricotta and mozzarelle
of various kinds) as well as grating cheeses and *ricotta
salata,* a very reliable source is **Alleva. (Cheeses of All
Nations,** as far west as you can get on Chambers St., is
fun but highly unreliable. If you want something
strange, however, they are sure to have it, and even the
ordinary stuff can be okay.)

Chocolates and Candy

To get the best of everything, you have, as usual, to run
the length and breadth of the city. For marzipan in all
forms, fresh chocolate-covered nuts, and reasonable
prices, go to **Elk.** For truffles go to **Teuscher:** some of
them seem to have a hazelnut-sized lump of butter in
the middle! Their variations on praline are excellent too.
Kron is somewhat overrated and overpriced, but if you
like his little shopping bag you can find what to buy to
put into it. **Le Chocolatièr** is run by a tailor and exists
behind his tailoring shop: good, honest French-style
chocolates and a warm welcome. In a pinch, **Godiva** is
respectable and you can get them all night and on
Sundays at the otherwise loathsome **Richoux of
London** in Citicorp Center. For the best in all-American
hand-dipped chocolates, take the Jamaica elevated train
out to **Davies** and buy the ones with a layer of caramel
and a thick layer of fresh, soft marshmallow: in the
large size (much gooier and better than the small size)
that confection is far more satisfying than almost any
other in the world. It makes you drool. Teuscher truffles
do not make you drool. If you have the energy, buy
Gaston Lenôtre's book on ice cream, jam, and candy

(published in English by Barron's) and make your own: very messy, but potentially better than any you can buy in New York.

Cigars

You can't exactly eat them with milk like shredded wheat, but they *can* form part of a splendid meal. In fact, on days when I am looking to eat nothing, or next to nothing, I often replace dinner with a big strong cigar. An hour and a quarter of dizzy-making savor. Don't listen to people who tell you that Havanas are no good any more: when you buy a good one from a good merchant, there is nothing like it. But, of course, you can't get them in the United States and can't even bring them in with you when you travel (except from Cuba itself—although all indications are that a box of cigars is not worth the otherwise uninspiring trip to our island neighbor). So what do you do? **J & R Tobacco** sells a first-rate weed under the suspiciously hyped-up name of "the ultimate cigar." They compare them to **Davidoff's** Havanas, which is silly; but they are excellent cigars none the less. Also very good are **Dunhill's** Montecristos (better than the ubiquitous Montecruzes). The other "Cuban" names (Partagas, H. Upmann, Romeo y Julieta, Punch, and so forth) can be very nice too if they are well stored by the merchant. I used not to think Jamaican Macanudos worth wasting a good match on, but someone gave me one recently and it was excellent. People smoke those dry Dutch things, which are not to my taste, although they do obviate the problem of humidified storage; a good brand is Schimmelpennick.

Coffee

If you don't drink coffee at breakfast time and have no moral or religious reason for this, you may as well not get out of bed (which is not a bad idea anyway). The best coffee I know about is sold by Alice Rowen at **Carriage House.** It is a bean from the Indonesian island of Celebes, called Celebes Kalosi. A few other stores sell it, and cheaper, too, but Ms. Rowen buys hers especially carefully; it is roasted to perfection and in small quantities, as are all her coffees, each of which is

just what it should be. **Zabar's** sells a lot of coffee, and
you can often get glorious stuff there, including
(occasionally) your actual Blue Mountain bean from
Jamaica, which is nectar if fresh and properly roasted.
But then again I've had mediocre coffee from Zabar's
too. In the Village, **Schapira's** and the **Porto Rico
Importing Company** are good bets. For house blends,
Cofféa is fine (their Brown Label blend is excellent),
and they are now selling unblended beans as well.

Eggs

Eggs have always been good for you, even during the
few years when certain gullible people actually believed
that their circulatory systems would become clogged
with congealed egg white or something. You can get
good eggs at the **Greenmarkets,** from **Salvatore
Cangelosi,** and from **Vineyard Poultry,** and
sometimes at the live poultry markets (see POULTRY).
And between you and me, I've had perfectly nice eggs
from the supermarket.

Fish

I've never been in a fish store where *everything* looked
nice, so I have no fish store I can recommend
unreservedly. Big selection at **Central Fish Market.**
Excellent stuff at good prices there, and at **Citarella.**
Balducci's sells fresh Dover sole (for a lot of money,
but I don't know any other source for it). **The Lobster
Place** gives a good deal on lobster, live or cooked.
Pisacane is pretty reliable and sometimes wonderful.
As with vegetables, lots of new places are opening up
run by Orientals. They are on the whole very good
indeed, and there is probably one near where you are.

Fruit and Vegetables

With the welcome proliferation of farmers' markets and
Oriental-owned greengrocers, you can find decent
produce everywhere. Not everything all the time, but go
shopping with an open mind and buy what's good. If
you want fresh wild mushrooms, go to **Dean and
DeLuca** or **E. A. T.,** but telephone first because these
are seasonal things (each with its own three-day season,

or so it seems). At E. A. T. I once got some chanterelles,
from France yet, and bought the biggest damned morels
I've ever seen (they came from New Jersey) at Dean
and DeLuca. We may as well mention truffles here. If
you want to flavor something with truffle, and you can't
get a fresh one (or one gently preserved: it will say
première cuisson on the jar or tin), either forget it or do
the cheapest possible thing: use Urbani's truffle paste,
packed in a tube and sold at Dean and DeLuca, or buy
a tin of peelings. If you are looking to use them for
show, don't bother. During their brief season you can
get them fresh (relatively fresh anyway) at E. A. T.,
Dean and DeLuca, **Balducci's,** and **Todaro's** (which is
generally cheaper than anyone else). For local produce,
shop at the **Greenmarkets** and try to put pressure on
the farmers to pick their fruit when it is ripe. Or go to
Fairway, which is an especially good source for apples.
Balducci's is famous for its produce, and sometimes it is
very good, sometimes so-so, always fairly pricey. Keep
your eye on the *Times'* Wednesday "Living Section" for
odd things coming and going in the seasonal
kaleidoscope, but act quickly. One year, just as I was
hankering to make some marmalade, the *Times* told me
that I could get Seville oranges somewhere or other. I
tarried ere I sallied forth, and there were none left.

Herbs and Spices and Things out of Sacks

Most people think that flour should be sifted to get the
lumps out; that is only partly true. Flour purchased
from supermarkets will almost never be wormy
(although once you've opened it and left it on a shelf for
a while, beware—especially if it's whole-wheat flour).
But certain flours are hard to find neatly packed in
little five-pound bags, flours like rye, semolina, etc., and
wheat flours for cake and pastry. For these you will
probably have to go to a dealer who sells them by the
pound. Health-food stores will often have such things,
but my favorite source for flours and dried beans of all
kinds, as well as paprika, freshly ground poppy seeds
(which freeze well, incidentally), and esoteric seasonings
is **H. Roth.** For dried herbs (culinary and "medicinal") I
like **Herbier de Provence; Fairway** and **Dean and
DeLuca** are the most likely sources for fresh herbs in
season (with parsley, dill, mint, cilantro, and basil being

widely available in vegetable stores). Dean and DeLuca
is also good for dried herbs and all sorts of spices for
Western cooking. For seasonings proper to non-Western
cuisines, see the listing under OUTLANDISH ITEMS. Other
nice sources for grains, beans, flours, seasonings, and
such are **Paprikas Weis** and **Gillies.**

Ice Cream

Down on the Lower East Side you can buy a Salton ice-
cream maker for about $16, and with a book like the
one by Gaston Lenôtre (published here by Barron's) you
can make wonderful ice cream at home. That, however,
is a nuisance and results in small quantities. For most
purposes, you can get by very nicely indeed with one of
the premium brands available throughout Manhattan
and beyond. My favorite is the preposterously named
Häagen-Dazs. You can buy it prepacked in
supermarkets, but their own shops have more flavors,
including a deep chocolate positively infested with
roasted almonds. (So what, you say: chocolate almond.
But *these* almonds are themselves chocolate-coated.)
Also a very subtle maple walnut (sweetened only with
maple syrup) and an equally subtle macadamia nut.
Alpen Zauber and Früsen Glädje are almost as good,
but their names are not as ridiculous. Out in "the
neighborhoods," there are several ice-cream parlors,
survivors of the old days. They are great fun, but the
Nordic impostors make better ice cream. Sorbets from
New York Ice, which taste, as sorbets should, of the
fruit from which they were made, can be purchased here
and there, including at **Artichoke. Dean and DeLuca**
has a good line, too, as does **Bloomingdale's.**

Jam

Question of style. The best English-style jams (jams,
that is, that never run off the bread, but which, at the
same time, achieve their consistency without the use of
anything beyond fruit and sugar) are those of Wilkins of
Tiptree, Essex. They are widely available. Frank
Cooper's Oxford marmalade is a fine old product, and it
too can be bought all over the place. French-style jams,
whose consistency varies from runny to English,
depending on the maker and the fruit, used not to be
very easy to find in New York, but there are a few good

ones around now. They include **Silver Palate's** line,
which is sold at their own little shop (along with other
good but often superfluous products) and at **Macy's,
Fay and Allen's,** and several other places in town.
Dean and DeLuca has a very big selection of jam from
all over the world, as do many "gourmet" shops and
departments. **Cofféa** may be the best place of all for
French jams; their Hédiard line is not a product of
genius, but it is dependable, and available in 20 million
flavors. It is also the best value for money of them all.
Alain Chapel sold a few hundred jars of his jam to
Bloomingdale's. I didn't buy any, but I have eaten his
jam: it *is* a product of genius, or rather the product of *a*
genius, the point being that while Chapel is superhuman
he is also capable of selling an odd-tasting jar of
raspberry jam from time to time. **Crabtree and
Evelyn** sells gimmicky jams, with booze in them; they
are well made but not what I call jam. Prune and
apricot lekvar you should get from **H. Roth,** and **Mrs.
Herbst** puts up very nice, friendly apricot and plum
jams.

Meat (Meat, Smoked Meats, Sausages, Deli)

For fresh meat, what can I say? Go to your
neighborhood butcher and nag him until he satisfies
you. Or you can travel around to one of the fancy
butchers like **Fitz's, Lobel's,** or **Macy's** (!), or a
semifancy butcher like the **Nevada Meat Market** or
the **Jefferson Market.** Or you can go to **Balducci's.**
Or **Schaller and Weber.** Or **Kurowycky.** Or
Ottomanelli. Or **Akron** (check their sales out from
time to time; I've had some of my best moderately
priced meat from them when I've shopped carefully). It
really depends what you want. Steak, go to Jefferson
Market. Sausage, go to Ottomanelli. Home-smoked ham,
baked or for baking (as well as kielbasa and other such
sausages), go to Kurowycky. Heavily aged beef, go to
Fitz. Hot dogs? Schaller and Weber. Give a call to
Piccinini and find out if he's got a beautiful piece of
what you want. For the awfullest offal, wander up and
down Ninth Ave. in the upper thirties and lower forties
and get a bargain in goat tonsils. Or you can go to your
local supermarket. (You could be in for a pleasant

surprise, because there is *gorgeous* meat in
supermarkets but not always and, heaven knows, not at
all supermarkets.)

What about cooked meat, in the Jewish deli line? For
the best pastrami and excellent corned beef and tongue,
the obvious place is **Pastrami and Things** (*not* the one
in Rockefeller Center, which is simply no good). For
Gentile cooked meat, Kurowycky is fine, and the deli
departments of the big stores like **Bloomingdale's** and
Macy's have nice stuff too. **Zabar's,** of course, has it all.
They've smoked everything in their time and sold it by
the pound. A lot of it is terrific, some of it miscalculated
(the miscalculations disappear from the line when
consumer displeasure is manifested over a period of
time), but you can never be burned, as they will hardly
let you buy without tasting first. Should you want
English-style sausages (made with bread filler and
mildly seasoned, but inimitable), you can get a good
version from **Country Host,** along with other British
things.

Oil and Vinegar

In a Great Restaurant of France one vacation-time, I
asked the boss what kind of wonderful vinegar he had
used to deglaze a little fry-up of foie gras. He replied,
"Just vinegar; you can get it at **Bloomingdale's.**"
Right; there it was on the shelf: Troisgros vinegar, and
Chapel vinegar, and a whole range of flavored vinegars
from Paul Corcellet (whose dowdy Paris grocery store
sells things like frozen lion steaks and boa constrictor
stew). Flavored vinegars I have little use for; anyway it
is a cinch to macerate anything in vinegar at home. But
if you like them you can find a good array, along with
various red and white wine vinegars, sherry vinegar,
cider vinegar, and other vinegar, at **Artichoke,
Balducci's, Dean and DeLuca, E. A. T., Zabar's,
Coffea** (good buy for the Hédiard brand), and a
surprising number of little shops wherever you go. A
nice all-purpose white wine vinegar at a reasonable price
(not at all reasonable when you figure that you can buy
nasty vinegar for thirty cents a bottle!) is La Marne. It
is made from champagne, but don't hold that against it;
it's not chi-chi and is pretty widely available.

Oil. Where it needs to be tasteless, use a neutral

blended oil, whichever one your mother uses. Be more particular when it comes to olive and nut oils. To my mind, the nicest olive oil around is the one sold for lots of money by **L'Herbier de Provence.** There are glorious, fruitier Italian oils, too, like Badia a Coltibuono and Poggio al Sole. A somewhat less expensive, French oil is J. B. et A. Artaud Frères; it is extremely good. The same places I have mentioned in connection with vinegar are good for oil, apart from Coffea. Nut oils are harder still, because they get rancid about thirty seconds after they are pressed. The Troisgros walnut oil at Bloomingdale's is good but costly. But then all walnut, hazelnut, and almond oils are costly apart from the health-food store kind, which are cheap and putrid.

Outlandish Items

My favorite Indian store is **Foods of India.** I buy nuts there, too. In Chinatown I get daunted by the smaller shops and so stick to supermarkets: Two good ones are **Kam Man** and **Kam Kuo.** To the extent that I buy Japanese goods, I usually find what I need in Chinatown or go to the **Katagiri Company,** which also sells good fresh fish for sushi. See the entries on HERBS AND SPICES and MEAT for some sources for European exotica.

Pasta

There are new shops selling fresh pasta opening every day. As of this writing there is one such shop for every three men, women, and children in the City of New York, or nearly. My favorites are **Raffetto's** and **Piemonte Home Made Ravioli Company,** but the Marcella Hazan stand at **Bloomingdale's** is excellent, and fine pasta can be had from **Pasta and Cheese** and **Zabar's,** too. Probably the best brand of *dried* pasta is De Cecco, and it is available in many places, including **Todaro's** and **Dean and DeLuca's.** Apart from the quality of the noodles, which is high, I favor Raffetto's because of the machine that cuts them. It does not use the usual revolving cutters and makes a noise like a jackhammer—I won't describe it because you have to see it to believe it.

Pastry and Cake

The best pastry man in New York, one of the best in
the world, is Maurice **Bonté**. Cakes include chocolate
(with a bit of raspberry among the various chocolate
butter creams), blackcurrant, hazelnut, Grand Marnier,
mocha, a cakelike mousse of passion fruit, a beribboned
triangular meringue confection, and a chocolate
charlotte. Sometimes lemon, sometimes chestnut cake
(and all year round, chestnut mousse). Turkey-shaped
cakes for Thanksgiving, egg-shaped cakes for Easter,
and Yule logs for Christmas. Blackcurrant mousse in
chocolate cups. Babas of various kinds. All the expected
small pastries from simple fruit tarts to mille-feuilles.
Quiches and, at the end of the week, meat pies and
savory open tarts of tomato and anchovy. Cookies.
Madeleines. Lady fingers. Meringues. The most
beautiful cakes for Occasions (he once did a little
wedding cake for friends of mine with two sugar-work
doves flying around it). Croissants, brioches, and their
subdivisions. All of the absolute highest quality both in
terms of ingredients (I've seen the place croissant- and
brioche-less because he didn't like the look of the butter
one day) and execution.

For Danish pastry **Dumas** is king of the mountain.
Buy a lot more than you think you need because people
get crazy when eating Dumas coffee rings; in the shop
they will ask you whether you want a pecan ring or an
almond ring. Answer, "Both, please." Trust me.
Dumas's other pastries and cakes are good, but they are
not inspired by angels (I swear I saw an angel
whispering into Maurice Bonté's ear one day). They do,
however, make terrific cookies, especially the long ones
with chocolate cream inside and almonds outside.

If you have a yen for Central European pastry, you
might wander over to E. 86th St. and stroll up and
down between Second and Lexington aves. You will be
tempted by handsome-looking cakes of all descriptions
in the windows of such *Konditoreien* as **Café Geiger**
and the **Kleine Konditorei.** Quality varies from
acceptable to lovely, but you can have great fun
experimenting.

That should really do you for cake. If it doesn't, other
good places are **Pâtisserie Lanciani** and, sometimes,
for some things, **William Greenberg, Jr. Desserts.**
Brownies from **Word of Mouth**. Italian pastries from

DeRobertis or **Veniero's** (Veniero's cheesecake is eggy cheesecake). Middle Eastern pastries from **Le Baklava;** sweet or savory, they are all made with a care for excellence that puts them in a higher class than any similar pastries I've tasted. I almost forgot to mention **Délices la Côte Basque.** That would be a pity; they make light, eggy Danish pastries, and their French pastries are not half bad. Also, they serve a very good cup of coffee. I also nearly forgot to mention **David's Cookies,** which are now a part of daily life here in New York. Sometimes a 2½-square-inch David's cookie will consist of 2 square inches of chocolate and just enough dough so they can call it a cookie rather than a candy bar. As with Dumas's Danish, people get piggy with David's cookies, so never buy less than a pound and a quarter.

Poultry

There's an old *New Yorker* cartoon of a butcher holding an imperious-looking turkey under his arm, showing it to a customer. He (the butcher, not the turkey) is saying, "A magnificent fowl, madam—note how he looks you straight in the eye." If you like to stare your dinner down before you roast it, there are still a handful of live poultry markets left, which sell chickens, guinea fowl, ducks, rabbits, and the odd pigeon and goose (but not everything all the time). Especially if (a) you are used to supermarket chicken's textureless tenderness and (b) you cook the victim too soon after it has squawked its last, you may find the flesh on the fibrous side. Flavor varies, unfortunately, and if you are unlucky, the flesh may be fibrous *and* tasteless. Generally, though, the slaughtered-before-your-eyes fowl will have plenty of taste. Here are some live poultry markets (not all of which I have tried, although I've bought from most of them at one time or another): **Antzi's, Cocozello's,** and **Village Live Poultry.** The *Times* did a chicken tasting a while ago and liked the chickens distributed by the Bell and Evans Company best; they are indeed very nice and can be found in many butchers around town, including **Jefferson Market, Fitz's,** and the uptown **Ottomanelli.** Ask your local butcher before you go running; he just might carry them. I sometimes buy poultry (including lovely capons) from **Vineland Poultry;** you have to order at least a day in advance because they only slaughter and bring into the city what they need each morning. Good fresh eggs there, too, every day, and the boss, Mr. Mansfield, is a charmer who will tell you about all the ritzy customers who buy his chickens and no others. Fresh ducks are problematical: **Akron** from time to time, Vineland, or go down to Chinatown. You can get good chickens (and pigeons) in Chinatown, too, but try to ascertain whether the chickens are raised on Chinese farms or are bought from Frank Perdue; try to avoid the latter!

Tea

There are whole peoples who drink tea with breakfast. Even if they *are* wasting their time, most of the good coffeehouses will sell them what they want. Sometimes wonderful exotic teas turn up in small quantities, and **Carriage House** usually gets a pound or two. But such teas are not for breakfast; they are to be drunk by delicate boys and girls with gilded eyelids, out of cups through whose translucence you can see other lands.

Akron Prime Meats, 1414 Third Ave. (81 St.), 744-1551

Alleva Dairy, 188 Grand St. (Mulberry St.), 226-7990

Antzi's Live Poultry Market, 1355 Amsterdam Ave. (126 St.), 662-6773

Artichoke, 968 Second Ave. (51 St.), 753-2030

Le Baklava, 325 E. 48 St. (First Ave.), 751-1377

Balducci's, 424 Sixth Ave. (10 St.), 673-2600

Ben's Cheese Shop, 181 E. Houston St. (Orchard St.), 254-8290

Bloomingdale's, 1000 Third Ave. (59 St.), 355-5900

Au Bon Pain, Citicorp Center (Lexington Ave. and 53 St.), 838-6996

Bonté Pâtisserie, 1316 Third Ave. (75 St.), 535-2360

Salvatore Cangelosi, 72 E. 7 St. (Second Ave.), 475-5993

Carriage House, 251 E. 82 St. (Second Ave.), 744-1185

Central Fish Market, 527 Ninth Ave. (40 St.), 279-2317

Le Chocolatièr, 843 Lexington Ave. (64 St.), 249-3289

Citarella Fish Market, 2135 Broadway (75 St.), 874-0383

Cocozzello's Poultry, 512 Broome St. (Thompson St.), 925-1089

Cofféa, 2349 Broadway (85 St.), 496-7200, *and* 982 Third Ave. (58 St.), 750-9733

Country Host, 1435 Lexington Ave. (94 St.), 876-6525

Crabtree & Evelyn, 30 E. 67 St. (Madison Ave.), 734-1108

David's Cookies, *several locations; call* 888-1610

Davies Chocolate, 101-07 Jamaica Ave. (101 St.), Richmond Hill, Queens, 849-7750

Dean and DeLuca, 121 Prince St. (Greene St.), 254-7774

Délices la Côte Basque, 1032 Lexington Ave. (74 St.), 535-3311, *and* in Olympic Tower, Fifth Ave. and 50 St., *and* at Zabar's (*q.v.*)

DeRobertis Pastry Shop, 176 First Ave. (12 St.), 674-7137

Dumas Pâtisserie, 1330-A Lexington Ave. (88 St.), 369-3900, *and* 116 E. 60 St. (Park Ave.), 688-0905, *and* 1042 Madison Ave. (79 St.), 744-4804

Alfred Dunhill of London, 620 Fifth Ave. (50 St.), 481-6950

E. A. T. Is Owned By Eli Zabar, Inc., 1064 Madison Ave. (81 St.), 879-4017 (New store to open at Madison Ave. and 72 St.)

Eclair, 141 W. 72 St. (Broadway), 873-7700, *and* First Ave. and 54 St., 759-5355, *and* Grand Central Station, Lower Level, 684-8877

Elk Candy Company, 240 E. 86 St. (Second Ave.), 650-1177

Fairway Fruit and Vegetables, 2127 Broadway (75 St.), 595-1888

Fay & Allen's Foodworks, 1241 Third Ave. (71 St.), 794-1101

A. Fitz & Sons, 944 First Ave. (51 St.), 753-3465

Foods of India, 120 Lexington Ave. (28 St.), 683-4419

Gillies 1840, 160 Bleecker St. (Thompson St.), 260-2130, *and* 1494 Third Ave. (85 St.), 861-5299

Godiva Chocolatièr, 701 Fifth Ave. (55 St.), 593-2845
(*and sold in many outlets*)

William Greenberg, Jr. Desserts, 1377 Third Ave.
(78 St.), 535-7118, *and* 17 E. 8 St. (Fifth Ave.),
674-6657

Greenmarkets, *various locations* (*seasonal*); *call Barry
Benape,* 477-3220

Isadore Guss, pickles, 42 Hester St. (Essex St.),
477-1969

l'Herbier de Provence (St-Rémy), 156 E. 64 St.
(Lexington Ave.), 759-8240

L. Hollander & Son, pickles, 35 Essex St. (Grand St.),
254-4477

Iron Gate Products, 424 W. 54 St. (Tenth Ave.),
757-2670

J & R Tobacco, 219 Broadway (Vesey St.), 233-6620,
and 11 E. 45 St. (Fifth Ave.), 869-8777

Jefferson Market, 455 Sixth Ave. (10 St.), 675-2277

Kam Kuo, 7 Mott St. (Bowery), 349-3097

Kam Man, 200 Canal St. (Mulberry St.), 571-0330

Katagiri & Company, 224 E. 59 St. (Second Ave.),
755-3566

Kron Chocolatièr, 506 Madison Ave. (52 St.),
486-0265, *and* 764 Madison Ave. (66 St.), 288-9259

Kurowycky Meat Products, 121 First Ave. (9 St.),
477-0344

Lanciani Pâtisserie, 275 W. 4 St. (Perry St.), 929-0739

Lobel Brothers Prime Meats, 1096 Madison Ave. (82
St.), 737-1372

The Lobster Place, 487 Amsterdam Ave. (84 St.),
595-7605

Macy's, 34 St. and Sixth Ave., 971-6000

Murray's Sturgeon Shop, 2429 Broadway (89 St.),
724-2650

Murray's Cheese, 42 Cornelia St. (Bleecker St.),
243-2387

Nevada Market, 2012 Broadway (69 St.), 362-0443

Orwasher Bread, 308 E. 78 St. (Second Ave.),
288-6569

Ottomanelli Brothers, 1155 First Ave. (63 St.), 355-4413

Ottomanelli's Meat Market, 281 Bleecker St. (Jones St.), 675-4217

Paprikas Weiss Importers, 1546 Second Ave. (81 St.), 288-6117

Pasta & Cheese, 1375 Third Ave. (79 St.), 988-0997, *and* 1886 Broadway (62 St.), 977-8782, *and five other locations*

Pastrami & Things, 297 Third Ave. (23 St.), 683-7185 *not Rockefeller Center or other locations*

Petrossian Caviar, *at Bloomingdale's* (*q.v*)

Piccinini Brothers, 633 Ninth Ave. (45 St.), 246-8277

Piemonte Home Made Ravioli Company, 190 Grand St. (Mulberry St.), 226-0475

Pisacane Mid-Town Seafood, 940 First Ave. (51 St.), 752-7560

Porto Rico Importing Company, 201 Bleecker St. (Sullivan St.), 477-5421

Raffetto's, 144 W. Houston St. (MacDougal St.), 777-1261

H. Roth and Son, 1577 First Ave. (82 St.), 734-1110

Russ & Daughters, 179 E. Houston St. (Orchard St.), 475-4880

Solomom Saperstein, 108 Rivington St. (Essex St.), 477-4515

Schaller & Weber, 1654 Second Ave. (86 St.), 879-3047, *and* 56-54 Myrtle Ave., Ridgewood, Queens, 821-7068, *and other stores*

Schapira Coffee Company, 117 W. 10 St. (Greenwich Ave.), 675-3733

Silver Palate, 274 Columbus Ave. (73 St.), 799-6340

SoHo Charcuterie, 195 Spring St. (Sullivan St.), 226-3545 *and at* **Ann Taylor,** 3 East 57 St. (Fifth Ave.), 832-1246

Todaro Brothers, 555 Second Ave. (31 St.), 532-0633

Les Trois Petits Cochons, 17 E. 13 St. (Fifth Ave.), 255-3844

Veniero Pastry, 342 E. 11 St. (First Ave.), 674-7264

Village Live Poultry, 205 Thompson St. (Bleecker St.), 727-3666

Vineland Poultry Farms, 512 East 80 St. (York Ave.), 288-1571

Word of Mouth, 1012 Lexington Ave. (73 St.), 734-9483

Zabar's, 2245 Broadway (80 St.), 787-2000

Anthony Zito, 259 Bleecker St. (Cornelia St.), 929-6139

Collector's Record Shops

New York has the largest number of unusual, interesting—and sometimes very inexpensive—record stores in the country. Almost any recording released in the world can be found somewhere in New York—from esoteric antique vocal recordings through the latest, limited edition rock single. Certain stores have made reputations for their vast selection of available recordings, and you never know what you will be able to find.

Discophile (26 W. 8 St., 473-1902) is probably the most professional record store in Manhattan. Almost every available classical recording (whether imported or domestic) can be located here. Founded over 20 years ago by the late Joe Greenspan, Discophile has been in the hands of long-time employee Franz Jolowicz for the past few years. There are also selections from the jazz and rock catalogues, although these are less well represented than at some other record stores. **Music Masters** (25 W. 43 St., 840-1958) not only stocks a variety of esoteric recordings but also has a special taping service available for many old and private discs.

J & R Music World (111 Nassau St., 349-8400) has a good amount of classical and jazz recordings, all at competitive prices. **The Soho Music Gallery** has a strong new music selection, as well as the best in jazz and obscure pop recordings (26 Wooster, 966-1637).

Two Manhattan bookstores feature a good selection of inexpensive, used LP's, mainly from the fifties and sixties: **Gryphon Books** (216 W. 89 St., 362-0706). Prices at the tiny **Jolly Roger** bookstore (190

Columbus Ave., 877-1836) are a little higher, but their records tend to be in slightly better condition. And for a good price on current releases, **The Record Hunter** (507 Fifth Ave., 697-8970) is still the best place in town—both in selection and price, especially during one of their frequent storewide sales. A careful browser can often find some bargains at **Sam Goody** or **King Karol** stores, although both outlets have slipped lamentably in recent years.

New York's vanguard record dealer remains the **New Music Distribution Service** (500 Broadway, fourth floor, 925-2121). Founded in 1972 by jazz musicians Carla Bley and Michael Mantler, NMDS is an outlet for recordings of artists and music that might prove too esoteric for commercial companies. NMDS, a not-for-profit organization, represents these musical pioneers and sells their recordings—both to single customers and in bulk to adventuresome record stores.

"Our personal judgment of a record's quality doesn't enter into it," says Taylor Storer, office manager for NMDSA. "We will take anything that is independently produced and can be loosely described as new music. Once we agree to distribute a record, we'll do so forever, or until the owners stop supplying us. Poor sales don't bother us a bit. We have records that sell only one copy per year."

NMDS represents 210 different labels, some boasting only one or two releases. Roughly 2,000 titles are stocked by NMDS, roughly divided between jazz and new music (sometimes a very difficult distinction to make). Among the specialties: an album consisting entirely of the sounds of different glasses being rubbed or struck; offerings from a group called Mother Mallard's Portable Masterpiece Company (on Earthquack Records, no less!), records by groups with names such as the U.S. Steel Cello Ensemble, the Nihilist Spasm Band, and the Residents, as well as recordings by a variety of whales and seals. In the more traditional mode, there are recordings of music by Charles Wurionen, Philip Glass, David Loeb, Milton Babbitt, John Adams, and Ingram Marshall. Prices are generally quite inexpensive, and the help is courteous and informed, always glad to point out interesting new releases to the sometimes overwhelmed customer.

Rock Record Shops

Brad's Records, 3756 White Plains Rd., Bronx,
654-3618

Founded in 1969 by Glenn "Brad" Osbourne, this Bronx
shop specializes in reggae and other Caribbean music
but also stocks most current pop, soul, and even country
releases. Additionally, Brad's sponsors two reggae-
oriented labels of its own, Grand Groove and Clock
Tower, and acts as a wholesale distributor of numerous
others based in both Jamaica and New York. Brad,
Mike, and David will gladly spin selected sounds at a
customer's request. Store hours are 11 A.M. to 9 P.M.
every day; from Manhattan the #2 train (Seventh Ave.
Express) will take you to the 219 St. stop, just a few
yards from Brad's door.

Bleecker Bob's Golden Oldies, 179 MacDougal St.,
475-9677

Cantankerous, controversial Bleecker Bob has been
dealing rare vinyl in Greenwich Village since 1965. In
1975 he moved to his present MacDougal Street location
and began the transition from oldies to punk, new wave,
and imported product. A punk fashion boutique
occupies the upper level, but the main floor bins are
crammed with everything *but* mainstream Hot 100
recordings: punk and progressive rock, reggae,
rockabilly, fifties and sixties R&B, electronic music,
collector's items (including bootlegs and promotional
rarities), and scores of hard-to-find independent
releases. Golden Oldies also carries a complete line of
English and American rock publications, numerous
smaller fanzines, and a selection of rare rock posters.
Despite increased competition, this is still the best-
known specialty record shop (especially for punk/new
wave) in New York. Hours are noon to 1 A.M. daily, 3
A.M. on Fridays and Saturdays, and Bob's hard-working
counter men will play your requests if they're not too
busy.

Downstairs Records, 20 W. 43 St., 354-4684

This midtown retailer once occupied a hallowed space in
a Times Square subway arcade, previously the site of
Slim Rose's legendary Times Square Records. Since
moving above ground in 1980, partners John Kulish and

Claude deKrechewo have expanded their already impressive oldies section (with a special emphasis on sixties soul and seventies disco collectibles), while maintaining a complete cross-section of contemporary rock and soul releases, though not much reggae or ethnic music. Some of the walk-in purchases are astonishing: $500 for an early Beatles single on German Polydor; $1,500 for an Elvis Presley promotional disc on RCA. Downstairs offers mail-order service, and their catalogue is available for $1.25, postage included. The staff will air requests when store traffic allows, and business hours are from 10 A.M. until 6:30 P.M. Closed Sundays.

99, 99 MacDougal Street, 777-4610
This basement-level shop, half record vendor, half punk boutique, was opened in 1978 by Ed Bahlman and Gina Franklyn. Its most notable characteristic is its selection: 99 doesn't stock *any* records on American major labels. But its selection of English imports, American indies (especially local New York releases), and reggae LP's and singles is excellent, and 99's prices are often lower than those of neighboring competitors. The staff will spin selected sounds for the curious shopper, especially if they're 99 records, which has already issued critically acclaimed sides by the Bush Tetras, E.S.G., and Glenn Branca. 99 is closed Tuesdays, but otherwise open from 1 to 7 P.M.

Record City, 734 Broadway, 533-3683
"It's a permanent sale here!" exclaims Record City's Rob Friedman. "Any two single albums, including imports, for $9.99—indefinitely!" This kind of crazy but canny thinking is characteristic of the man who, in the midst of a 1980 industry slump, chose to open a second capacious outlet in Newark. (Business is reportedly booming in both locations.) Friedman's success can be attributed not only to low prices but also to the sheer size and variety of his stock, the best of any single store on this list: jazz, blues, country, new and old rock, reggae, ethnic, and classical may all be found here in copious quantites. And those are just the *new* records. There are also hundreds of miscellaneous singles selling for 75 cents apiece, and used LP's ranging from 25 cents to $3.99. Open from 11 A.M. to 7 P.M., Monday through

Saturday, Record City offers the best one-stop record
shopping in Lower Manhattan.

St. Marks Sounds, 20 St. Marks Place, 677-3444
This small but vital East Village store opened in 1978
and quickly established itself as *the* used record center
in the area. St. Marks pays top dollar for good-condition
records (nonclassical LPs only), and resale prices range
from 25-cent daily specials to $3.99 for unplayed copies
of new releases. A solid selection of import LPs and
singles (mostly punk, reggae, and roots-rock reissues) is
maintained, and you can scan the walls for assorted
collector's discs at assorted prices or recent cutouts at
an average of $2.99. Mitch and Binky, among other
personnel, will play your requests (singles preferred) if
they're not too busy. The doors are open from noon to
10:30 P.M., Monday through Saturday, and from noon to
8 P.M. on Sundays

V.P. Records, 170–21 Jamaica Ave., Queens,
291-7058
Any reggae or Caribbean records you can't find at
Brad's you will surely find at V.P. This large, well-
stocked store is an offshoot of Randy's Records in
Kingston, Jamaica; like its parent store, V.P. also acts
as a distributor and wholesaler of reggae and calypso
labels like Sonic's and Tuff Gong. Chin is the top man
here, and V.P. is open six days a week (closed Sundays)
from 11 A.M. until 8 P.M. From Manhattan, either the E
or F train will carry you to the nearest stop, at 169 St.

Dayton's Records, 824 Broadway, 254-5084
This old, established outlet caters primarily to an older,
more established generation of record buffs with its
high-priced selection of rare pop, jazz, and soundtrack
recordings. Rock collectibles take a definite back seat
(the selection is random, the prices eyebrow-raising),
and punk never got in the door. But Dayton's might be
the place to find that Frank Sinatra or original
Broadway cast album you've been looking for. Don't
bother asking to hear anything—you'll only annoy the
middle-aged jazz fans behind the counter. It's open
from 10 A.M. to 6 P.M., until 5 P.M. Sat., and closed Sun.

Hall Place, 41 E. 7 St., 982-1604
Max Becker has dealt in used books and records from

this same crowded, dusty shop for 17 years. Two factors guarantee a high turnover in his stock: one, his Lower East Side neighborhood is filled with struggling artists and musicians who often must sell their collections to make the rent; two, the majority of Hall Place records are priced at $2 to $3. Of course, Max is no dummy, and his rare jazz, classical, and soundtrack albums run higher (though not as high as those at Dayton's and other specialists), but he's not averse to bargaining. There aren't any new, sealed records here, so don't go looking for them; Max doesn't have a record player in the shop, so don't ask to hear anything. But there are still bargains to be found in those jam-packed shelves and crates, assuming you can take the time to flip through piles of discs in no particular alphabetical or other order. Hall Place is open from 12:30 to 8 P.M. every Mon., Tues., and Thurs., and from 1 P.M. to 9 P.M. on Fri. and Sat. Max stays home on Wed. and Sun.

Special Specialty Stores

It's been said that "you can find anything in New York." And it's probably true, too. This section of the guide presents some stores that carry very specific merchandise, and it also tells you about some unusual places offering items a little out of the ordinary.

Caswell-Massey, 48 St. and Lexington Ave., 755-2254, is "the oldest chemist and perfumer in America." Established in 1752, this pharmacy has the largest selection of imported and rare toiletries, cosmetics, and health aids.

Herbs for cooking can be found in the Food chapter of this book, but what about herbs for medicinal purposes or even witchcraft? Besides several places in Chinatown, **Il Hwa Korean Ginseng** has herbal products for the health: 401 Fifth Ave. (686-3546). On a weirder note, **The Magickal Childe/Warlock Shop,** at 35 W. 19 St. (242-7182), is the store for buying herbs as potion ingredients, and the incantation books to go with them. They're serious about witchcraft and voodoo here . . . be careful.

There are several gift shops stocking uncommon giftware. Try **Cardier,** 212 Third Ave., 473-7971, especially for its unusual greeting cards. **Gemma's Dilemma,** at 145 Seventh Ave. So., 675-0858, carries handmade jewelry and miniatures. **Mythology,** 370 Columbus Ave., 874-0774, and **R.S.V.P.,** 162 E. 22 St., 982-8115, sell the trendier gifts, including handmade ones. Some gift shops stick to a more specific theme. **Only Hearts,** 281 Columbus Ave., 724-5608, sells exactly that: only items that are heart-shaped or that have hearts on them. **Unicorn City,** 55 Greenwich Ave., 243-2017—you guessed it: Its merchandise strictly adheres to the unicorn motif.

Rita Ford, 19 E. 65 St., 535-6717, and **Nathaniel's Music Box,** 200A Front St., 227-3232, are two places that sell nothing but music boxes, from the tacky to the collector's item.

People serious about glass art (stained and leaded) should go to **Glassmasters Guild,** 621 Sixth Ave., 924-2868. It is a department store of supplies and a gallery of glass objets d'art.

One wonderful shop is **Old Buttons,** a place devoted to old (clothing-type, not political-type) buttons, located at 143 E. 62 St. (753-8741). You can find Civil War, colored glass, and other antique fasteners.

New York has some unusual pet stores: **Exotic Aquatics** specializes in "pets that don't need to be walked," amphibians, reptiles, and tarantulas (272 Bleecker St., 675-6355). **The Parrot Jungle II,** 717 Lexington Ave., 752-0443, carries all species of birds. **Fish Town U.S.A.** is unique because of its size; it's like a marine museum to browse through (513 Third Ave., 889-3296).

Dollhouses (not just for kids) and their furnishings can be bought at **Doll House Masters,** 1650 Third Ave., 534-1012, and **Tiny Doll House,** 231 E. 53 St., 752-3082. For special repairs on loved ones, the **Manhattan Doll Hospital** is at 176 Ninth Ave., near 21 St. (989-5220).

Costumes for masquerade parties can be rented or bought at **Animal Outfits for People,** 252 W. 46 St., 840-6219, or **Universal Costume,** 1540 Broadway, 575-8570. There are several places to purchase theatrical makeup for such occasions, including **Bob Kelly,** 151 W. 46 St., 245-2237, and **Zauder Brothers,** 902 Broadway, 245-4155. For masks and disguises, try **Times Square Shoppers World,** located at 201 W. 49

St., 765-8342. **Wig Town,** 62 W. 14 St., 675-1649, is *not* the place to get an elegant coif, but for a silly change of styles, they even carry hairpieces in pink, green, or a patriotic red, white, and blue stripe.

Toy stores are in no shortage in Manhattan. The best for young children is **Childcraft,** with two locations: 155 E. 23 St. (674-4754) and 150 E. 58 St. (753-3196). Best for any age (especially kids-at-heart) is **F.A.O. Schwarz,** Fifth Ave. at 58 St. 644-9400. **The Train Shop,** 23 W. 45 St., 730-0409, stocks everything for model railroads.

For magic tricks, see **Hornmann,** established in New York since 1856, at 304 W. 34 St., 279-6079, or the very large **Magic Towne House,** 1026 Third Ave., 752-1165.

Unusual, especially out-of-season flowers can be bought at the **Cultured Seed,** 284 Columbus Ave., 874-4520. The plant and flower district, wholesale and retail, is located on and near Sixth Ave., from 23 to 29 St. For more exotic plants, check out **Bonsai Dynasty,** 851 Sixth Ave., 695-2973; **Paradise Palms,** 120 W. 28 St., 924-3776; or **Persephonie,** 1373 Third Ave., 734-1536.

There are many sporting goods stores, and some are devoted exclusively to individual sports; but did you know that there are several fencing equipment stores in the city? Two of them are **Rohde's,** 169 E. 86 St., 534-9170, and **Santelli,** 412 Sixth Ave., 254-4053. Horse saddles and riding gear are available at two places, and both have been in business since the turn of the century: **Kauffman,** 139 E. 24 St., 684-6060, and **Miller's,** 123 E. 24 St., 673-1400.

Art supplies are best bought at **Pearl Paint,** 308 Canal St., 431-7932, or at one of the **Sam Flax** stores (for locations and information, call 620-3000). Craft supplies are available at **Allcraft Tool & Supply,** 22 W. 48 St., 246-4740, and many other specialty dealers on Broadway and Sixth Ave., from 21 St. to 33 St. For a huge selection of yarns, go to **Yarn Center,** 866 Sixth Ave., 532-2145, or try **Needlemania,** 71 Broadway, 269-0939.

Many, many stores sell nothing but photographic equipment, but your best bet is the world's largest photography store, **Willoughby's,** 110 W. 32 St., 564-1600.

Comic books, new, used, and rare (and not for the

kiddies), can be found at **Comic Art Gallery,** 132 E. 58 St., 759-4861, and at **West Side Comics,** 107 W. 86 St., 724-0432.

Sheet music of the classical variety is best bought at **Patelson's,** 160 W. 56 St., 582-5840. **Schirmer's,** 586 Fifth Ave., 752-3800, also carries popular sheet music.

Untitled, 159 Prince St., 982-2088, is a very special postcard store—not your run-of-the-mill souvenirs, but art, unusual, and collector's item cards, in a wide variety.

Autographs can be purchased at **Lion Heart,** 12 W. 37 St., 695-1310, or at **James Lowe,** 667 Madison Ave., 889-8204.

The Collector's Cabinet, 153 E. 57 St., 355-2033, specializes in butterflies and seashells. **Captain Hook's Marine Antiques and Seashells,** 10 Fulton St., 344-2262, near the Fulton Fish Market, carries shells, sponges, and sea specimens.

A place that carries nothing but quilts is the **Continental Quilt Shop,** with two locations: 129 E. 57 St., 752-7631, and 7 W. 49 St., 757-3511. **Deutsch,** 196 Lexington Ave., 683-8746, sells everything made out of wicker and rattan, including larger-than-life gorillas, camels, and giraffes. They stock some small rattan goods and a complete line of wicker furniture.

The **Connoisseur Pipe Shop,** 51 W. 46 St., 247-6054, is recommended for the serious tobacco-phile, featuring handmade and custom-made pipes and fine tobacco mixtures.

The Erotic Baker features an assortment of anatomically accurate lollipops, gingerbread people, and cakes; most of the items are tasteful, and taste good. Their three locations are: 117 Christopher St., 989-8846; 246 E. 51 St., 752-9790; and 73 W. 83 St., 362-7557.

Here is a list of places selling those items politely referred to as "marital aids." Check out the **Pink Pussycat Boutique,** 161 W. 4 St., 243-0077, or the **Pleasure Chest** (several locations, for addresses call 242-4327). Naughty lingerie can be purchased at **Naughty Lingerie,** 99 Nassau St., 732-9099, or at **Playmate Lingerie,** 40 E. 34 St., 532-1333. Two other stores—which, if you can't guess what they sell, you have no business there—are the **Marquis de Suede,** 321 Bleecker St., 675-8463, or **Scarlet Leather,** 96 Christopher St., 255-1155.

THE PERFORMING ARTS

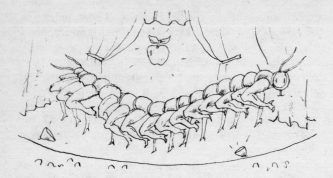

Concert Halls

New York City, arguably the music capital of the world, has many concert halls. But the most famous jewel in this fine and varied collection is the legendary **Carnegie Hall,** thought of by most performers as the best and most important hall in America and one of the three—with the Musikverein in Vienna and the Concertgebouw in Amsterdam—most distinguished in the world.

Carnegie, located on the southeast corner of Sixth Ave. and West 57 St., was financially backed by industrialist Andrew Carnegie. Completed in 1891, the hall was scheduled for demolition in the early 1960s, when Lincoln Center's Philharmonic (now named Avery Fisher) Hall went up. A group of concerned citizens, led by the forceful violinist/activist Isaac Stern, foiled that plot, however, by supporting a deal whereby the city of New York bought the property and rented it to a not-for-profit corporation, of which Stern was named president. Today the hall, its interior a splendor of red, white, and gold, infuses the city's cultural scene with performances on practically every night of the week by artists of international repute. The 1980–81 season saw the presentation of 336 concerts in the main hall and 471 in its neighboring, much smaller, Carnegie Recital Hall. "In many respects," wrote *New York Times* music critic Harold Schonberg in a piece noting its ninetieth birthday, "Carnegie Hall has remained . . . *the* hall in

New York, the one with glamor and tradition." The
ghosts of concerts past include performances by Arturo
Toscanini, Gustav Mahler, Tchaikovsky (who, with
Walter Damrosch, conducted Carnegie's opening night
concert), Paderewski, Rachmaninoff, Stokowski,
Koussevitzky, Fritz Kreisler, and Jascha Heifetz.

Carnegie Hall has witnessed, and helped stimulate,
the coming of age of American cultural life. When it was
built, notes author Richard Schickel in *The World of
Carnegie Hall,* there was only one truly professional
symphony orchestra in this country and virtually no
American musicians or composers. Now Carnegie Hall,
in its ninth decade, coexists with a myriad of
performing arts spaces throughout America and a
steadily growing number of such centers in New York
City alone.

The most glamorous of these is **Lincoln Center.** A
conception of the renowned former New York City
Parks Commissioner Robert Moses, Lincoln Center is,
for better or worse, largely responsible for the
realization of that builder's vision of "a reborn West
Side, marching north from Columbus Circle, and
eventually spreading over the entire dismal and decayed
West Side." According to journalist Robert Caro, 7,000
low-income families and 800 businesses were displaced
in order to build the cultural complex, which
represented, according to the American Institute of
Architects Guide to New York City, an initial
investment of more than $165 million early 1960s
dollars—mostly in private contributions—along with
federal aid in acquiring the site and a state contribution
to the New York State Theater.

The halls of the complex—**Avery Fisher,** the **State
Theater,** and the **Metropolitan Opera**—are, in the
words of *New York Times* architecture critic Ada
Louise Huxtable, "lushly decorated, conservative
structures." The plazas surrounding the halls attract a
comfortable number of visitors—tourists as well as New
Yorkers on their lunch hours. In warm weather, one can
sit in the outdoor café beside Avery Fisher Hall or
brown-bag it around the plaza's fountains. In summer,
Lincoln Center Out-of-Doors sponsors free concerts.

The **New York State Theater,** located on the
southeast corner of Lincoln Center on Columbus Ave.
between W. 62 and W. 63 Sts., was designed by

architects Philip Johnson and Richard Foster and completed in 1964. This 2,800-seat theater is the home of the New York City Opera Company, now directed by Beverly Sills, and George Balanchine's New York City Ballet. The annual December performances of Tchaikovsky's "Nutcracker Suite" by the latter ensemble are among the most popular constants on New York City's cultural calendar.

The **Damrosch Park Guggenheim Bandshell,** on the southwest corner of Lincoln Center, was designed by the architectural firm of Eggers & Higgins and completed in 1969. It provides, as it was intended to do, a space for free concerts; many of the ones presented there are part of the Lincoln Center Out-of-Doors program mentioned above.

The **Metropolitan Opera House,** located on the west side of Lincoln Center between W. 63 and W. 64 Sts., was designed by Wallace K. Harrison and completed in 1966. The house is most easily recognized by the Chagall tapestries that hang in the lobby, which faces the plaza, and the dramatic, red-carpeted stairs provide ticket holders with all the physical glamor associated with a night at the opera. The sight of the Austrian crystal chandeliers inside the hall rising to a gold-leafed ceiling never fails to evoke an admiring gasp from visitors.

Avery Fisher Hall is the home of the New York Philharmonic. Originally called Philharmonic Hall, but renamed to honor the man who donated $10 million for an overhaul of what were the auditorium's singularly unsuccessful acoustics, it was rebuilt several times in attempts to solve those acoustical deficiencies. The most radical reconstruction was completed in 1976, to the general satisfaction of both acoustical and architectural critics.

The **Juilliard School,** located on Broadway between W. 65 and W. 66 Sts., on the west side of Lincoln Center, is, like the other constituents of the complex, built of a light-colored limestone. The structure holds two fine concert halls: the 1,096-seat **Alice Tully Hall** was designed for chamber music and is the home of the Chamber Music Society of Lincoln Center. The 277-seat **C. Michael Paul Hall,** opened in 1970, is wider in relation to its length than Carnegie Recital Hall, which is only a little larger. The hall is paneled in cherry wood, and the pipes of a 50-rank Holtkamp organ hang over the stage. The acoustics, very live but clear, were designed by Heinrich Keilholz, who was also responsible for the acoustic design of Tully Hall.

The newest concert hall in Manhattan is the **Merkin Concert Hall** in the Abraham Goodman House, located on 67 St., one block north of Lincoln Center. Opened in December 1978, the 457-seat auditorium is a little less than half the size of Tully. During its 1980–81 season, it offered half a dozen concert series, including ensemble programs with the Tokyo String Quartet, Tashi, and the Beaux Arts Trio, and three evenings of contemporary music, known as Music Today, organized by Gerard Schwarz. A special Tuesday matinee series featured instrumental chamber music.

The most active concert halls on Manhattan's East Side are the Metropolitan Museum of Art's 700-seat **Grace Rainey Rogers Auditorium** on Fifth Ave. and 82 St., and the **Kaufmann Concert Hall** of the Young Men and Women's Hebrew Association (known as the 92nd Street Y), located on the southeast corner of Lexington Ave. and E. 92 St. Grace Rainey Rogers Auditorium opened in 1954, and the 1981–82 season, a representative one, included concerts by the Jupiter Symphony Chamber Players, the Music Aeterna Orchestra, the Waverly Consort, the Juilliard, Cleveland, and Guarneri Quartets, and the Beaux Arts Trio, as well as series of sonata, early-music, and vocal-music programs.

The 916-seat Kaufmann Concert Hall of the 92nd Street Y offers the most varied programming in all of Manhattan. During the 1980–81 season, its renowned Poetry Center, established in 1939 because practically no institutions outside the university offered poetry readings, included among its guests the 1980 Nobel Laureate Czeslaw Milosz, Erica Jong, John Updike, Jules Feiffer, John Cheever, and Grace Paley. An economics roundtable included John Kenneth Galbraith, Alan Greenspan, George Gilder, Robert Lekachman, Leonard Silk, and Robert Heilbroner. This YM–YWHA also sponsored series on lyrics and lyricists and on critics and criticism, and one called "Opera: From Score to Stage," as well as programs of American Jewish theater and Jewish film. The Y has established its own orchestra, the distinguished Y Chamber

Symphony, conducted and directed by Gerard Schwarz.
The performance of all of Bach's Brandenburg Concerti
by members of this musical organization during the
Christmas/New Year's season has become so popular
that the 1981–82 season saw that event scheduled five
times. A series featuring the Guarneri, Concord, and
Cleveland Quartets included all the quartets of
Beethoven, Bartók, and Brahms.

Carnegie Hall and Carnegie Recital Hall, Seventh
Ave. at 57 St., 247-7459

Lincoln Center: Alice Tully Hall, 362-1911; **Avery
Fisher Hall,** 874-2424; **Metropolitan Opera House,**
580-9030; **New York State Theater,** 870-5570

Merkin Concert Hall, Abraham Goodman House,
129 W. 67 St., 362-8719

Metropolitan Museum, Fifth Ave. and 82 St.,
570-3949

92nd Street Y, on Lexington Ave., 427-4410

Dance in New York

No question about it, New York has given the world the
most innovative dancing of the twentieth century. And
the wide array of performing spaces here—from the
grandest theaters to the humblest of lofts—parallels the
diversity of the dance activity itself.

There is no central institution that presents dance in
New York, which has meant that there's no one central
type of accepted dance, no acknowledged standard, and,
therefore, more experimentation is possible. On the
other hand, the haphazard availability of theater space
for dance has meant that dancers have had to make do,
performing in many types of spaces, none of them ideal,
and many are more decrepit than adequate. For the
smaller modern companies, it's all they can muster
financially to present one or two weekends of concerts a
year. There are so many practicing choreographers in
New York that the audience never wants for a
constantly changing calendar of dance events.

The closest thing New York has to an institution is
Lincoln Center. The **New York State Theater**
(877-4727) houses the New York City Ballet for six
months a year. This theater was designed with dance in

mind—much to the dismay of opera-goers who suffer the house's acoustics the other half year, when the New York City Opera is in residence there. But it's a glorious setting for the city's glorious dance company.

Across the plaza, at the gaudily opulent **Metropolitan Opera House** (799-4420), the American Ballet Theater has become resident dance company, though for only a few months a year. During the summer, the Met has gotten into the habit of importing foreign dance companies—mostly classical ballet, the likes of the Royal Ballet or the Stuttgart Ballet. Ticket prices there are high, matched only by the prices on Broadway, where top-ranked companies occasionally perform.

It's ugly and sight lines are awful; nevertheless, **City Center** (131 W. 55 St., 246-8989) is the only other large uptown theater where dance is a regular attraction. In addition to the Ailey and Joffrey companies that call City Center home, a "Masters Of Contemporary Dance" series brought such companies as those of Merce Cunningham, Alwin Nikolais, and José Limon to the house. For better or for worse, City Center has become the only large theater that's affordable for dance companies and that encourages their bookings.

The Brooklyn Academy of Music (30 Lafayette Ave., 636-4100, Brooklyn) is a largish theater that regularly features dance. The subway ride is almost compensated for by the charming opera house and the delicious snacks for sale in the lobby. BAM has sponsored a mix of dance styles, from experimentation toward polite ballet companies.

There's "uptown" dance and "downtown" dance, though these terms refer more to aesthetics than to geography. What we now call postmodern dance had its genesis in the experimentation that got its start in the early sixties at the Judson Church in Greenwich Village. This was a time of "happenings" and the Living Theater, and the choices that dancers made were closely related to this vibrant art scene. They said no to theatricality, yes to closer audience involvement in the work. The type of space in which a dance performance was situated became an integral part of the choreography and of the choreographer's statement. The large open loft spaces that were beginning to gain currency at that time could be used like clean canvases;

the audience could be participants through close proximity to the performers, with the freedom to look at anything momentarily interesting.

Today there are a number of loft-theater spaces used by dance companies. These spaces tend to be small, informal environments located in out-of-the-way crevasses of lower Manhattan. Don't expect comfort, unless sitting on a square of thin foam rubber is your idea of gracious living. And don't expect an even standard of quality, for it varies from the terrible to the transcendent. The thing about loft spaces, though, is that when you do come upon a good performance, the intimacy of the environment can make the experience seem like a treasure.

Though **Judson Church** (55 Washington Sq. So., 477-0351) is where postmodern dance got its start, it doesn't present dance more than occasionally now. **Washington Square Church,** however, located close by at 133 W. 4 St. (777-2528), offers a grand setting for modern dance. If you just don't want to stray far from Washington Square, there's always the **New York University School of Education Theater** (17 E. 4 St., 598-3232). This moderately-sized house offers a proscenium setting for more modernism.

American Theater Laboratory (219 W. 19 St., 924-0077) is one converted loft theater where the quality of events is uniformly good. This means that you can go there any weekend and usually see a fine performance. The space is run by Dance Theater Workshop, a service organization for dancers, and technically is quite sophisticated—for a loft. There's a gallery area in the lobby, and you can usually find dancers of all types drinking coffee there at intermissions.

Merce Cunningham uses his top-floor studio at the artists' complex **Westbeth** (463 West St., 691-9751) for performances of his own company. (It's probably the best place to see them perform.) At other times, assorted choreographers rent the space. With its bank of windows that overlook a glittery Manhattan skyline— you never know what color the Empire State Building will be—there's always *something* worthwhile to look at.

The Kitchen (484 Broome St., 925-3615) presents mostly video and music, but once a month it manages to book some of the most reliably interesting dance going

on. A sport of dance-watching at the Kitchen is to spot
how each choreographer will deal with the pillars that
divide the room.

Close by are the **Performing Garage** (33 Wooster
St., 966-3651), a square, cavernous kind of place with
bleachers; **Eden's Expressway** (537 Broadway,
226-8988); and the **Trisha Brown Studio** (541
Broadway, 925-6031), where one can find a regular
stream of postmodern loft dance events.

Danspace, at St. Mark's Church (10 St. at Second
Ave., 674-6377), has reopened since fire damaged the
church, and performances have once again begun. The
center has a long history of fostering artists in many
media, and—in dance, as well—you can find what's
avant-garde entrenched at St. Mark's.

The Riverside Dance Festival at Riverside Church
(490 Riverside Dr., 864-2929) is a six-month-long affair
that books a lively assortment of modern companies,
some non-New York troupes, small chamber ballet
groups, and some ethnic and jazz dancing into its
proscenium stage auditorium. Don't expect to find
experimental dance here, yet the quality of attractions
is solid, if uninspired at times. On a much less regular
basis, **Marymount Manhattan Theater** (221 E. 71 St.,
472-3800) is a similar space that books similar
attractions.

The Dance Gallery (242 E. 14 St., 685-5972),
Theater of the Open Eye (316 E. 88 St., 534-6363), **St.
Clement's Theater** (423 W. 46 St., 246-7277), the
Cubiculo (414 W. 55 St., 265-2138), and the **Emanu-el
Midtown Y** (344 E. 14 St., 673-2207) are all established
nonestablishment dance theaters.

Many ethnic dance companies flow into Manhattan,
ranging from spectacles like the Moiseyev Troupe from
the Soviet Union to the grand scale Kabuki Theater
from Japan. You'll find attractions like these at the Met
or at the **Beacon Theater** (2124 Broadway, 874-1718).
For reliable quality, always high, and uniqueness, the
ethnic troupes sponsored by the Asia Society are not to
be missed. They import visiting troupes from obscure
mountaintops—at least it seems like it—several times a
year, usually presenting them at theaters like **Carnegie
Hall** (154 W. 57 St., 247-7459), or the **American
Museum of Natural History** (Central Park West and
79 St., 873-1300). **Japan House** (333 E. 47 St., 371-

4758) also hosts dance events, classical Japanese or American dance based on Japanese themes.

The proliferation of dance in New York is astonishing. On any given weekend, from fall through spring, one can choose from a hearty list of dance events. Though you can't predict quality (with rare exceptions), you *can* get a sense of what type of work to expect from the type of space in which the performance is taking place. And it's all happening here!

New York Film Revival Houses

The revival house has been a New York tradition for almost fifty years by providing a small, intelligent, and discerning movie-going audience with the finest in foreign, silent, rare, or esoteric films; films that, because of their timeless entertainment value, deserve to be reshown, or recent films of merit that may have been buried because of limited audience appeal.

Prices and admission policies vary but remain considerably less expensive than those at first-run theaters, and many offer further price reductions to members or frequent customers.

Remember, many theaters offer a double bill that changes daily, so pick up one of their schedules, check the newspaper, or call ahead.

The Bleecker Street Cinema, at 144 Bleecker St., is a small picturesque theater located in the center of Greenwich Village, with numerous cafés and restaurants in the immediate area. The Bleecker shows a fine mix of American and foreign films with frequent specials and series such as a recent very popular and long-running Japanese series on Tuesdays. Telephone: 674-2560

The Carnegie Hall Cinema at Seventh Ave. and 57 St., located in one of New York's most famous buildings, exudes a feeling of class unequaled by most other revival houses. The Carnegie stresses foreign films and foreign specials as well as important and popular American films. Telephone: 757-2131

The 8th Street Playhouse, at 52 W. 8 St., is another popular Greenwich Village theater located in a bustling neighborhood of shops, late-night cafés, clubs, and restaurants. The 8th Street Playhouse has an erratic revival policy, alternating between extended runs of first- and second-run films with more traditional revival and offbeat series. They also cater to the campy, cult, and bizarre-for-the-sake-of-being-bizarre film audience by offering a different midnight show nightly. Telephone: 674-6515

The Cinema Village, at 22 E. 12 St., is located in a quieter more residential area of Greenwich Village, a short walk from cafés and restaurants. The Cinema Village is a typical revival theater in a pleasant neighborhood showing a solid mix of the more popular foreign and American films. Telephone: 924-3363

The Hollywood Twin Cinemas I and II at Eighth Av. and 47 St. are located on the edge of the Times Square porno belt in an area nothing short of sleazy. It is laudable that the Hollywood Twin Cinemas I and II have adopted an excellent revival policy with a strong accent on American double bills blended with the more popular foreign films. Telephone: 246-0717

The Olympia Quad, on Broadway at 107 St. is a popular spot near Columbia University. A few restaurants and bars dot the area, with the Balcony next door being as good as any place else. Recently divided into four separate theaters, the Quad now devotes one theater to showing a strong but uninspired program of foreign films mixed with the more tried and true American revival house standards. If you live in the area, visit them, but unless you are of an impetuous nature, or have little time in the city, don't travel. The same films will be shown somewhere else. Telephone: 865-8128

The Regency, on Broadway at 67 St., lies in perhaps the most comfortable and civilized area of the West Side. It is a short distance from Lincoln Center, and there are several good bars and restaurants nearby. The Regency is an American film revival house noted for its ambitious series and glowing film tributes. Broad themes, such as comedy, mystery, drama, or extensive selections of films from the major studios are the traditional Regency fare. Telephone: 595-0012

The Thalia, at 95 St. just west of Broadway, lies in what some feel to be an uncomfortable Upper West

Side area. For years the area has been improving, but progress has been slow. There are virtually no places to go after a late show except home or another neighborhood. Despite the area's mixed reputation, the Thalia has remained a vital New York tradition for over 50 years, making it the oldest foreign film-revival house in the country. The Thalia remains the quintessential revival house, offering perhaps the most inspired, adventurous, offbeat, and oft-copied programming of any New York revival house. Telephone: 222-3370

The Theater 80 Saint Marks, at 80 St. Marks Pl., is another theater in an area with an undeservedly bad reputation. This East Village theater has many nearby restaurants and bars. The Theater 80 Saint Marks specializes in showing some of the more obscure as well as popular American films from the thirties and forties. Telephone: 254-7400

Other Music Spots in New York

The Brooklyn Academy of Music, 30 Layfayette St., Brooklyn, 636-4100
BAM (as this historic concert hall is commonly referred to) is a short subway ride into Brooklyn. Its programming is eclectic and daring—1981 featured the New York City premiere of Philip Glass' *Satyagraha,* and there have been many other highlights here. Besides BAM's strong commitment to the avant-garde, it also hosts the home concerts of the Brooklyn Philharmonia. Well worth a trip if you are interested in the program—a nice hall, well kept, and not inconvenient to Manhattan.

Carnegie Tavern, 165 W. 56 St., 757-9522
Located within Carnegie Hall, but a separate entity, the Carnegie Tavern features the splendid Ellis Larkins on piano many evenings. Composer Alvin Curran once called Larkins the "Webern of stride piano." The tavern serves good, if overpriced, food, and houses an unfortunate stuffiness at times. But Larkins is great.

Ear Inn, 326 Spring St., 226-9060
A popular hangout for downtown experimental musicians, the Ear Inn serves good food and presents

unpredictable music. Very comfortable and pleasant. Friendly, especially if you're a musician.

Inroads, 150 Mercer St., 226-6622
Another spot to catch experimental jazz, rock, and new music. Call for details—Inroads often has some very interesting performers. No booze.

The Kitchen, 484 Broome St., 925-3615
New York's most established center for the avant-garde. The Kitchen—which serves neither food nor drink— offers dance, video, performance, and musical evenings. Call ahead to find out what is on; it's usually interesting. Located in the heart of Soho.

Michael's Pub, 211 E. 55 St., 758-2272
A snazzy, expensive midtown East place, but well worth it for Woody Allen, who plays clarinet here Monday nights. It's a mob scene, of course, but fans of the comedian will have to try to get in. *Not* cheap.

Other End, 149 Bleecker St., 673-7030
Quintessential Village folk/rock/light jazz hangout. Lots of bohemian atmosphere, not terribly friendly.

Roulette, 228 West Broadway, 431-1022
Run by two transplanted midwesterners, Roulette has established itself in the last two years as a very good place to hear New Music. Nothing fancy—the concerts are held in the owner's loft, but there is often fine music, some complimentary wine and lots of downtown atmosphere.

Soundscape, 500 W. 52 St., 581-7032
On the far western edge of "Swing Street," this club offers good experimental jazz and a solid professional environment. Well worth a visit.

Stilwende, 225 West Broadway, 431-1133
A funky, pleasant downtown bar that has lately begun some adventuresome programming. One evening you might find hard rock, the next evening new wave, the next evening avant-garde jazz, and the next New Music. Unpredictable and exciting.

Symphony Space, 2537 Broadway, 865-2557
Symphony Space is located in what used to be one of the Upper West Side's largest movie houses. It is now public territory, offering a space to numerous performance groups of all stripes, from the Group for Contemporary Music to the New York Gilbert and

Sullivan Players. A lot of different material passes through the Symphony Space. Give them a call; there might be something that interests you.

Trude Heller's, Sixth Ave. and 9 St., 254-8346
A popular cabaret/nightclub with a mixed clientele; located in the heart of the Village, and very chic.

Village Gate, Bleecker and Thompson Sts., 475-5120
Another historic Village night spot—folk, jazz, cabaret, or rock, depending on who is performing.

Village Vanguard, 178 Seventh Ave. So., 255-4037
Still, after all these years, *the* jazz spot in New York City. The Vanguard is a smoky, cavernous dive, but that just adds to the appeal for jazz lovers, who still pack this subterranean establishment to hear some of the best music in the city. Very Greenwich Village, and, in its own way, very romantic—if you like pipes.

Performance Art

• The place is **Carnegie Hall.** David Van Tieghem, a tall angular man in a snap-brimmed fedora, is manipulating dozens of objects that cover the surface of a long table and spill over onto the floor. Pots and pans, children's toys, he sounds each in turn, creating a musical performance in which what is seen is as important as what is heard.

• The place is the **Franklin Furnace** in Tribeca. Rose English, dressed in a man's Elizabethan doublet and hose, is seated on a makeshift platform ringed with theatrical lights. As she unpacks the contents of her costume truck, she improvises a nonstop hour-long monologue that moves back and forth between the relationship of humor and fetishism and the expectations of audience and performer. All seen afresh in the context of contemporary feminism.

• The place is an office building in the Wall Street area. Vanalyne Greene, costumed in what-the-well-dressed-secretary-will-wear, is at her desk. She talks directly to her audience, mostly neighborhood office workers, about problems she encounters in her job. Later, everyone is invited for coffee and discussion.

These three solos are among the best and simplest performances to take place in New York in recent months. Other have made use of casts of thousands and elaborate technology. Their durations have been as short as a minute and as long as a year, and their locations have been private homes, the street, galleries, museums, concert halls, clubs, and theaters, as well as spaces devoted specifically to what has come to be called performance.

Located on the boundaries of all established art media, performance glories in the adversary position. For this reason it is difficult to define. Come up with a working definition and you can be sure some performance makers will go out of their way to negate it. The basics are surely someone to "perform" an activity and someone to witness the performance; however, these two disparate roles can be combined in one person as in "I perform taking the A train to 59th Street." In this hypothetical performance, the boundary in question is the one between art and life; here, performance becomes an attitude.

Although most performances are more visible than this one, they are not always easy to find. Despite the attention it has been given by the media in the past decade and its promotion by the art gallery system, performance remains an economically marginal activity. Performance is attractive to young artists partly because their own bodies are the cheapest material they can use. However, as there is no lasting object to be bought or sold, little income is generated. Performance centers, dependent on the vagaries of private and public funding, lead precarious existences.

The oldest and most active is the **Kitchen Center for Video, Music, Dance, and Performance.** Finding out what's cooking at the Kitchen is a sure way of getting a toehold on the circuit. Other places to check out are the **Franklin Furnace, Just Above Midtown (JAM), Artists Space,** and the **Mudd Club,** all in Tribeca; the **Performing Garage** in Soho; **P.S. 1** located in a refurbished schoolhouse in Queens; and **Fashion Moda** in the Bronx. Established galleries and museums are occasionally the sites of performance activity as well.

Since most performance is centered in lower Manhattan in Soho, Tribeca, and the East Village, a glance at posters plastered on lampposts and walls in those neighborhoods should provide some good leads.

The Kitchen, 484 Broome St. 925-3615

Franklin Furnace, 112 Franklin St., 925-4671

Just Above Midtown (JAM), 178 Franklin St., 966-7020

Artists Space, 105 Hudson St., 226-3970

The Mudd Club, 77 White St., 227-7777

The Performing Garage, 33 Wooster St., 966-3651

P.S. 1, 46-01 21 St., Long Island City, Queens, 784-2084

Fashion Moda, 2803 Third Ave. (near 147 St.,) 585-0135

Poetry Readings

Besides being the center for commercial publishing, New York City has become a focal point for poetry readings as well. On any given evening in the fall or spring, you're likely to find up to ten different readings taking place throughout the five boroughs, with an even greater spread as to style and quality. They're to be found at colleges, bars, bookshops, libraries, museums, art galleries, churches, theaters, parks, restaurants, lofts, and the living rooms of apartments. With the exception of a few "benefits," prices are reasonable, usually under $4. Keep in mind, though, that price here is no indication of the quality of the readers. Readings at libraries, for example, are often among the best, and always free.

At one end of the quality scale, you'll probably find at least one "open reading" per night, where everyone is welcome to come and read a poem or two. At the other end of the scale are the two mainstays of the established poetry community: the **YMHA Poetry Center** and **The Academy of American Poets** (which sponsors readings at the Donnell Library and, for its most prestigious writers, at the Guggenheim Museum). Both these series feature top names in American poetry, well-published younger poets, and distinguished foreign writers (always with distinguished translators as well).

One of the most interesting poetry series is to be found at **St. Mark's Church.** Here a regular Wednesday night reading series includes a wide range of readers, from Allen Ginsberg and John Ashbery to people whose names will be unfamiliar to all but the avid poetry reader. The series was begun over 20 years ago as an alternative to the establishment series: they've kept up the tradition of focusing on more experimental writers. In addition, St. Mark's sponsors a Monday night reading series, which usually presents younger writers, and they have free writing workshops on other nights.

A few highly recommended reading series that run through a good part of the year are listed below. But since many series are short-lived, it would be useless to list them here. The *Poetry Calendar,* available free at many bookshops, contains a full monthly listing of readings. Be sure to check neighborhood papers for what other readings might be going on.

The Academy of American Poets
(sponsors readings at
the Donnell Library, 20 W. 53 St.
and the Guggenheim Museum, 89 St. & Fifth Av.),
427-5665

Books & Co.,
939 Madison Ave. (at 75 St.),
737-1450

Ear Inn,
326 Spring St.,
226-9060

Manhattan Theater Club,
321 E. 73 St.,
472-0600

The Public Theater,
425 Lafayette St.,
598-7150

The St. Mark's Poetry Project,
10 St. and Second Ave.,
674-0910

The YMHA Poetry Center,
92 St. and Lexington Ave.,
427-8000, ext. 176

Where to Go on Off-Off-Broadway

It was a steamy summer night, and I was at the
Performing Garage on Wooster St., feeling miserable.
Not because of the heat—the garage was air-
conditioned—but because of the stupefyingly banal
performance art piece that was droning on before my
eyes. Just as I was cursing the fact that there was no
intermission during which one could politely escape, I
felt a rustling at my elbow. Two women sitting next to
me were leaving, so I attached myself to their party and
snuck out. Outside we commiserated. My fellow critics
consisted of a well-dressed suburban housewife and her
teen-aged daughter, and the mother said, "We wanted
to see something wild and experimental, and someone
suggested this was a good place to go. I guess they were
wrong."

Actually, they were right—the Performing Garage is
one of the main places to go for experimental theater.
But the nature of experiments is that some are failures.
And when you're sailing forth into what may be for you
the uncharted waters of Off-Off-Broadway, the most
you can hope is that—failure or no—the experiment you
select will be interesting. With a little study and
preparation, however, you can increase your chances of
seeing the best of Off-Off-Broadway. And the best of
Off-Off-Broadway is, nine times out of ten, more
thoughtful, more exciting, more intimate, and far more
inexpensive to attend than any Broadway theater. In
recent years, in fact, a hefty percentage of the shows
that hit Broadway have come from smaller, not-for-
profit theaters Off- or Off-Off-Broadway. And it's
almost always more pleasant to see a play in a 200-seat
theater for $5 or $8 than to see the same play with the
same cast in a 1,000-seat theater for $20 or more; and
there's always the cachet of being able to say, "I saw it
when it was on East Fourth Street." Still, Off-Off-
Broadway offers shows that will never make it to
Broadway yet are unforgettable experiences; even when
a show on the whole doesn't make it, often there will be
a single performance so striking that it makes it all
worthwhile. And the economic consideration can't be
overstressed—when tickets cost $3 up to $10, how can
you go wrong?

Okay, say you're sold. You're from out of town or you're a native novice, and you want to see some Off-Off-Broadway theater. How do you know where to go? There are so many shows to choose from, and most don't have the money to advertise in the papers telling you how great Rex Reed thought they were. Here are a few general hints to steer you in the right direction.

1. *Read reviews.* But you have to know how to read them the right way. Bear in mind that everybody has an opinion, and many people publish theirs. So unless you've followed a critic for some time, his or her opinions probably won't mean much to you. What's more important is to read the description of the play and decide for yourself; if it sounds interesting to you, follow your instincts. The most thorough and reliable Off-Off-Broadway coverage appears in the *Village Voice; Other Stages,* a biweekly paper distributed free at theaters, is exclusively devoted to Off-Broadway theater and also carries a lot of useful information.

2. *Consider the source.* There are theaters that have been around long enough to become institutions, and these institutions are more likely than not to produce good work. **The New York Shakespeare Festival,** better known as the **Public Theater** (425 Lafayette St., 598-7100), the **Manhattan Theater Club** (321 E. 73 St., 288-2500), and the **Phoenix Theater** (221 E. 71 St., 730-0787) are sufficiently professional and well funded so that almost any production there is worth seeing. Theaters such as **La Mama ETC** (74A E. 4 St., 475-7710), the **Performing Garage** (33 Wooster St., 966-3651), **Theater for the New City** (162 Second Ave., 254-1109), and the **Ensemble Studio Theater** (549 W. 52 St., 247-4982) usually produce a large quantity of work each season, but you have to be a little more careful to separate the wheat from the chaff. Here is where reviews or word-of-mouth can help; another tip is to check the names of the playwright, the director, and the actors: if there's someone there who has given you pleasure before, that's a good sign, and, likewise, if the director is someone who gave you one of the dullest evenings of your life, take that into account.

3. *Avoid like the plague.* The obverse of number 2 is that there are numerous Off-Off-Broadway theaters whose shows can usually be counted on to be dreadful— pathetically poverty-stricken, hopelessly amateurish,

unimaginative, unattractive, uncomfortable. No one
likes to admit it, but these places usually house either
vanity productions or cheap, dreary revivals: the **AMDA
Studio I** in the Ansonia Hotel, the **Drama Committee
Repertory Theater,** the **Force 13 Theater
Company,** the **13th Street Theater,** the **Quaigh
Theater,** the **New York Theater Ensemble,** the
Apple Corps Theater, American Theater of Actors,
and the **78th Street Theater Lab.** Very occasionally
something good might appear at these theaters, but
unless you hear reliably otherwise, stay away. Let's put
it this way: you may think you want to go see *The
Importance of Being Earnest* at the Drama Committee
Repertory Theater, but you don't.

4. *Consult the reference books.* Not that there are
many. The closest thing to a Michelin guide to Off-Off-
Broadway is a book called *New York's Other Theatre*
published in 1981 by the Off-Off-Broadway Alliance. It
gives addresses, phone numbers, and thumbnail
sketches of more than 75 theaters, as well as handy
directions on how to get to them and recommended
restaurants nearby.

These are merely guidelines. Of course, the spirit of
Off-Off-Broadway suggests that you be creative and
take a chance.

Inexpensive Theater Tickets

Imagine a club that provides you with free tickets to
hundreds of concerts at major New York halls and half-
price tickets to more shows than you can possibly sit
through in a year. Now deduct half the tab for dinner at
restaurants all over town, add reduced rates at several
movie houses, and you may begin to suspect that
Norman J. Seaman's Concert/Theatre Club is the
biggest bargain in the Big Apple. The price tag confirms
this suspicion. A one year, double membership will set
you back (ready for this?) $25. Memberships for four
are even cheaper at $35. To get yours call 595-0351, or
write to: Norman J. Seaman's Concert/Theatre Club,
2067 Broadway, N.Y., N.Y. 10023.

If there's even one among you who doesn't know what
the letters TKTS stand for, then I consider the
explication of that acronym to be my sacred duty. For
the unwashed, these four letters represent theater

tickets available on the day of performance at half price plus a $1 service charge.

TKTS are available at two Manhattan locations. The **Times Square Theatre Centre** (Broadway and 47 St., Duffy Sq.) is open 7 days a week from 3 P.M. to 8 P.M. On matinee days, the Centre opens at noon to accommodate afternoon audiences. On a given day as many as thirty shows, including top hits, may be offered. Since half-price tickets are made available subject to the strength of a theater's advance sales, offerings change daily.

Providing fewer shows, but greater convenience to downtowners, the **Lower Manhattan Theatre Centre** (100 William St.) is open Monday through Friday from 11:30 A.M. to 5:30 P.M. and Saturday from 11 A.M. to 3 P.M. The policy here is the same as at Duffy Square. All tickets are half-price plus $1, though only evening performances are available.

The **Theatre Development Fund,** in addition to its sponsorship of TKTS, offers cut-rate tickets to a wide variety of performing arts events through its huge mailing list. Inclusion on TDF's list is restricted to students, teachers, performing arts professionals, union members, retirees, members of the clergy, and members of the armed forces. To find out if you qualify, send a stamped, self-addressed envelope to: Theatre Development Fund, 1501 Broadway, New York, N.Y. 10036.

Even opera tickets can be had for a song. The **Metropolitan Opera** (Broadway and 64 St. at Lincoln Center) offers standing-room tickets on the day of performance at $6, tops. The box office opens at 10 A.M., but be forewarned: Standee tickets are limited, so get there *early* for the more popular dates. In addition, only one ticket per customer is allowed. If you need four, better bring three bodies to stand in line with you. For performance times and ticket availability, the number at the Met is 580-9830.

A Guide to New York Video Art

"Video in the eighties," a young video artist recently confided, "is like candlemaking in the sixties.

Everybody's doing it, but nobody knows that much about it."

As true as that might be, video is still the answer to the eighties artist's prayers. For the visual artist, it's a chance to explore time, kineticism, and technology. For the filmmaker, its equipment is less expensive, more portable, and more accessible. For the performance artist, it's a chance to document one's work and to experiment with what a little editing can do. For musicians, it provides an opportunity to sync music up with visual images.

But what does it provide for the layman?

Not only entertainment and some possible insights (like all other art forms), but the possibility of mass communication on the aesthetic level—everybody's got a TV. And a whole new way of watching that little electric box that more often, in the real world, tends to anaesthetize rather than aestheticize.

Although many universities and art schools are teaching and using video equipment, and despite flourishing video scenes in Los Angeles, San Francisco, and Chicago, New York is the capital of video art. In the beginning (1966) there was a lone SONY Portopak (portable video camera) and behind it was Nam June Paik, a Korean conceptual artist, who almost single-handedly gave birth to video art, here in Manhattan. Most of the other early video artists—Vito Acconci, Joan Jonas, Lynda Benglis, Doug Davis, Richard Foreman—were visual or conceptual artists, who used it to extend their work in other media. Yet, for about ten years, video was not taken seriously as a possible art form by critics, art journals, and, particularly, laymen. The Castelli–Sonnabend Gallery showed some of its stable of artists' video tapes, but there was nowhere else to see it.

Video art now plays a big part at the **Museum of Modern Art,** the **Whitney,** the **Kitchen Center** (in Soho), the **Anthology Film Archives** (also in Soho), the **Mudd Club,** on occasional nights other video/rock clubs, and some younger galleries, and on Cable TV. Occasionally, some experimental art video even trickles on to the likes of PBS. Sophisticated New York audiences pack into halls to see the newest video works just the same way they would to see an important gallery show or the hottest band.

In fact, video art has gained enough prominence and

popularity to be deemed with recognizable dividing genres: image processing, which means the images are manipulated electronically; landscape video, the title of which is self-explanatory; performance video, popularized by the documentation of performance art and theater; punk video, usually brash or pop culture images set to new wave music; dramatic narrative tapes, in which artists tell some sort of stories, usually abstracting a bit for meaning or effect; comedic video, which is humor combined with a very interesting or bizarre sensibility; and television language tapes, wherein the artist plays with the archetypal TV images, often ridiculing prime-time TV.

And each of these genres has its own accomplished stars—Gary Hill, Shalom Gorewitz, and Maureen Nappi work with technology and music to create bright, abstract, image-processed material. Bill Viola and Davidson Gigliotti, both part of last year's Whitney Biennial, are the pioneers of landscape video (Gigliotti's most recent was shot from a hot-air balloon). Julia Heyward, Joan Jonas, and Erika Bechman, performance artists, make fine performance tapes. Dara Birnbaum, always a big draw in shows, is the reigning queen of television language tapes. Louis Grenier, Michael Smith, and Mitchell Kriegman make very funny (and very marketable) tapes. And the stars of the New York video scene, John Sanborn and Kit Fitzgerald, make dramatic narrative tapes, mostly cut to musical scores, which sometimes involve the use of image processing.

Here's a rundown of the best places to see the best video art:

The Kitchen, 484 Broome St., 925-3615. Not only are there evening screenings about three or four times a month, but there's a daily viewing schedule in the Kitchen's video room, of their monthly shows (usually made of works by four or five artists), curated by Tom Bowes. Some of the freshest, newest talent is often on view here, plus new works by established artists. One can also request tapes from the Kitchen's well-stocked tape library.

Anthology Film Archives, 80 Wooster St. (226-0010), is an alternative film space that has weekly video shows of relatively well-known individual artists. A good place to get some recent video history.

The Whitney Museum, 75 St. and Madison Ave.

(570-3676), has several video shows a year, ranging from single tapes by artists to large multi-channel installations. Somehow or other, video seems "artier" here.

The Museum of Modern Art, 53 St. off Fifth Ave., also has several video shows per year, ranging from the likes of Wendy Clarke's *Love Tapes* (a series of individuals exposing their feelings on that subject on tape) to Margia Kramer's video documentation of the actress Jean Seberg. The programming here tends to be more eclectic and less "arty."

The **Donnell Library,** across from the Museum of Modern Art, does not have regular viewings of their tape library (which consists of the work of early and current established artists), but you can call and reserve screening time and fill some gaps in your video education.

Soho TV, a project of the Artists TV Network, run by Jaime Davidovich and Robin White, aired on Manhattan Cable every week since 1978, is the only artists' video on television thus far. During its half-hour span, it might show tapes by three different artists, or a half hour of one artist, or artists interviewing artists, etc. It is *the* pioneer video art programming by Cable.

The Mudd Club, 77 White St. (227-7777), was the first of the rock clubs equipped with video to abandon rock video in favor of art. About two years ago, Wendy Chambers, a music/performance artist, began programming four-hour video art marathons, plus early evening screenings of artists' work. It put the Mudd Club on the art world map, and the video set thronged to the club's second floor when a screening was announced.

Some of the other rock clubs will turn up with a video art screening now and again (**Peppermint Lounge,** 128 W. 45 St., 719-1973, and the **Ritz,** 119 E. 11 St., 278-8080), but mostly they show old and new rock promo tapes, most produced by record companies for the purpose of selling records. However, a lot of artists' techniques are getting incorporated into these slicker and slicker productions, and watching them, one can learn a great deal about the new video.

Rocks in Your Head, a record store in Soho (Prince

St. off West Broadway, 228-4557), has a soda fountain with a video monitor, and they show a wide selection of rock tapes.

Jefferson Market Library (243-4334) offers public facilities for video artists to work on and edit projects. It's located in the village at 425 Sixth Ave. Reasonable fees.

ART GALLERIES

One of the most important breakthroughs in the postwar art scene was the emergence of the Upper East Side galleries as the place where the world's most exciting art was being introduced. By the mid-1970s, the situation had changed somewhat, and the art had changed a great deal: the hottest galleries in New York, and, thus, many of the hottest galleries in the world were turning up in a former warehouse district in Lower Manhattan: Soho. With the further upscaling of Tribeca as an artists' community, the downtown art axis was solidified, and downtown, as far as Art is concerned, has become the world center uptown once was.

Artists Space, 105 Hudson St., 266-3970;
Tues.–Sat., 11–6
One of New York City's first "alternative spaces," Artists Space opened in 1972 as the gallery of the Committee for the Visual Arts, a government-funded organization set up to offer struggling artists grants and guidance. Director Linda Shearer, a former Guggenheim Museum curator, has sought to maintain the gallery's unique commitment to new artists without gallery affiliation and new trends still fermenting in downtown lofts. It was at Artists Space that Laurie Anderson and Jon Borofsky, among others, made their New York debuts, and it is here where dealers and museum people still venture to see the shape of things to come.

Blum Helman, 20 W. 57 St., 245-2888;
Tues.–Sat., 10–6

During the seventies, dealers Irving Blum and Joe Helman worked out of a charming little East Side townhouse, content to sell work by several blue-chip artists who came to prominence in the sixties and to promote quietly a few younger painters and sculptors. In the fall of 1980, however, the two greeted the new decade with a markedly new direction: Blum Helman moved to 57 St.'s gallery row, opened an elegant exhibition space, began hosting parties at the Mudd Club, and lured to its stable a few of the city's most talked-about emerging artists. Those shown by Blum Helman include Richard Diebenkorn, Bryan Hunt, Neil Jenney, Steve Keister, Ellsworth Kelly, Bruce Robbins, Richard Serra, Donald Sultan, and Hap Tivey.

Mary Boone, 420 West Broadway, 966-2114;
Tues.–Sat., 10–6

Mary Boone raised some eyebrows in 1978 when—just a gallery assistant in her mid-twenties—she rented half the ground floor in Soho's prestigious "420" building and began to show a handful of raucous, if unheard of, painters. The only faces being made today are those of some critics and collectors who can't believe the attention (and prices!) the hottest of these painters now command. If tough, new-expressionist painting is the art scene's latest religion—and for now, at least, it seems to be—then this tiny gallery may be its Mecca. Among the painters represented here are Ross Bleckner, David Salle, Julian Schnabel, Gary Stephan, and Robin Winters.

Leo Castelli, 420 West Broadway (Annex for large-scale works at 98 Greene St.), 431-5160;
Tues.–Sat., 10–6

As cool as his long, white-walled gallery, as refined as the work it displays, Leo Castelli (now in his seventies) is the uncontestable *doyen* of dealers. With one eye ever following the vagaries of art world taste, and the other fixed on art history, Castelli has shaped not only a fortune but the very way we look at and comprehend the art that followed abstract expressionism: neo-dada, pop, color-field, minimalism, conceptualism, and so on. And as even the briefest Saturday afternoon visit to his bustling back room will confirm, the center is still holding. Castelli artists include Richard Artschwager, Dan Flavin, Jasper Johns, Donald Judd, Ellsworth Kelly, Joseph Kosuth, Roy Lichtenstein, Robert Morris,

Kenneth Noland, Claes Oldenberg, Robert
Rauschenberg, James Rosenquist, Richard Serra, Frank
Stella, and Andy Warhol.

Paula Cooper, 155 Wooster St., 677-4390;
   Tues.–Sat., 10–6
Paula Cooper opened the very first gallery in Soho (on
Prince St. in 1968), and her current basketball-court of
a space on the neighborhood's northern edge continues
to chart some of the most important courses in
postminimal art. When Cooper managed the seminal
Park Place "co-op" gallery in the mid-sixties, she
insisted it be more than walls for paintings; the same
holds true in her own place. Throughout the season, she
hosts assorted poetry readings and New Music concerts,
and every New Year's Eve, the gallery serves up what's
come to be a genuine Soho tradition: an all-night
reading of Gertrude Stein's *The Making of Americans.*
Artists regularly shown include Carl Andie, Jennifer
Bartlett, Lynda Benglis, Jon Borofsky, Elizabeth
Murray, and Joel Shapiro.

Dia Art Foundation, 393 West Broadway, 925-9397;
   141 Wooster St., 473-8072; call for times
The art world holds many mysteries, and one of the
biggest is surely the Dia Art Foundation. Very quietly—
with money from the oil-research fortune of the De
Menil family, and aesthetic guidance from onetime
German dealer Heiner Friedrich—Dia funds the work of
a handful of artists, most prominently (and lavishly) the
gargantuan undertakings of earth-artist Walter de
Maria. In Soho, the foundation has sponsored two
wondrous, and permanent, De Maria installations. On
West Broadway the artist has filled a capacious ground-
floor space with his *Broken Kilometer:* row upon
regimental row of glistening brass bars, each a meter
long. And north on Wooster St. in the original
downtown branch of the Friedrich gallery, there is the
New York Earth Room: an entire floor of a typical loft
building filled untypically enough with tons of topsoil.

Drawing Center, 137 Greene St., 982-5266;
   Mon.–Sat., 11–6; Wed. until 8
Before opening the Drawing Center in January 1977,
Martha Beck had spent a career preparing for it—
studying under distinguished historian Erwin Panofsky
and working at the Museum of Modern Art with

William Lieberman, then director of the museum's nonpareil drawings department. Beck takes the all-inclusive view that a drawing can be nearly any sort of "work on paper," and in its first years the Center has shown everything from Gaudi's architectural studies to musical manuscripts to artists' postcards. There's also a regular program of lectures and workshops, and an ongoing "Selections" series devoted to works by new artists who take drawing to the edge.

Fashion Moda, 2803 Third Ave. (near 147 St.), 585-0135; call for hours

It was nearing the end of the seventies, and Stephan Eins, an expatriate Viennese artist, had had it with Soho. For several years, he had been running 3 Mercer St., a lively storefront-*cum*-alternative space, but now he wanted to set up shop beyond the boundaries of the city-recognized and increasingly boutique-beset artists' district. His interests, to say nothing of his courage, led him to the South Bronx, where he opened a ramshackle storefront in 1978. Eins, who oversees Fashion Mŏda with help from Joe Lewis, a young black artist, likes to refer to it as a "museum of science, technology and fantasy." With its street-smart shows devoted to graffiti and angry political art, and its emphasis on introducing young downtown artists to those of the surrounding Bronx blocks, Fashion Moda could well be the most truly experimental art center in the city.

Franklin Furnace, 112 Franklin St., 925-4671; Tues.–Sat., 12n–6

Among the progeny of conceptual art has been the artist's book—the small-format, mass-produced, moderately priced volume through which artists are able to control not only form and content but also distribution. That these publications, designed to circumvent the system, might actually be lost to art history worried a young performance artist named Martha Wilson. In 1976, having moved into a Tribeca loft complete with ample storefront, she founded Franklin Furnace (the name is owed to a sign she uncovered on the premises) as an archive for artists' books. Moreover, for those who couldn't be bothered binding their ideas or images, she offered space for exhibitions and performances. To date, more than 2,000 books have been filed away for safekeeping, and the schedule of shows and events is as crowded and *au courant* as any in town.

Institute for Art and Urban Resources: The Clocktower, 108 Leonard St., 233-1096; Wed.–Sat., 1–6; **P.S. One,** 46-01 21st St., Long Island City, 233-1096, Thurs.–Sun., 1–6

In London in the late sixties, several artists, with help from the city government, took over a seedy waterfront warehouse and turned it into a thriving center for artists' studios and exhibition space. Several years later and thousands of miles west, Alanna Heiss founded the Institute for Art and Urban Resources to test the concept in New York. Today, the Institute runs two flourishing spaces! At The Clocktower, located atop an old, city-owned office tower, the Institute organizes shows of mostly overlooked contemporary art directly beneath a long-broken, four-faced clock. And at P.S. (Projects Studio) One—an abandoned, block-long public school in Queens—the Institute offers inexpensive studios to artists, has classrooms-*cum*-galleries for special projects, and mounts surveys of new art (often guest-curated) in a roomy ground-floor space.

Phyllis Kind, 139 Spring St., 925-1200; Tues.–Sat., 10–6

Yes, Virginia, there is art after New York, and some of the funniest and funkiest of it hails from Chicago. Dealer Phyllis Kind is from Chicago (she's pretty funny and funky herself), and in her offbeat gallery she champions the naughty, cartoony, surrealism-inspired painters and sculptors of the Second City. Kind has also got a thing for the naïve, reclusive artists of our time, and when she unveils the overlooked creations of a new one, it usually ranks among the art season's more memorable events. Artists who show at Kind include Roger Brown, Jim Nutt, and Ed Paschke.

Light Gallery, 724 Fifth Ave. (near 57 St.), 582-6552; Tues.–Sat., 10–6

New York, like everywhere else, experienced a photography boom in the seventies; where once there wasn't a photo gallery that could meet the rent, there now thrive more than a dozen. The foremost of these, in terms of the range of high-quality photographs exhibited, as well as the care and thought brought to bear upon them, is the Light Gallery. Founded in 1971, Light is committed to showing the work of

contemporary image makers who confront not only their
subjects but also the aesthetic issues of the medium
itself: whether the strict formal considerations so
debated in recent years or the growing interest in color
prints and Polaroids. From time to time, Light will also
mount historical surveys of work by those not part of
the gallery stable. Among photographers regularly
shown here are Ansel Adams, Harry Callahan, Lee
Friedlander, Nicholas Nixon, and Gary Winogrand.

Metro Pictures, 169 Mercer St., 925-8335;
Tues.–Sat., 10–6

One of Soho's newest, most vanguard galleries, Metro
Pictures was opened in 1980 by Helene Weiner,
longtime director of Artists' Space, and Jennelle
Riering, formerly of Castelli Gallery. The artists
represented here are young, pop-cultured types, and the
art they make tends to reflect a certain fascination with
the mass media—specifically, the steady flow of riveting
if ultimately ambiguous imagery it serves up. The
approach of these artists—cool, distanced, once-
removed—is similar to attitudes found on the new wave
scene, which emerged around the same time. Among
those showing at Metro Pictures are Troy Brauntuch,
Jack Goldstein, Thomas Lawson, Robert Longo, and
Cindy Sherman.

New Museum, 65 Fifth Ave. (at 14 St.), 741-8962;
Mon–Fri., noon–6; Sat., noon–5

When Marcia Tucker lost her curator's post at the
Whitney Museum in 1976, she did what couldn't be
done: started her own museum. With a gallery in a
branch of the New School for Social Research, a tireless
staff of young art historians, and a sincere commitment
to show, collect, and write about the art that's been
made since 1970, the New Museum is among the city's
most unusual art institutions. And with its timely,
provocative exhibitions—one was devoted to "Bad
Painting," for instance—it has also proved among the
most important.

Holly Solomon, 392 West Broadway, 925-1900;
Tues.–Sat., 10:30–6

Although her first love was acting, Holly Solomon and
her husband Horace began collecting modern art in the
early 1960s. Later in the decade, Holly founded 98
Greene St., a freewheeling venue for poetry,
performances, and painting, including, among the latter,

work that drew upon fabric design, wallpaper, and non-Western art for its style and substance. These "pattern painters," along with other artists with an interest in the "New Decorativeness," were among the first Holly showed when she opened her gallery in 1973. Some of them have since gone on to be recognized as leading artistic lights of their generation. Among the artists exhibiting regularly at Holly Solomon are Nicholas Africano, Laurie Anderson, Brad Davis, Donna Dennis, Robert Kushner, Kim McConnel, Ned Smyth, and William Wegman.

Sonnabend, 420 West Broadway, 966-6160; Tues.–Sat., 10–6

Ileana Sonnabend, raised in Bucharest and once married to dealer Leo Castelli, opened her first gallery with husband Michael in Paris in 1961. Ten years later, she opened her Soho space with an abstruse performance by Gilbert and George, Britain's conceptual-art answer to Laurel and Hardy. Conceptual art from Europe as well as from this country remains the gallery's staple, complemented regularly by some of the finest "art" photography to be found in New York. Gallery artists include Vito Acconci, John Baldessari, Mel Bochner, Bevan Davies, Gilbert & George, Jan Groover, David Haxton, David Hockney, Barry Le Va, and Robert Morris.

Sperone Westwater Fischer, 142 Greene St., 431-3685; Tues.–Sat., 10–6

Having previously worked for dealer John Weber and served for several years as managing editor of *Artforum,* Angela Westwater became the managing partner of her own Soho space in 1975. Gianenzo Sperone and Konrad Fischer were already prominent dealers abroad (Sperone in Rome and Turin; Fischer in Düsseldorf), and so it was only natural that the gallery became the American outlet for many of the most important European artists of the 1970s—minimalists and conceptualists in particular. More recently, Sperone Westwater Fischer has brought to these shores the eccentric, expressive canvases of several young, highly touted Italian painters. Among the artists represented here are Sandro Chia, Francesco Clemente, Enzo Cucchi, Hanne Darboven, Richard Long, and Gerhard Richter.

MUSEUM ALTERNATIVES

All right, you've been in New York now *how* long? And you're beginning to feel like you practically *live* at the Guggenheim and the Whitney? Well, cheer up! Though not as well known as the Met, or MOMA, the following may give a new sense of purpose to even the most jaded museum-goer.

Alternative Museum, 17 White St., 966-4444;
Wed.–Sat., 11–6 (call for events and prices)
In operation since 1975, the Alternative Museum has occupied its present White St. space since January 1980. Exhibits here emphasize nonmainstream, nonestablished artists, more than sixty of whom have donated their work to the museum. This "permanent collection," which is constantly expanding, ranges from works on paper and photographs to small three-dimensional objects in mixed media. Special exhibits, featuring a particular stylistic theme, are also mounted monthly.

The main gallery at the Alternative Museum is also the site of frequent concerts of unusual interest and merit. Folk music and other musics from around the world are presented in a relaxed, informal atmosphere, encouraging contact with the performers.

Brochures and booklets detailing exhibits and concerts at the museum are obtainable in person or by phone.

Soho Center for Visual Artists, 114 Prince St., 226-1995; Tues.–Sat., noon–5 (closed August); Admission: free

For the most comprehensive collection of new art in the city, the blocks between Broadway and West Broadway, Spring and Prince Sts. are unbeatable. Of the dozens of galleries in the area, one of the most consistently interesting is the Soho Center for Visual Artists. A nonprofit organization, the Center is sponsored jointly by the Aldrich Museum of Ridgefield, Connecticut, and Mobil Oil. Here, emerging Manhattan artists whose work has not previously been displayed are given the opportunity to stage group exhibitions.

The Ukrainian Museum, 203 Second Ave., 228-0110; Wed.–Sun., 1–5; Admission: adults, $1; students and seniors, 50 cents

Since it first opened its doors in 1976, the Ukrainian Museum has afforded visitors a uniquely concentrated look at Ukrainian folk art and culture. Now the collection is more than triple its original size and includes everything from embroidery to Easter eggs, woodcarving to weaving. Most of the objects displayed date from the 19th and early 20th centuries.

Recent exhibits have included a selection of "Rushnyky," unique ritual cloths, some from the 18th century, and a variety of ceramics, metal, and woodwork from the Carpathian Mountain region of the Ukraine.

Scheduled for 1982 is a very special exhibition, "Lost Architecture of Kiev." Commemorating the founding of that city 1,500 years ago, the exhibit will feature photographs, slide shows, and relics of both existing and no longer existent landmarks.

In addition to its exhibits, the museum sponsors workshops in a number of popular Ukrainian crafts. From early fall through December, people of all ages and skill levels have the opportunity to learn such arts as embroidery, woodcarving, and the design of Christmas ornaments. Most workshops are held on Saturdays, and places can be reserved by phone.

Museum of American Folk Art, 49 W. 53 St., 581-2474; Tues., 10:30–8; Wed.–Sun., 10:30–5:30; Admission: adults, $1; students and seniors, 50 cents; under 12, free

Open since 1963, the Museum of American Folk Art was founded "to foster, promote, and increase appreciation of the American folk arts." Still the only museum of its kind in the city, it has splendidly achieved its goals.

The museum's permanent collection consists of paintings, sculpture, furniture, ornaments, and functional crafts of the 17th to 20th centuries. All are the work of American "folk artists"—that is, artists who lacked formal training in their discipline.

Recent exhibits of particular interest were "Small Folk: A Celebration of Childhood in America," and "Anonymous Beauty," an exhibition of approximately sixty American folk art textiles from the 18th and 19th centuries.

In addition to its exhibits, the museum also publishes a beautifully illustrated quarterly magazine, *The Clarion,* for its members.

The Museum of Broadcasting, 1 E. 53 St., 752-7684; Tues.–Sat., 12n–5, Thurs. till 7:30; Admission: adults, $2; seniors and children, $1

Since its inception in 1976, the Museum of Broadcasting has managed to compile the most extensive collection of radio and television tapes currently available for public use. Duplicates of any of the museum's thousands of tapes are available for viewing and listening on any one of twenty-three private consoles. There, visitors can relive the greatest moments in broadcast journalism, comedy, music, sports, popular series, and variety shows. Such highlights as FDR's first fireside chat, the Kennedy-Nixon debates, and the comedy routines of Ernie Kovacs and Jack Benny are all here.

Complementing the tape library are two theaters showing changing, special exhibits. Recent features have included "The Museum of Broadcasting's Midsummer Revue," an anthology of musical, dance, and comedy performances from 1957 to 1980, and "In Celebration of U.S.," a one-hour show of highlights of the American bicentennial.

The Museum of the City of New York, Fifth Ave. at 103 St., 534-1672; Tues.–Sat., 10–5, Sun., 1–5; Admission: free

While it might be argued that Manhattan is itself an island museum, the city does have its own official collection near the northeast corner of Central Park. Originally opened in 1923 at Gracie Mansion, the museum moved to its present Colonial Georgian structure some ten years later. Here in four floors of exhibits is presented the whole history of the city.

Starting on the first floor you can walk from a life-sized reproduction of an early 17th-century Dutch fort, through to the transplanted fifth-floor bed and dressing rooms of John D. Rockefeller. A quicker trip through nearly four centuries is hard to imagine.

In between can be found an impressive array of paintings, artifacts, and multimedia displays featuring everything from the stock exchange to Broadway theater. There's even a collection of rare and antique dolls and dollhouses, one of the best anywhere.

Recent special exhibits have included a salute to designer Vera Maxwell, and a group show of contemporary color photographs of the Big Apple. Slated for 1982 are exhibits of the photography of John Albok, and the "Bard on Broadway," a retrospective of Shakespeare in Manhattan's theaters.

The Jewish Museum, 1109 5th Ave., 860-1888; Mon.–Thurs. noon–5, sun., 11–6; Admission: adults, $1.75; children, $1

Quick, what's the largest Jewish city in the world? Did you say Tel Aviv? Nope. Jerusalem? Wrong again. It's New York, and, not surprisingly, we have the world's largest collection of Hebrew art and artifacts right here in Manhattan. The two floors of permanent exhibits at the Jewish Museum feature religious objects from both the synagogue and home, including displays illustrating the full year of Jewish holidays and celebrations.

An additional floor of changing exhibits focuses on themes and issues in contemporary Jewish life both in Israel and elsewhere.

Jacques Marchais Center of Tibetan Art, 338 Lighthouse Ave., Staten Island, 987-3478; Sat.–Sun., 1–5; Admission: adults, $1; children, 50 cents

This recreation of a Buddhist temple is the legacy of a Mrs. Harry Klauber, who died in 1948 leaving her enormous collection of Tibetan art to the center. The center itself consists of a working library, an elaborate altar, and the surrounding gardens.

The altar and gardens have been meticulously designed with authenticity in mind. The gardens are inhabited by numerous stone-carved animals, Buddhas, and live birds, which enhance the birdhouses, lotus pool, and wishing well on the grounds. The altar presents a gaudy array of religious objects: statues, musical instruments, wall hangings, incense burners, and much more. In the library, Mrs. Klauber's own collection of books on various Oriental subjects are available for casual perusal or serious study.

American Museum of Immigration, Liberty Island; Ferries leave Battery Park, Mon.–Sat., 9–4; Sun., 9–5; Admission: free

The American Museum of Immigration might be more appropriately housed on Ellis Island, but its inclusion in the base of the Statue of Liberty is certainly a convenience. Ellis Island, as many American readers of this guide know, is where your fathers' and grandfathers' names were changed from Jacobovsky to Jacobs, Stanislawski to Stanley, when they arrived in this country at the turn of the century. But no matter. The museum's extensive collection of photos, audiovisual presentations, artifacts, and dioramas depicting all phases and aspects of immigration into this country are ample compensation.

In addition to these permanent exhibits, recent special exhibits have featured individual ethnic groups and their particular contributions to American society.

THE NIGHT LIFE

Bars

Joe Allen's 326 W. 46 St., 581-6464
This is one of *the* Broadway institutions—a popular
hangout for theater-goers, thespians (both famous and
aspiring), tourists, and students. Located on Restaurant
Row, one block west of the theater district, Joe Allen's
is open until 3 A.M. The atmosphere is casual—old
photos and posters adorn the brick walls. A *must* for
theater buffs.

Angry Squire, 216 Seventh Ave., 242-9066
This good ol' Chelsea pub has a nautical decor and
draws an eclectic clientele—all ages, all walks of life.
Notables such as Arthurs Miller and Clarke have been
known to drink here; Halston has thrown parties here.
However, it's not really that strong a lit/glit scene, even
a bit of a dive—in a nice way. Live jazz keeps the place
hopping on Friday and Saturday nights, when there is a
reasonable minimum. If it gets too crowded upstairs, try
the basement bar for a quieter retreat.

Barnabus Rex, 155 Duane St., 963-9693
This is a hot downtown bar and has been hot since its
opening some years back. When Barnabus opened, it
was one of the only watering holes within blocks for the
burgeoning Tribeca scene; today it is one of a handful
but has many charms. There is a good jukebox and a
lively crowd—not too artsy, not too rowdy.

Beaubern Cafe, 42 W. 28 St., 725-9380

There's nothing really unique about Beaubern's, but it is one of very few bars within that strange no-man's-land between the garment and flower districts. Unescorted women will feel comfortable here; everybody will feel welcome. A friendly, happy joint.

Blarney Stone/Blarney Castle, various locations
The Blarney chain is a New York institution. These bars, located in all sorts of neighborhoods—rich and poor—really proliferate in midtown. They offer the cheapest drinks in town, and the chance to really drink at a *bar,* with barflies, charismatic drunks, and talkative Irish bartenders. Not the place for a quiet date, but you may find the Blarney bars suitable for many other purposes.

Bradley's, 70 University Pl., 228-6440
After 9:30 P.M., live jazz is one of the features of this charming bar and restaurant. But that's not the only reason to pay Bradley's a visit. The Continental food is worthwhile; dining and quiet drinking is best done on weekdays when the jazz is at a comfortable background volume. But if you really enjoy music and don't have claustrophobia, go on the weekend, when the place is packed and loud.

Broome Street Bar, 363 West Broadway, 925-2086
This is one of the most popular of the old Soho bars. By old, we only mean 7 or 8 years, but that's a whole generation in Soho language. The bar is filled with students, artists, musicians, and members of this colorful neighborhood, who come to drink the many beers available or to eat the best hamburgers in Soho. Worth a visit.

Buffalo Roadhouse, 87 Seventh Ave. So., 242-9028
This former gas station was converted into a popular Village bar. There is often a wait for tables and lots of singles action at the bar. The clientele is diverse but basically Villagey: artsy, literary, or students. Kitchen open until 3 A.M.; bar open until 4.

Caliban, 360 Third Ave., 689-5155
A sophisticated neighborhood bar, Caliban is a touch of the Upper East Side but with the friendliness of the Middle East Side. There is some singles action at the bar, but the dimly lit Caliban caters to a comfortable mix of scenes. Caliban's drinks are always made with

premium stuff, and the wine list is good. You may have
to look for Caliban—only a tiny sign on the door lets
you know it is there—but it's worth the hunt.

Cedar Tavern, 82 University Pl., 929-9089
This was once the hangout of Jackson Pollock, Larry
Rivers, and crowd, so art fanciers will have to pay a
visit to the Cedar. But there's more than just history
here, and the restaurant upstairs serves some good,
simple American fare. Help is a little surly until they
get to know you, in classic Village-bar fashion.

Chipps, 150 Columbus Ave., 874-8415
This is one of our favorite after–Lincoln Center
hangouts—friendly, inexpensive, and *very* West Side.
The talk is intellectual, literate, but mainly musical—
your waitress may be an aspiring cellist and that gang of
kids at the next table may be from the nearby Juilliard
school. The food is good and unpretentious. We love the
Grolsch beer—Holland's best.

Chumley's, 86 Bedford St., 675-4449
Chumley's has changed barely an iota since its
speakeasy days: it's in an out-of-the-way location and
has no sign to mark the entrance. It's a truly historic
literary hangout; Millay drank here often, as did Dos
Passos, Lardner, and Steinbeck. Today, Chumley's
draws mainly young people—especially those who love
their nostalgia with a touch of poetry.

P. J. Clarke's, 915 Third Ave., 759-1650
Within the giants of Third Avenue in the fifties, P. J.
Clarke's, only two stories tall, strikes one as an amiable
dwarf. This famous bar's fortune was made when they
shot the late-forties classic film *The Lost Weekend*
here. Many weekends have been lost here since, but
P. J. Clarke's is also a great place to find oneself on a
Sunday morning, with the hair of the proverbial dog
and a burger.

Colonnades, 432 Lafayette St., 473-8890
Located in a magnificent old townhouse, the Colonnades
is directly across the street from the Public Theater.
The ambience and service make a visit very
comfortable, and this is an ideal place for a long
conversation with somebody you like. The bar fills up
with downtown theater-goers both before and after
showtime. At other times, the Colonnades caters to the

diverse range of artists, writers, and students living in the surrounding neighborhoods—Soho, the East Village, and what is now called Noho.

Jimmy Day's, 192 W. 4 St., 675-9793
This well-established saloon seems as if it's been part of the Village scene for years, but it is in fact comparatively new. Clientele comprises NYU students, Villagers, and some tourists. In the summer, there is an outdoor café, ideal for people-watching. Food is pretty good.

Donohue's, 174 W. 72 St., 874-9304
This is a nice folksy joint smack in the middle of W. 72 St., halfway between the Park and the River. It gets all kinds of people, from elderly men who have been coming here for years to young people who prefer a quieter atmosphere than that found at some of the singles bars. There is a gigantic stuffed marlin on the wall, lots of trophies—it's like walking into 1955, and we mean that in an entirely positive sense. If you're under 35, the waitresses will call you "dear."

Fraunces Tavern, Corner of Pearl and Broad Sts., 260-0144
Established in 1763, Fraunces is the oldest ongoing tavern in New York. The walls are decorated with flags, colonial art, and other Americana. George Washington may not have *slept* here, but we know that he frequently dined at Mr. Fraunces' original tavern. Fair food at expensive prices is not the main attraction; go for a drink.

Green Derby, 978 Second Ave., 688-1250
Just about as Irish as you can get—the walls are covered with Irish flags and memorabilia, and most of the waitresses and bartenders are of Irish descent. The Derby attracts the singles set as well as the serious drinkers. Note: Like all Irish bars, the Green Derby is best avoided on St. Patrick's Day, unless you like *real* circuses.

Hanratty's, 732 Amsterdam Ave., 864-4224
This is a real outpost here in a seedy, somewhat dangerous section of the Upper West Side, south of Columbia University, and miles from the "Fashionable West 70's" crowd. But it's a hip place; the burgers are great, and the selection of imported beers is a delight

for the guzzler. The East Side branches of Hanratty's (opened recently) lean more toward the singles crowd and are not yet as distinguished.

Hell's Kitchen, 598 Ninth Ave., 757-5329
Named for the infamous precinct in which it's located, Hell's Kitchen is a small contribution to the gentrification of a tough neighborhood. Up front there's a modern, friendly bar. The back table area is decorated as though imitating the city outside: weathered brick walls, some covered in graffiti, others with clothesline, hung with laundry. For some, Hell's Kitchen may be a little too cute; after all, Columbus Ave. doesn't start for a few more blocks north.

Holbrook's, 1313 Third Ave., 734-2050
Finely polished wood and etched glass dominate this Upper East Side restaurant's decor. Drinking is usually restricted to the bar at Holbrook's, but boy, can they make drinks. Service is sometimes slow, but that's because the bartenders are kept busy making their specialty: fancy drinks, especially those made with ice cream, and tropical concoctions. For such a classy place, Holbrook's is surprisingly friendly.

The Lion's Head, 59 Christopher St., 929-0670
This is one of the classic Village writer's bars, and anyone who ever thought he was a poet—even for a moment—owes it to himself to pay a visit. Food is great at the Lion's Head, but the important thing here has always been drink, drink, drink. Lots of writers hang out at the Lion's Head, when off the wagon. Service is not terribly friendly, but that's part of the charm. Tourists are despised here, so act artsy but macho, and keep that chip firmly on your shoulder.

The Locale, 11 Waverly Pl., 674-0860
Formerly the "Local," and most New Yorkers still pronounce this famous bar's name without the "e." It is situated just off the NYU campus and Washington Square, and the scene is collegiate and made up of actors, artists, and writers. The Locale combines the atmosphere of a neighborhood bar and a Village coffee-and-cake place. Open until 4 A.M.

The Marlin, 2844 Broadway
This old bar has long been part of the Columbia neighborhood, but until recently it was a hangout for

old drunks and street people. No more. Suddenly, the
Marlin is *the* happening spot above 96 St., filled with a
variety of musicians, Columbia students, would be
punk-rockers, and old drunks and street people. There
is an undeniable energy here these days, cheap drinks,
and very friendly service.

McSorley's, 15 E. 7 St., 473-8800
Until the early seventies, McSorley's was the last
"Gentlemen Only" hangout in New York. But it
accepted "liberation" cheerfully, and now men and
women stand side by side, pouring ale and whiskey
down their throats. It's the oldest alehouse in the city,
and it attracts one of the most diversified clientele—
basically young. Check McSorley's out if you happen to
be in the East Village.

No Name Bar, 621 Hudson St., 243-8012
Our favorite Greenwich Village bar. The No Name is a
friendly, relaxed West Village spot, with a great crowd.
Here you'll find gays, actors, career folk, stockbrokers,
anarchists, and every other type of New Yorker
standing by and drinking some of the best drinks in the
city. Prices are reasonable; there's some good chili
available, and not a bad jukebox. Introduce yourself to
owner Danny Lettieri, a good man and a fine host. He'll
make sure you feel at home.

Once Upon a Stove, 325 Third Ave., 683-0044
The hodgepodge decor is antique *kitsch;* bits and pieces
of miscellany, only related because of age. This
restaurant is divided into several rooms, some hidden,
one with a secret panel. The atmosphere is fun, the
patrons young, theater-oriented, and professional.
Singles and couples mingle freely. Once Upon A Stove
has a generous happy hour.

Phebe's, 361 Bowery, 473-9008
This is a popular East Village place that stays open late,
serves good food, feeds a variety of musicians, actors,
writers, and artists, and always makes everyone feel at
home. It's a real oasis from the strange Bowery life
outside your window, and well worth a visit. Drinks are
good; the price is right.

Puffy's, 81 Hudson St., 766-9159
Another of the original Tribeca bars, and this is a gem.
There is a great jukebox, with everybody from Enrico

Caruso to the Talking Heads on it, and a lively artistic crowd gathers here. We like Puffy's, which has been a bar for a long time and many years before the birth of the downtown arts scene, and has a certain ambience that manages to be very new and very old at the same time.

Ruppert's, 1662 Third Ave., 831-1900
Ruppert's is one of the friendliest night spots in town. The soft live jazz never drowns out conversation, and Ruppert's decor mixes old world with ultramodern, and it works. The dimly lit bar sometimes gets crowded, and the food is a little overpriced, but Ruppert's is a romantic and comfortable place to have a drink . . . or six.

Shakespeare's, 176 Macdougal St., 777-2540
One can guess Shakespeare's decor simply from the title, and one would not be wrong. It's an English pub, and the walls are covered in Shakespeare-related posters. The crowd is young, and the atmosphere is casual. The bar is packed on weekends but has a rather large seating capacity; the choice tables overlook 8 St. Shakespeare's is an institution by now, and quite inexpensive.

Tenth Avenue Bar, 140 Tenth Ave., 675-5604
This would be a typical Chelsea dive, but it has been remodeled in what might be called *echt* Soho style. The Tenth Avenue Bar has quite a bit of charm, and its snazziness hasn't interfered with its friendliness. It's a small place, serving good simple food, and a good spot to have a drink if you are in the Chelsea area.

T.G.I. Friday's, 1152 First Ave., 832-8512
This is one of the quintessential singles bars—a classic boy-meets-girl rendezvous that continues to attract a steady crowd. It's basically "young dentist meets young stenographer"—very professionally oriented—but the drinks are good, and the hustling's fine. If singles bars are your thing, this is one of the best.

Tin Pan Alley, 220 West 49 St., 246-9356
This bar attracts some sharply contrasting customers—primarily young folks: students, artists, rock 'n' rollers, and some junior execs. Great jukebox, and the back-room pool table and pinball machine see some heavy action. Now and then prostitutes and pimps stop in—

this *is* the red-light district—but this is basically a relaxed and pleasant place in a seedy area.

Top of the Park, Gulf and Western Plaza, Columbus Circle, 333-3800

On a good day you can see four states from this 43-floor hideaway. Even on a bad day, you should have a superb vision of midtown and the Upper West Side. The bar is only open from 5 to 11 P.M., but it is a *must* for visitors. The restaurant is not really worth the high prices, but there is a spectacular view of Central Park available. Jacket is required.

Top of the Sixes, 666 Fifth Ave., 757-6662

The Top of the Sixes is on the 39 floor of one of New York's most prestigious buildings, and it provides a breathtaking panorama of the city. Come here only for a drink—they are expensive, but the view is worth it. Jackets are required for men . . . and don't get superstitious about the address.

Trader Vic's at the Plaza, 59 St. and Fifth Ave., 355-5158

Ever heard of a drink called the Samoan Fog Cutter? Well, it's available here, along with many other extravaganzas. Trader Vic's is expensive, but the amazing tropical drinks, usually rum-based, are worth it. As Baudelaire once said, "Get Drunk!" And as an ad man once said, "Nothing unimportant ever happens at the Plaza."

West End Café, 2911 Broadway, 666-8750

Malcolm Lowry drank here. So did Kerouac and Allen Ginsberg. So do Columbia freshmen, and therein lies the rub. We love the back room at the West End throughout the summer, when the kids are away, but during the year, the place is *packed!* There is good jazz in the side room, old big-band greats come to play for you.

Wine Bars

Wine bars haven't yet caught on in New York the way they have in London, but here are six that are alive and well in the Big Apple. The principal attraction of each is that they offer fine wines by the glass; wines that would normally be available only by the bottle. This

makes experimentation cheaper and simultaneously
eliminates the problem of selecting a wine to suit all
palates at your table. *A votre santé!*

Washington St. Café, 433 Washington St., 925-5119
About twenty wines, on average, available by the glass.
Most, $2.50 to $4. List changes frequently.
Recommended: Red—Château Puy Blanquet, '75;
White—Lambert Bridge Chardonnay, '79

Vintages, 216 Columbus Ave., 496-7059
Approximately twelve wines by the glass. Most, $2 to
$3. List changes every two to three weeks.
Recommended: White—Château St. Jean Riesling

The Wine Bar, 422 West Broadway, 431-4790
Thirty-three wines, on average, by the glass. Most, $2.25
to $4. On weekends, more costly wines are offered.
Recommended: Red—Beaujolais-Villages Drouhin, '79;
White—Gewurtztraminer Trimbach, '79; Port—Calem
'66

Jacquelines, 132 E. 61 St., 838-4559
Only champagne bar in the city. Five to 6 champagnes,
as well as a number of still wines, available by the glass.
Most, $2.50 to $5.50. Recommended: Sparkling—
Codorniu Blanc de Blancs

Au Grenier, 2867 Broadway, 666-3052
Approximately ten wines by the glass. Most, $2.50 to
$3.50. Recommended: Red—Château de la Chaize
Brouilly and Daniele Pinot Noir

Stevens Wine Bar, 103 W. 70 St., 595-2600
About thirty wines by the glass. Most, $2 to $4.
Recommended: Red—Château D'Angludet, '77; White—
Heitz Chablis

Happy Hours

There's a lie going around that says the happy hour
bunch consists exclusively of 9-to-5-ers looking for a
snack and a few drinks after work. But look more
carefully and you'll find a lot of the out-of-work and
"free-lance" set to whom this kind of cheapo food-and-
drink extravaganza appeals most fervently. Whoever
they're for, happy hours are a pleasant diversion and a
great opportunity to parlay a few croquettes and a piece

of breaded tuna into a full dinner. Dozens of restaurants
have initiated this as a way of encouraging bar business
and bringing in new customers. Here are some of the
most notable:

The Cattleman, 5 E. 45 St., 661-1200
The buffet here is one of the most generous, with
shrimp, chili, rice, and pot roast all available on a good
day. People have been known to get away with ordering
a single ginger ale and pigging it up at the food table
continually from 5 to 8—not a bad deal, by any means.
On top of all this, you get a honky-tonky pianist singing
"New York New York" and such—but mercifully you'll
be too busy guzzling down hors d'oeuvres to even know
he's there.

Company, 354 Third Ave., 532-5222
The appetizers vary—one day it'll be meatballs, the
next quiche rolls, some days both. The important thing
is that you get a dollar off every drink you order, from 5
to 8 weekdays. The ambience is mixed, but primarily
gay and cruisy, and willing patrons have been known to
go home with more hors d'oeuvres than they bargained
for.

Fonda los Milagros, 70 E. 55 St., 752-6640
This Mexican restaurant promises small plates of
nachos, tacos, and guacamole dip, but all we had were
taco chips and hot sauce before we gave up waiting. At
least drinks are cheap (well, cheaper) from 4:30 to 7
weekdays.

George's, 18 W. 33 St., 564-7284
Everything here has "leftover" stamped all over it, but
quantity isn't lacking, and if you're not looking for
haute cuisine, you can make a reasonably appealing
meal of it. On a sample day, the buffet included
tunafish, meatballs, cold cuts, kasha, croquettes, bread,
and onions.

Harley St., 547 Second Ave., 685-9659
The main attraction here, from 5 to 7 weekdays, is that
you can order clams on the half shell at a cut rate—
three for $1. While you're waiting, nibble on crackers
and cheese and guzzle cheap drinks. Then order some
more clams.

Izakaya, 43 W. 54 St., 765-4683
The Japanese specialties aren't very Japanese (the day

we visited, there was breaded tuna and something
resembling french fries), but they're cute and so is the
atmosphere in this popular after-work hangout. On
Tuesday, "Ladies night," drinks are $1.25 for women,
and they're $1.75 for everyone on other weekdays,
5 to 7.

Molly Mog's Pub, 65 E. 55 St., 593-0535
This is the best happy hour in town, with a plentiful
carving board that features ham, corned beef hash,
salads (green, macaroni, potato), rice, beets, and kidney
beans. There's a two-drink minimum, but that doesn't
prohibit people from swarming the place after work like
bees to the hive. Hungry bees, we should add.

Richoux, 153 E. 53 St., 753-7721
The fried clams and scallops here don't look very
desirable, but one glance at the real menu prices at this
or any Citicorp restaurant is consolation enough.

Tandoor, 40 E. 49 St., 752-3334
If you order enough drinks at this ritzy Indian
restaurant during happy-hour time, you'll be rewarded
with a plate of Indian fried chicken, crispy Indian
bread, and Indian potato appetizers. It's all Indian, in
case we haven't mentioned.

Teheran, 45 W. 44 St., 840-1980
It's strictly *le grande bouffe* time at this American-
Italian-Persian restaurant, which fills up daily with
rambunctious patrons who enjoy pint-sized spare ribs,
pizza, chicken, croquettes, and lots more. It starts at
4:30, and it may never end.

The Clubs

The nightclub scene in New York is probably the most
exciting—and most volatile—in the world. Clubs
presenting the whole range of musical styles stay open
late, and not only are there after-hours clubs, there are
after-after-hours clubs. The guide below is indicative of
the New York club scene at the time of writing; it is
subject to change and probably will.

A-7, 7 St. and Ave. A, 279-1980
This little dive features an unsavory atmosphere well
watched by its clientele. The bands that play here have

generally only recently been formed and have yet to play anywhere else. Usually of the crudest variety, though with some surprises.

Bottom Line, Mercer and W. 4 St., 228-7880
This tastefully dull cabaret features far less rock 'n' roll than it used to, but it is a comfortable, well-run change of pace from the freneticism of the other New York clubs. Drinks and food are expensive, and the bands booked are usually well established dullards half of whose tickets are distributed by their record companies, but the seats are comfortable, the sight lines are good, and its two shows a night both start on time. Tickets are sold in advance, with some SRO tickets available the night of performance.

CBGB, Bleecker St. and the Bowery, 982-4052
The birthplace of punk rock, CB's is by now a tourist's must-see. And with good reason. Though gone are the Hells Angels/Talking Heads days of old, CB's still features the best sound system in New York, the best sight lines of any club, and listings of avant-garde New Music, established NYC punk-rockers, and occasional surprise "name" acts. The ambience is punk rock apotheosized. The beer is expensive. Good times are had by all, from the preppies in from the Ivy's, to the junkies who crawl up from CB's infamous toilets.

Danceteria, 30 W. 21 St., 620-0790
New York night-life legends Jim Fouratt and Rudolf have reappeared on the scene with a reincarnation of their popular club on the premises of the former Interferon. And just in time, for we were all beginning to miss that Danceteria lady (on the club's logo), whose sharp waitress's uniform and pert smile promise to serve up the best in music and entertainment. The new Danceteria, inspired by the tenets of "pantropicalism," contains three floors of bars, dancing, and performance areas, plus a video lounge and a restaurant that serves from 9 P.M. to 5 A.M. ("so you can dance all night.") With an encyclopedic booking policy (including earlier sets for non-nighthawks) and the staging of special "events," Danceteria has once again become a fabulous destination on the club circuit.

Maxwell's, 1039 Washington St., Hoboken, N.J., 201-656-9632
Though technically not in New York, Maxwell's is but a

ten-minute PATH train ride from Penn Station, and its heart is in the city. There is a boring restaurant attached, and so the majority of those who make it into the little back-room rock 'n' roll club are adventurous New Yorkers there to see the best of local or visiting bands play in an uncrowded but supportive atmosphere. Drinks are cheap, the crowd is friendly, and what's more, Maxwell's is the finest unobtrusive rock club left in the city.

Mudd Club, 77 White St., 227-7777
Still the late-night spa for would be scene-sters, this snobby little club is a load of fun. Multitiered, and separated along lines of New York rock 'n' roll hierarchy, it can either totally offend you—if you get in—or make you feel you're on the last outpost of beatnik decadence. Bands—often unannounced—don't go on until *very late,* and the place really doesn't even get going until after 2:30. Still, a must stop if you're visiting the Big Apple for the lure of its rock 'n' roll clubs.

Peppermint Lounge, 128 W. 45 St., 719-3176
Yes, it's the same Peppermint Lounge your parents remember, only not quite. This incarnation of the Peppermint Lounge features the best of local and visiting rock 'n' roll bands, with imaginative booking. A blend of the downtown clubs with the comfort and commercialism of such lamented uptown clubs as Hurrah, the Peppermint Lounge is a well-run, enjoyable club. There's dancing downstairs, seats upstairs, and plenty of nooks and crannies for thee and thine to get away from it all. The two bands a night usually each play twice, on a prompt schedule of 12 P.M., 1 A.M., 2 A.M., and 3 A.M.

The Ritz, 119 E. 11 St., 228-8000
Though initially suffering from bad vibes and a bad sound system, the Ritz has, through sheer volume of good bands that have played there, wormed its way into the city's heart. There is no doubt about it: the Ritz has the best lineup of bands in the city today, and it is an increasingly palatable late-night palace. Though there sometimes are problems at the door, these can be avoided by buying tickets in advance (advisable especially for any of the many British bands that the Ritz books). There is seating upstairs, a large dance

floor with giant video screen downstairs, and various
bars all over the place. This is a club you can't avoid if
you want to have fun in New York.

S.N.A.F.U. 21 St. and 6 Ave., 691-3532
This lively little club occasionally features up-and-
coming New York rock 'n' roll bands, as well as cabaret,
jazz, and theater. Though darkly lit and intimate, it is
cheerful, friendly, and fun.

Squat Theater, 256 W. 23 St., 691-1238
Squat is a precariously financed little hall that features
the best of avant-garde jazz and rock. To say it is
informal is to understate: the bar consists of a card
table and a couple of coolers of beer. But the music is
always fine, there are occasional real surprises, and it's
cheap.

Tramps, 125 E. 15 St., 777-5077
Across the street from Irving Plaza, Tramps is a cozy—
though expensive—little bar that features old blues
singers, modern reggae stars, and the occasional
resurrected soul star. It is also a club with a fine
ambience, an eclectic crowd, and a pleasant mix of rock
club standing, bar leaning, and cabaret seating.

Trax, 100 W. 72 St., 799-1448
From its carpeted floor to its expensive seating, Trax is
about as dull a place as fine rock 'n' roll has ever been
created in. Used by record companies as a nervous
halfway house to launch out-of-town acts, Trax has a
fine mainstream booking policy and is courteously run.
It is, however, no place to see a band in if you can
possibly help it.

Discos

The death of disco has been proclaimed so many times
it's about time to proclaim its rebirth. Not surprisingly,
all the funereal hype was exaggerated. While the equally
hyped rock invasion put an end to the opening of too
many new discos, a lot of the clubs that were around in
disco's heyday are still going as strong as ever. There
are still people who aren't ashamed to admit they love
disco, and some who, in fact, thrive on it.

Disco started as a largely gay and black movement,

but it's gone aboveground to the point where everyone
goes to discos and there's a disco for everyone. Now,
even new-wavers can go to discos, which have modified
their style to incorporate danceable rock and even all-
rock nights. In most cases, though, the well-intentioned
synthesis doesn't work; people come for the
uninterrupted hypnosis of that thumping disco beat.
Beyond the music, the other features of a club—decor,
image, door policy—are essential. Large, lavish places
with many levels and numerous diversions abound in
New York, all vying for the disco-goer's attention with
more and more glamor and gimmickry.

Disco will never die, so you might as well get used to
it.

Bond's, 1526 Broadway, 944-5880
The best thing to be said about this home of Third
World radio station parties is that it's big.

Copacabana, 10 E. 60 St., 755-6010
Once a classy place where showgirls named Lola
strutted their feather boas, the Copa is now notable for
featuring top cabaret talent, and not-so-notable for its
disco-dancing swarms of businessmen and borough
people, who've infested the place like desperate insects.
Like disco in general, the club has seen better days.

The Electric Circus, 100 Fifth Ave., 989-7457
Three levels, with dancing, light shows, and live rock
groups—but don't think for a minute that this is any
kind of avant-garde multimedia complex. The crowd
could tell you how to get there from Brooklyn faster
than they could tell you their names, and the ambience
is generally not very ambient: tacky, actually. "Circus"
is very apt, as anyone with sophistication or taste is
likely to feel like a big Bozo here.

The Funhouse, 526 W. 26 St., 691-0621
If the Circus isn't tasteful enough, don't dare approach
the Funhouse—a cheap-looking, cavernous place with
juvenile balloon stands, popcorn machines, and lots of
bubblegum-popping to drown out the music. If polyester
really causes brain damage, the teen set that fills this
place is in big trouble.

Ice Palace 57, 57 W. 57 St., 838-8557
An offshoot of the Ice Palace on Fire Island, this one
somehow doesn't quite fit into its 57 St. milieu, with its

hordes of young, attractive gays lining up a block away from Carnegie Hall. Interesting high-tech decor and good music makes for a reasonably energetic and very youth-oriented club that especially comes alive for Sunday tea dances (at which absolutely no one sips tea, by the way).

Magique, 1110 First Ave., 935-6060
On the former site of a used-car showroom, this club tries to recreate the magic of a past disco era with inept, arrogant door service and an upstairs, glass-enclosed VIP room, fronted by even more inept, arrogant service. Frequent special events (Disco Sally's wedding anniversary) make for diversion, at least, and the oval dance floor surrounded by banquettes and studded by neon is tasteful enough, but the sense of Upper East Side desperation forces the club to live down to its nickname: Tragique.

Paradise Garage, 84 King St., 255-4517
Third World gays convene here for ultra-low chic and high-energy body pumping and thumping. The overall ambience is about as genteel as a tribal dance in Zimbabwe. As well as being *the* place to let off dancing steam, the Garage is also a showcase for disco talent, which goes on at approximately 4 A.M., when the crowd peaks. They continue until daybreak, and the energy never relents.

The Red Parrot, 617 West 57 St., 247-1530
It's ironic that the newest and hottest thing in disco is something as new and hot as the big-band sound, but anyone who's been to this club—the size of a city block and replete with a 20-piece orchestra—can't deny the excitement of having DJ music alternate with the live swing. By 6 A.M. you don't even notice the difference. The big band also does country hoedowns and practically anything else you might imagine, and the actual live cockatoos wisely keep to themselves. At press time, this is *the* place.

Regine's, 502 Park Ave., 826-0990
French jet-setter Regine Zilberberg started this club (one of an international chain) in order to capitalize on the need for a touch of Continental elegance in New York. To get in, you must conform to the stringent dress code (black tie for men, dresses for women). Order a drink and be prepared to close out your bank account.

Talk to a stranger and be prepared to learn French, Spanish, German, Italian, or Dutch. The dance floor is really much too small for anything too wild, but that's the point. You come here to be seen in ornately elegant surroundings, not to be madcap and carefree. Inevitably, Regine's has lost some of its snob appeal over the years, but no one's come along to top it.

The River Club, 491 West St., 924-6855
Steven Cohn took over the defunct 12 West and made it into a reborn gay disco filled with West Village musclemen pulsating to the beat of a different drum. Send in the clones . . . don't bother, they're here.

Roseland, 239 W. 52 St., 247-0200
The schedule alternates between ballroom dancing to the tune of two live big bands and disco for the younger set, who can toss each other around the huge, old-fashioned ballroom space with reckless abandon. The place is a little too steeped in art deco tradition to sustain its schizophrenic identity—the disco crowd never really wanted to take advantage of that grand space—but it's still one of the few places to dance cheek to cheek, as they say.

Roxy Roller Rink, 515 W. 18 St., 675-8300
If you've got wheels on, you might as well head toward the Roxy. The rink is large, the neon fixtures fall appealingly just beyond the range of gaudiness, and there's food served at the bar. Spin around here for a few hours and you'll lose all sense of time, place, and identity. A better recommendation for a disco doesn't exist.

Studio 54, 254 W. 54 St., 489-7667
Once the dazzling doyenne of discos, this club has since gone through so many identity crises the doormen virtually have to sweep people in from the streets on off nights. The illusion of exclusivity is still there, as is the awesome decor—complete with descending lights and an immense balcony—but the magic is gone. Occasionally a celebrity birthday party will bring out a starry crowd, but chances are that when that happens, someone will have to call the paparazzi from the public phone and tell them to rush over. Not much has really changed except the times, but at this point Studio 54 reeks uncomfortably of necrophilia.

Underground, 860 Broadway, 254-4005
Literally overnight, a fading gay club in Andy Warhol's
Factory building on Union Square became the new rage,
with hordes of would-be revelers randomly shouting
doormen's names ("Mark! Steve?"), only to be told they
have to be on the list to warrant admission to this
palace of fabulousness. If you get beyond the rude door
treatment, you enter a two-level disco done in a brick
and prison-bar motif, but definitely several notches
above any State Pen you've ever danced in. The music
is retro disco, with an implicit understanding that no
matter how many trends may pass by, Donna Summer
is still queen. The crowd answers the question
"Whatever happened to all those old Studio people?,"
especially at special events, which are plentiful. New
wave Wednesdays, gay Sundays, and Ruby Tuesdays
haven't helped this club hold its own against the not-so-
underground Red Parrot.

Wednesday's, 210 E. 86 St., 535-8500
The format—a disco/bar/restaurant in the form of a
block-long underground village—may seem a bit quaint
for most, but not for the Upper East Side swingles set,
who find it the perfect ambience for dancing and
romancing, and not just on Wednesdays, either. Ah well,
to each his own.

Xenon, 124 W. 43 St., 221-2690
Entrepreneurs Howard Stein and Pepo Vanini opened
this major club 4 years ago and have surprised everyone
by keeping it open and popular beyond the hump of
disco's descent. Founded as a rival to the exclusive
hotsy-totsiness of Studio 54, Xenon's always seemed
like a competitor—the place you ended up at if you
didn't get into 54. Now it's one of the few large, mixed,
respectable discos around, so it commands its own
crowd. A converted theater, the place has the built-in
voyeuristic bonus of a balcony, from which one can
watch a series of disco special effects and effective disco
people.

The Gay Scene

New York has long been the Eastern mecca for gay men
and lesbians. In the past few years—since the advent of

gay liberation—New York has come out in a big way. The following is a selected listing of lesbian and gay bars and discos in Manhattan.

The Anvil, 500 W. 14 St. at Eleventh Ave., 924-0528
A private club, though easy to crack if you look the part. An almost circus-like atmosphere prevails. Drag shows and specialty acts nightly atop the circular upstairs bar. A lower catacomb features sex between patrons. Best very late after all the other bars have closed. Open until the early morning hours on weekends.

Uncle Charlie's South, 581 Third Ave., at 38 St., 684-6400
A popular East Side singles spot representing the sweater and slacks set of young gays with a decent 9 to 5 job who spend their money on clothes and a classy studio apartment.

Uncle Charlie's Downtown, 56 Greenwich Ave., 255-8787
A little bit of the Upper East Side in Greenwich Village. Very popular, with a restaurant in back. Imitates San Francisco's famous Midnight Sun with strategically placed video screens showing scenes from old TV and movies.

The Ice Palace, 57 W. 57 St. off Sixth Ave., 838-8557
See "Discos."

Crisco Disco, 15 St. and Ninth Ave.
A different kind of disco for the after-hours crowd. Technically private but easy to crash if you don't mind being frisked at the door. The DJ sits atop a giant can of Crisco. Pinball arcade and very large dance floor. Gets crowded very late.

Julius', 159 W. 10 St., at Waverly Pl., 929-9672
One of the oldest and most consistently popular gay bars in New York. Was used as a set for *Next Stop Greenwich Village* and the film version of *The Boys in the Band.* Great hamburgers and very relaxed. A New York landmark.

The Eagle's Nest, 21 St. at Eleventh Ave. 929-9304
Once strictly leather, this longtime favorite is now more relaxed but still very butch with a leather/western veneer. Has the best music in New York and good,

cheap hamburgers until 4 A.M. Located on the waterfront circuit, down the street from The Spike, a heavier leather bar.

The Saint, Second Ave. at 6 St. 674-8369
The ultimate disco of the eighties, with a full-sized planetarium dome and special effects to rival those in *Close Encounters.* You must be a member or enter with a member. Weekends only, and very expensive—but worth it if you can get in. No liquor. Open until 7 A.M.

The Duchess, 70 Grove St., at Sheridan Sq., 242-1408
A rarity—a lesbian cruising bar and disco. Fair prices and very friendly. Women only.

Marie's Crisis, 59 Grove St., off Seventh Ave., 243-9323
Theatrical singalong bar in which patrons crowd the piano and join in the fun. Worth a visit on weekends when most rowdy. Extremely friendly, outgoing attitude. Gay men mainly, though women welcomed.

Nickel Bar, 127 W. 72 St., 874-9858
One of the few predominantly black gay bars in New York and very crowded on weekends. Good music and not very expensive.

Ty's, 114 Christopher St., 924-7414
One of New York's oldest pose bars. Popular by virtue of the fact that it's located in the heart of the "ghetto," but a waste of time to most New York gays.

The Ninth Circle, 139 W. 10 St., 243-9204
Gay teenagers' heaven. Double-level bar with outdoor garden in summertime. Draws swarms of young gays who parade through Greenwich Village on weekends.

The Rawhide, 212 Eighth Ave., at 21 St.
Chelsea local western bar, draws a neighborhood crowd during the week and those on their way to and from the waterfront on weekends.

Boy-Meets-Girl (or Sex in the Big Apple)

New York can be the most difficult place to meet your mate. Although the city has over 3,500,000 women and 3,500,000 men, many of each sex are unattached. Some say this is because there aren't enough friendly social settings. In small towns, there are many such places: schools, church socials, and even soda shops. But these aren't meeting grounds for true New Yorkers. True, many "students" take courses to study their peers (a friend of mine calls this "making skin-ections"). But why pay for a course when all you want is the extracurricular activity? The bars are a meeting place, true. Many people go to singles bars, but be forewarned: these places are pretty desperate, they charge a fortune, and most customers seem to come from outlying boroughs or dreadful bedroom communities. Here, then, are some nice, free places where New York boys can meet New York girls (and vice versa):

Singles Bars

If you must go, the big singles bar area is First Avenue from 60 to 66 Sts. Three other bars to note: **Ichabods, Herlihy's,** and **Mad Hatter,** all near 77 St. at First or Second Ave. Many clubs and restaurants listed elsewhere in this guide are also good places to meet and greet. But regarding the singles bars, remember: they are a real racket. Fodder for tomorrow's Dear Abby column.

Block Parties

Mentioned elsewhere in this guide, block parties are one of the best social aspects of New York life. There are thousands of block associations, and they all seem to hold one or two block parties a year. These usually feature music, flea markets, and lots of food stands. Everyone has a good time; they're informal and they're free.

Bloomingdale's

(59 St. and Lexington Ave.) or **Macy's** (Herald Square, 34 St. and Broadway). These two stores are key meeting places, where everyone and anyone can meet. Like the stores themselves, you'll find the Bloomingdale's crowd a bit trendier, the Macy's crowd more varied.

Madison Avenue

From 42 to 50 St. is a preppie shopping turf, so you

might meet the same. From 60 to 96 Sts. is the home of
the city's best jewelry shops, boutiques, and art
galleries. The crowd is part preppie, part
ultrafashionable. Lots of money here, so if you find Mr.
or Ms. Right on Madison, remember: they flaunt it, and
expect you to do the same.

South Street Seaport

Located on the East River, north of Wall Street, this
popular maritime museum draws tourists and city folk
in equal numbers. The museum hosts a number of folk,
country, and sea-chanty music concerts. The crowd is
wholesome. Unpretentious.

West Broadway/Washington Square

On weekends, this gallery row on West Broadway and
Washington Square immediately to the north are
crawling with singles. Most are cute and arty, but
preppies are making inroads.

Libraries

That's right, singles meet at libraries. Not in among the
books but outside, on the steps. The two most noted for
this are: the **New York Public Library,** Main Branch
(42 Street and Fifth Ave.), and **Low Library** at
Columbia University (116 St. and Broadway). The
people here, as you might expect, are more educated
than the norm. They often enjoy good conversation. Be
intelligent and act smart if you want to score.

Museums

The scene is at the entrances, as with libraries, but the
crowds are more diverse. Three of note for singles
action: the **Metropolitan Museum** (82 St. and Fifth
Ave.), the **Museum of Modern Art** (11 W. 53 St.), and
the **Museum of Natural History** (Central Park West
and 79 St.).

Waiting Rooms/Lobbies

Major transportation hubs are also major meeting
places. Three major stations provide New Yorkers with

social opportunities, but you should be careful, as many of those you might meet may be doing their meeting for money. Nevertheless, check out **Grand Central Station** (42 Street and Park Ave. [note the information kiosk]), **Penn Station** (32 St. and Seventh Ave.), and the **Port Authority Bus Terminal** (41 Street and Eighth Ave.).

Running Tracks

Last but not least. Since running and jogging became popular, running and jogging tracks have also become key places to meet mates. Five popular tracks are: **the Reservoir in Central Park** (used in all seasons, entrance at 90 St. and Fifth Ave.); **East Drive or West Drive in Central Park** (best on warm-weather weekends, enter via 72 St. east or west); **East River Promenade** (best in afternoon and after rush hour, to catch local singles; enter from 80, 78, 70, or 63 Sts.); **West Side Elevated Highway** in the Village (good in all seasons, for all types, enter at Vandam or Chambers St.; note that highway may soon be dismantled); **Washington Square Park** (good in all seasons, for all types, around the outside of the park, at Fifth Ave. and Waverly Pl. or 4 St.).

24-Hour New York

If you're not in the mood for an all-night party or club, but you still can't sleep, here's a list of some 24-hour services in New York. Five of the better all-night restaurants are:

Brasserie, 100 E. 53 St., 751-4840 French and American cuisine; good omelettes. Dinner menu until 10:00 P.M.; supper served until 6:00 A.M., when the breakfast menu begins.

Empire Diner, 210 Tenth Ave. at 22 St., 243-2736 Continental fare and snacks served in fashionable deco diner.

Kiev, 177 Second Ave. at 7 St., 674-4040 A popular hangout, offering a wide variety of homemade food. Best are the blintzes and fresh breads. Coffee shop decor.

Richoux, Sixth Ave. at 55 St., 265-3090, is a bar, restaurant, and coffeehouse. Another Richoux, also 24-hour, is located in the Citicorp Center.

Sarge's, 548 Third Ave., at 36 St., 679-0442 Classic New York-style delicatessen, with everything from a takeout pastrami on rye to a complete sit-down meal.

We hate to recommend them, but if you must, you must. A few **Burger King** and **McDonald's** locations are open all night.

Delis

Smiler's and **7-11 Stores** have many locations in Manhattan. They're no bargain during the day but are very convenient convenience stores. Smiler's makes deliveries at all hours, too. Here are a few of their places:

107 Seventh Ave. So. (Christopher St.) 741-9092

293 Third Ave. (23 St.) 689-2703

686 Third Ave. (43 St.) 599-9093

924 Third Ave. (56 St.) 935-9170

850 Seventh Ave. (55 St.) 757-5871

Markets

On Broadway, just south of Columbia University, there are a couple of all-night markets. Of note is the fresh produce at **Cathedral Market,** at 110 St. Both the Cathedral and **Westside** markets have some convenience items, canned goods, beer . . . **Gourmet Shop I,** 877 Third Ave. (at 53 St.), features a variety of imported and domestic delicacies, makes deliveries, and is open 24 hours a day (486-0277).

Pharmacies

For fast relief, at any hour, the **Kaufman Beverly Pharmacy,** at 50 St. and Lexington Ave. (755-2266), handles emergency prescriptions. Its complete stock also includes cosmetics, sundries, and surgical supplies.

Florists

Two of the florists that stay open 24 hours are **Fantasy**

Flowers, 33 Greenwich Ave. (989-0060), and **Rialto Florist,** 707 Lexington Ave., near 57 St. (688-3234).

Hair Salons

There is even an all-night hair salon at 536 Madison Ave. (between 54 and 55 Sts.). **Larry Matthews** (246-6100) can provide a midnight manicure or 4 A.M. facial.

Game Rooms

The Game Room, retailer of chess sets and books, is open 24 hours daily. Chess, backgammon, and Scrabble played on the premises: 2130 Broadway (at 75 St.), 595-0923.

Parking Lots

Most parking lots in New York have early closing times, and if you're just a minute late, you may not see your car until morning. Here are three that are open and attended around the clock:

Perry Abingdon, 97 Charles St. (near Bleecker), 242-9723

Red Ball, 142 E. 31 St. (between Lexington and 3 Ave.), 683-2056.

Sutton Terrace, 450 E. 63 St. (near York), 838-5717

Newsstands

(See "Great New York Newsstands," page 188.)

Photocopying

The only place where we found a 24-hour photocopier was in the lobby of the General Post Office, Eighth Ave. and 33 St. Limited postal services available also.

Transportation

Some city buses and most subways run 24 hours, although nighttime service is less frequent than during the day. Taxis are easily found (or called for) at all hours. Very little is open (or advisable) at the bus and train terminals.

Looking for something to do that doesn't cost much? The Staten Island Ferry runs all night: a cheap-thrill view of the Statue of Liberty, New York Harbor, bridges, and the lower Manhattan and Brooklyn skylines. Accessible via subways 1, 4, 5, N, and RR and buses 1, 6, 15. Downtown is where some workers begin their day, in the middle of the night. The Fulton Fish Market: Get off at Fulton Street/Broadway–Nassau, and follow your nose toward the East River. The truckers and fishers load and unload as-much-as-you've-ever-seen of as-fresh-as-you-can-get seafood. The height of activity is just before dawn, when shipments are carried off to markets and restaurants. The retail store is at 18 Fulton St. (952-9658). Night Court is where the bar brawls and the *other* side of late night life end up. Great New York dramas that never sell out! Civil Court, 111 Centre St.; Criminal Court, 100 Centre St. (both are near Franklin St.). You could walk across the Brooklyn Bridge or just go uptown to a Sutton Place park bench (East River between 55 and 59 St.) and wait for the sun to rise . . .

Not Quite 24-Hour

In addition to all-night places, there are other establishments with later-than-usual hours.

By New York State law, alcohol cannot be sold after 4:00 A.M. Many English, Irish, and neighborhood bars serve until that time, but liquor stores (never open on Sundays) usually close around 10:00 P.M. A few exceptions have hours from 8:00 A.M. until midnight, 6 days a week:

Cambridge, 594 Eighth Ave., at 39 St. (947-3966)

House of Cheers, 261 West 18 St. (929-1924)

Schumer's, 59 E. 54 St. (355-0940)

76 Liquors, 1469 First Ave., near 76 St., (249-1700)

Some of the better downtown bookstores stay open until midnight or later, 7 days a week. These include:

Marloff Paperback Corner, 10 Sheridan Sq. (924-5864)

New Morning Book Store, 169 Spring St. (966-2993)

St. Mark's Bookshop, 13 St. Marks Pl. (260-7853)

On the Upper West Side, near Columbia University, there are a couple of good bookstores open until midnight. Of special note is **Papyrus Books,** 2915 Broadway at 113 St. (222-3350). Farther south on Broadway, **Gryphon Bookshop,** which also carries records, is open until 11:00 P.M. every day (216 W. 89 St.; 362-0706).

Colony Record and Radio Center, 1619 Broadway, at the corner of 49 St., not only has an extensive selection of recordings but also has hours until 3:00 A.M. daily, including Sunday.

For nighttime recreation, there are tennis courts and bowling alleys open late:

Gramercy Tennis and Racquetball club, Sixth Ave. at 23 St. (691-0110), and **Tower Tennis Courts,** 1725 York Ave. (between 88 and 89 Sts.), 860-2464, are both open from 7:00 A.M. to midnight, all week long. **Madison Square Garden Bowling Center,** at Penn Plaza (Seventh Ave. from 31 to 33 Sts.; 563-8160), is open from 9:00 A.M. to 1:00 A.M. **National Bowling Recreation Arena** (242-7675), at 270 Eighth Ave. (at 23 St.), is open nightly until midnight and closes at 2:00 A.M. on Fridays and Saturdays.

COMMUNICATIONS

Cable TV

Cable TV is currently available in Manhattan for a monthly fee of about $12 and a one-time installation charge of under $20, bringing viewers extra channels of unconventional programming as well as improved reception on all channels. Channels C and D are free public access (no commercials); L is municipal access (no commercials); J is leased access (yes, commercials); and Channel 10 is programmed by the cable company. The following programs, times, and channels are subject to change, owing to the raw, spontaneous nature of cable.

Crank Call Show, Saturday 11 P.M., Ch. C
Got a comment . . . on anything? A good joke? A bad joke? Or just an uncontrollable urge to swear or talk dirty on television? No problem. Poised and personable John-Who-Knows takes all calls. The First Amendment suffers not.

Sex

Ugly George, Tues., Wed., Thurs., 11:30 P.M., Ch. J
He prowls the city in search of willing, buxom women to disrobe for the prying eye of his video camera. A secluded alley, a deserted doorway, or his basement "studio" are the typical settings for his notorious exploits. His half hour of "truth, sex, and violence"

attracts approximately 40,000 viewers, or students, as
His Ugliness refers to them. If naked locals (New York's
finest?) are your bag, be sure to catch this one.

Midnight Blue, Mon., Fri., 12m, Ch. J
Al (*Screw Magazine*) Goldstein is the force behind this
program, which presents some artful, well-produced
documentation of slimy Times Square skin emporiums.
Porn stars, pin-ups, and professionals are interviewed in
tubs, in beds, and in various stages of undress. A great
way for the shy tourist to scope out the scene.

Interludes After Midnight, Sun., Tues., Thurs.,
12m, Ch. J
This live, phone-in show is hosted by Daniel Jay,
referred to as "The Rabbi" by many of his callers. He
conducts his talk show from mattresses on the studio
floor. He and his guests are quite naked and the show
opens with a mass of groping bodies. Sorry, no erections
or genital touching. His various topics, such as the
sexual nature of lesbianism, are generally discussed in a
serious, open, and honest manner. For the intellectual
erotic.

Robin Byrd, Wed., 12m, Ch. J
Bikini-clad Byrd, the self-proclaimed Goddess of
Erotica, does exercises, tells sex-laden bedtime stories in
a low, breathy voice, lip-syncs to "Baby Let Me Bang
Your Box," has guests and takes phone calls. If you tell
her how beautiful, sexy, and talented she is, she won't
hang up on you. For a special New Year's treat, she goes
topless, but if you miss the unveiling, don't fret, the
lady's got terrific legs.

Drugs

If I Can't Dance You Can Keep Your Revolution,
Wed., 10:30 P.M., Ch. D
Cannabis queen Coca Crystal is the hostess and star.
She raps with guests (you can too, via phone) and
smokes marijuana (you can too, if you have any). Also
featured are dope-related comedy skits—a middle-aged
woman pot peddler sells different kinds of pots and
pans—and the public service segment, done by an
executive-looking young man who reports on the quality
and cost of grass currently available in the city. Hey
man, the counterculture lives, ya know?

Music

Paul Tschinkle's Inner Tube, Sun., 11 P.M., Ch. C
Tschinkle haunts the clubs—CBGB, Max's, Irving
Plaza, Mudd, etc. and brings the best and/or strangest
of the hopeful local bands to your TV. Past programs
have included Richard Hell and the Void Oids, the
Angry Simones, DNA, the Dead Kennedys, and a
bizarre underground film, *They Eat Scum.*

Rock Variety Show, Wed., 5:30 P.M., Ch. C; Fri.,
12m, Ch. D
Carl Williams presents documentation of live, big-name
concerts from across the country and record company
promo tapes of the real biggies. Don Kirshner, à la
cable.

Esoteric

Soho Television, Thurs., 8:30 P.M., Ch. 10
Video art, which means tapes of almost anything,
ranging from computerized lines and colors to thought-
provoking or nightmarish quasi-reality, is gathered from
everywhere, even L.A. Watching this unusual offering
takes some effort and practice but it's worth it.

Political

Municipal Access, Wed., 7:30 P.M. to 11 P.M., Ch. L
Unlike the typical municipal access channel,
Manhattan's does not voice the city line, because it is
not funded by the city. Three live, phone-in programs
featuring elected officials, city agencies, and nonprofit
groups offer information, referral, and insight into some
of the skulduggery that goes on around here. Sometimes
dull, sometimes hot. Check it out.

Communications Update, Wed., 7:30 P.M.; Fri.,
3 P.M., Ch. D
From obscure, Third World-country wars to
questionable behavior of some members of the New
Orleans Police Department to the worldwide
information imbalance, exposing injustice is their
specialty. Sometimes a Yugoslav artist or stream-of-
consciousness linguist slips in, but it's hard to watch
this program without learning something. On TV, yet.

Great New York Newsstands

If your "must" reading includes magazines with names like the *Unmuzzled Ox,* or you want to buy a copy of the *New York Times* at 3:30 A.M., finding a newsstand that caters to your needs can be a problem. Although New York is the nation's media capital, most of the city's 4,000 newsstands keep limited hours and only carry a small selection of publications. But there are exceptions. Here are some stands to consider if you want the best of the Fourth Estate in New York City:

SohoZat, 307 West Broadway (north of Canal St.), Tues.–Fri., 11 A.M. to 9 P.M.; Sat., 11 A.M. to 1 A.M.; Sun., 10 A.M. to 6 P.M. Closed Mon.

Although the financial district has few great newsstands, the area between Canal St. and 14 St. has them in abundance. SohoZat's owner, Stan Bobrof, boasts his newsstand carries "the most complete collection of esoteric publications," and there is no reason to doubt him. Underground magazines flank the *New Yorker,* and gaudy adult comics jostle copies of the *Reader's Digest.* There is no better stand, if you're looking for alternative publications with titles like *Raw* or *Wet.* The diverse clientele includes artists, truck drivers, and security analysts. Bobrof doesn't cater to any single group. "My criterion," he says, "is to put information out and let people make up their minds."

Gem Spa, 131 Second Ave. (at St. Marks Place), 24 hours

The Gem Spa is a landmark, where purchasing a paper may take second place to watching the street life around it. Its shelves are reminders that the East Village is still a melting pot, with Hungarian, Polish, Russian, Yiddish, Spanish, German, Italian, Irish, and Caribbean papers on sale; there is also a wide selection of comics and local alternative papers. In addition, the Gem Spa has a soda fountain wedged in between tobacco and bric-a-brac; no visitor should leave without trying one of its famous egg creams.

Hotalings Foreign News Depot, 1 Times Sq. (Broadway side), Mon.–Fri., 8 A.M. to 9:30 P.M.

Hotalings is New York's greatest newspaper stand. It is also one of the oldest, founded in 1901 (since

remodeled). Homesick travelers take note: In the booth
by the front entrance, you can pick up copies of
virtually every major daily paper in the U.S. Inside,
there is a selection of over 800 foreign newspapers and
magazines. Because Hotalings is known for its large out-
of-town stock, there is often a line of customers waiting
to be served, so be prepared. The service is otherwise
excellent; the dealers know their business. Their motto:
"You mention it, we got it."

96 News, Broadway and 96 St. (southwest corner),
24 hours

The Upper West Side has some of the city's funkiest
newsstands, with major stands on Broadway at 72, 79,
and 96 Sts. (Interesting note: There are no comparable
stands in the Columbia University area further north—
but bookstores are another matter.) Buying a paper at
96 News can be an adventure, for the stand is located at
one of the city's liveliest intersections. The service may
be rude, but there is a selection of about 1,000
magazines and newspapers on the racks. The 96 News is
strong on sports and ethnic publications (it is the only
stand where this writer saw the Haitian paper
L'Observateur prominently displayed). It also carries an
impressive number of Third World papers.

Mitha Brothers, Inc., 1500 First Ave. (south of 79
St.), Mon.–Fri., 6 A.M. to 10 P.M.; Sat., 6 A.M. to 2:30
A.M.; Sun., 6 A.M. to 2 P.M.

It is still possible to speak German with some of the old
newsdealers on East 86 St., just as one could speak
Yiddish, Spanish, Italian, or Greek in other
neighborhoods. But the best stands on the East Side
cater to the new urban gentry that has moved into New
York in the past few years. One such stand, the Mitha
Brothers, has 2,000 publications on its shelves. It also
offers eccentric sidelines: cymbals, brassieres, and black
silk bow ties. The news emphasis is on fashion and
business publications, with music and sex magazines not
far behind. The Mitha brothers are the most
considerate salesmen this writer encountered: They
don't just say "thank you" when a customer plunks
down change. They add, "Have a most gracious,
beautiful day," in the soft lilting English of their native
Pakistan. All that, and the news, too. Not bad for 30
cents.

Press in the Big Apple

New York is a city that thrives on information: it became the nation's media capital because the locals have a tremendous need for diverse kinds of papers, magazines, and television stations. Contrary to popular opinion, the number of newspapers is growing here: For each general interest publication that folds, a dozen specialized magazines and newspapers spring up. If you are a straight WASP with a trust fund, looking to invest money in stocks and real estate, you will find the publications you need for business and pleasure. More significant: If you are a young, black Estonian lawyer who belongs to a socialist party and wants an acting job, you will find regularly published local newspapers catering to your interests. There's something here for everybody.

What follows is a selection of the local press. It isn't complete (the newspaper list alone takes up three closely spaced pages in the telephone book), but it does give you an idea of what's available.

General News Dailies (New York City Proper)

The *New York Daily News* (best feature: it carries Doonesbury), 949-1234

The New York *Post* (best features: the movie clock, the screaming headlines), 349-5000

The *New York Times* (best feature: it's the newspaper of record), 556-1234

General News Dailies (Suburban)

Bergen Record (best feature: good general reporting), 279-8484

Long Island *Newsday* (best feature: entertainment coverage on the Island), 490-7111

Staten Island *Advance* (best feature: it's not the Manhattan *Advance*), 981-1234

Today Newspaper (best feature: ditto), 563-5409

The *Yonkers Herald Statesman* (best feature: hard-hitting investigations), 914-965-5000

Magazines

New York (best feature: listings, including the old *Cue* movie clock), 880-0700

The New Yorker (need we say more?), 840-3800

Political/Professional

The Daily Worker (old-line Communist)

The *Guardian Radical News Weekly*, 691-0404

The *Journal of Commerce* (covers business news, manufacturing, and trade), 425-1616

The *National Law Journal* (a must for lawyers), 964-9400

New York Law Journal (ditto, more localized), 964-9600

Publishers Weekly (covers the Fourth Estate), 764-5154

Real Estate Weekly, 226-6500

The Sporting News (weekly sports paper), 391-8290

Variety (the thespian's bible), 582-0650

The *Wall Street Journal* (no-nonsense financial and general news), 285-5000

Women's Wear Daily (the fashion business and good, interesting general news), 741-4000

Worker's World (leftist weekly), 255-0352

Young Socialist (left, socialist weekly), 675-0510

Religious/Ethnic/National

Al-Islaah (Arabic paper), 925-8350

American Magyar Nepszava (Hungarian paper), 254-0397

Amerikan Uutiset (Finnish semiweekly)

Amsterdam News (greatest black-oriented newspaper, good Harlem, Third World news), 678-6600

Aufbau (German paper), 873-7400

China Daily News, 962-3271

China Post (daily), 431-3897

Christian Science Monitor (daily national news reporting, excellent features), 599-1850

El Diario/La Prensa (Hispanic daily tabloid, modeled on *Daily News,* Third World news), 553-0600

Filipino Reporter (Philippine daily), 255-7062

France–Amerique (French weekly), 534-5455

Haiti *Observateur* (Haitian weekly, in French), 877-6600

Harlem Weekly (black-oriented paper), 532-8300

Hellenic Times (Greek-language paper), 986-6881

Hungarian Weekly Nepszava (Hungarian weekly), 737-9370

Il Progresso (Italian-language daily, good sports coverage), 799-5500

Impacto (Spanish-language paper), 568-7266

Iran Times (Iranian newspaper), 682-3685

Irish Advocate (English-language weekly), 233-4672

Irish Echo (English-language weekly, best-known Irish paper), 582-5750

Irish World & Gaelic American Newspaper (English-language weekly), 677-6060

The Jewish Daily Forward (Yiddish-language daily), 889-8200

The Jewish Daily Morning Freiheit (Yiddish-language daily), 255-7661

Joong-Ang Daily News (Korean-language daily), 255-9600

New Al Hoda (Arabic-language semiweekly)

New Lebanese–American Journal (Arabic-language paper), 686-7398

The News–World (Rev. Sung Myung Moon's contribution to daily journalism, in technicolor), 532-8300

Novoye Russkoye Slovo (Russian-language daily), 564-8544

Peimei News (Chinese paper), 732-8950

Polish Daily News, 354-0490

The Post Eagle (Polish weekly paper), 201-473-5414

Staats–Zeitung und Herold (German-language weekly, good sports, European news), 786-1110

Svoboda (Ukrainian daily), 227-5250

Vaba Eesti Sona (Estonian weekly), 686-3356

Vienybe (Lithuanian semimonthly), 277-7257

Weekly/Community

Chelsea Clinton News (good coverage, 14 to 59 Sts., West Side), 989-4096

The Community Herald (good coverage, midtown, East Side), 777-6810

Co-op West (freebie in West Side co-op buildings), 222-2603

East Side Express (good coverage, East Side, 14 to 96 St., 989-4096

Heights and Valley News (good coverage, West Side north of 96 St.), 866-4332

Heights–Inwood Newspaper (good coverage, West Side north of 96 St.), 569-8800

Murray Hill News (good coverage in midtown, residential), 684-6728

The Other Paper (good coverage in East Village, counterculture remnant), 673-8959

Our Town (New York's largest community weekly, freebie, conservative), 289-8700

The Village Voice (best feature: the classifieds, especially apartments, personals), 475-3300

The *Villager* (conservative version of *Village Voice*, community paper), 929-7200

The *West Sider* (good coverage, West Side from 59 to 116 Sts.), 989-4096

New York Radio

Stations in the Spotlight

WBLS-FM (107.5 mhz) has revolutionized radio programming. Drawing upon the increasing mass appeal of disco in the mid-seventies, this black-owned station developed a sound that, while definitely black-oriented, appealed as well to whites. The station encouraged a tone of voice in the cool style of a jazz station with low-key DJs and avoidance of noisy hype, propelling itself into the number-one spot and remaining there for the last several years. WBLS-FM has recently backed off the all-disco sound, now playing "disco and more," but still maintaining their former style and good taste in programming.

WKTU-FM (92.3 mhz) dropped the "mellow sound" to do disco battle with WBLS in 1978. WRKS-FM (98.7 mhz) also known as KISS 98 has become the latest "urban contemporary" station.

WKHK-FM (106.7 mhz) was once WRVR, an all-jazz station. More recently it was a "jazz fusion" station, and for a while it sounded a lot like WBLS. Now they play "country music," a hot item in many radio markets around the country. So far WKHK has not exactly made a big splash in New York, but who knows? In time it may adopt a slogan such as "country and more," perhaps adding a dash of Rolling Stones and Bob Dylan to its western blend.

Whenever WPIX-FM (101.9 mhz) changes its rock format, which is every few years, they invariably call themselves the "new 102." For a while, they even attempted an all new-wave format. Now they are straight rock music with hardly a trace of rhythm and blues, or even rockabilly. On WYNY-FM (97.1 mhz) you'll hear the DJs say "YNY" a lot and play a mishmash of pop and not-too-raucous oldies. This format used to be called "chicken rock" and is in a nebulous limbo between top-40 and MOR (middle of the road). If you can stand all those DJs beginning and ending every sentence with the station's call letters, you may enjoy this station's format. Obviously somebody does, for WYNY's audience has been growing steadily in the last year.

Rock 'n' Roll

WCBS-FM (101 mhz) plays "oldies" (pop/rock since ca. 1954) and some new top-40 hits which the DJs refer to as "future gold." WNEW-FM (102.3 mhz) has an avant-garde approach to rock music programs. This "progressive" rock station plays cuts from albums, more or less ignoring the singles charts. This is where new-wave bands like Adam and the Ants, the Pretenders, and the Police are heard, along with standard album cuts from the past. WPLJ-FM (95.5 mhz) plays best-selling albums, making no attempt to break new ground.

Easy Listening

The older generation had its nerves shattered by World War II and Korea and quietly took to this type of music in the late forties and fifties. Commonly referred to as "elevator" or "dentist office" music, "Beautiful Music" stations have very large audiences in every part of the country. Aural Valium. In New York, the best station of this type is WRFM (105.1 mhz). WPAT-AM (930 khz) and FM (93.1 mhz), which originates from Paterson, New Jersey, is also a "Beautiful Music" station, but not quite *as* beautiful as WRFM. WTFM (103.5 mhz) plays regular pop hits in a relaxed version.

Jazz

Since WRVR changed its call letters to WKHK and its format to "country and eastern" a while back, there has been no commercial jazz radio in New York City. When one considers that even Boise, Idaho, has an all-jazz station, this is a shocking statistic. Fortunately, many college stations include a bit of jazz in their programming. WKCR-FM (89.9 mhz) leads them all in professionalism, as well as in the educational and entertainment value of their jazz programming. Whether it's a weekly jazz sampler or special programs, such as the annual Louis Armstrong marathon, the programs are good because the students care enough to research their material and are smart enough to let the music speak for itself.

Classical

Among the college stations, WKCR (Columbia University, see above, under "Jazz"), WNYU (89.1 mhz, New York University), and WFUV (90.7 mhz, Fordham University) all have some classical music programming. WKCR was recently given an entire library of rare classical recordings, and no doubt they will expand their programming to accommodate this gift. WBAI-FM (99.5 mhz), a listener-supported station, includes classical music in their highly diversified offering.

The two commercial classical stations in New York are WNCN-FM (104.3 mhz) and WQXR-AM (1560 khz) and FM (96.3 mhz). WQXR is the "station of the *New York Times*"; their record library is in excellent condition, and "Live from The Met" has become a national institution. In spite of their smooth announcers and live simulcasts, some people find their programming conservative, repetitive, and uninspired.

WNCN is usually held in higher regard. Although the records are sometimes more scratchy than those at WQXR, the programming is more interesting. WNCN will *try* things—like an all-Berg program or a birthday concert devoted to a composer or performer, whereas WQXR always plays it safe. Although both stations appear to have the same percentage of commercials, WQXR, for whatever reason, *sounds* more commercial; on WNCN these 30-second annoyances seem more incidental to the programming, not an integral part of it.

There are *no* commercials on WNYC-FM (94 mhz), and its programming is the most adventuresome of all. Its comprehensive classical programs give the privately owned stations a run for their money. Some old standards, but also 20-century and out-of-the-ordinary classical works are featured. WNYC, an affiliate of National Public Radio, airs cultural and New York current events programs as well. WNYC-AM (830 khz) offers music interspersed with public affairs and dramatic programs.

Noncommercial Radio

The Federal Communications Commission (FCC) has set aside 88 mhz to 92 mhz for noncommercial use. Most of these stations—such as WKCR, WNYU, and WFUV—are owned and operated by colleges and universities and programmed by students with varying degrees of expertise. Without a program schedule, which most of these stations will be happy to send to you, it may be difficult to figure out what and who is on when. This applies as well to WBAI and WNYC, both noncommercial stations that found their way into the area "zoned" for commercial use.

On AM

AM radio has been kicked into a category all its own in the last decade or so. This has been aggravated by manufacturers of hi-fi equipment complementing their exquisite FM receivers with poor quality AM receivers. These put out a far worse sound than AM actually deserves. AM, therefore, is practically ignored by people playing the radio on their home stereo systems but still hangs in there with the less discriminating clock and car radio crowd. As one Chicago programmer recently noted, "AM has to work a lot harder now" to gain listeners. News and information formats seem to be where AM is heading.

WINS (1010 khz) is New York's first all-news station and in spite of its Group W affiliation does not sound as polished as WCBS (880). WINS was formerly top-40 and home of the "Fifth Beatle," the late Murray the K. Another former top-40 station, WMCA (570), offers more casual talk, including interviews and call-ins from listeners. WOR (710) mixes a little music into its prime-time shows, but its main attraction is a full lineup of interview shows throughout the day. The hosts change every half hour. WHN (1050), formerly WMGM and another ex-top-40 station, plays a better blend of country music than its FM rival, WKHK. "America's original music and news station," WNEW-AM (1130), plays what it originally played—big-band and pop standards. WNEW is noted for its radio personalities. Two of them, Ted Brown and William B. Williams, are legends in the business.

WABC (770) and WNBC (660) are the top-40 stations, but WABC, in fact, is expected to go "all talk" in the near future. On WNBC, New York's most original DJ, Don Imus, and his "Imus in the Morning" feature a witty newsman and a cast of hilarious fictional characters. Recently WAVC brought the team of Ross and Wilson up from Atlanta to do battle against Imus with their own skillful brand of humor.

Don't expect to hear too much music on AM stations before 10 in the morning; news, traffic, weather, and comedy bits take up the bulk of the time.

WLIB (1190) plays West Indian music for the most part—reggae and beyond. Latin sounds are heard in Spanish on WJIT (1480) and WADO (1280). WWRI (1600) plays rhythm and blues, disco, jazz fusion, and the Reverend Ike, the most frightening preacher since Jonathan Edwards (Sunday night, 11 to 11:30). If you want to get some more Bible under your belt, you can try WWDJ (970), yet another of the top-40 stations that went the way of all-talk.

PERSONAL DETAILS

Finding an Apartment in NYC

It's not so tough to find an apartment in New York City . . . but an apartment that's affordable and livable is another story altogether. There are whole books devoted to this fine art.

Rule number one: Don't get discouraged. Prepare to pay the equivalent of two to four months rent, depending upon security deposits, utilities, and fees. Establish your limitations and preferences before you call the movers.

Rule number two: Safety and convenience, in the long run, are money-savers.

Rule number three: Manhattan is (for a good reason) the most expensive of the five boroughs. Many apartments in the other boroughs are safe and cheap. But if you're spending every waking hour in Manhattan, the commuting expense, wasted time, and migraines aren't always worth it. Size up prospective neighborhoods: Visit the areas during the day and at night, go bar-hopping, talk to locals, and shop. Look for anything that might influence the area's character—high schools, hospitals, and rock clubs make rather noisy neighbors. Single women should pay special attention in selecting a neighborhood.

The majority of rentals that you'll find are "rent-stabilized." This means that your exorbitant rent can only be raised by a fixed percentage when the lease expires. Nearly all apartments require tenants to sign a lease, usually one to three years in length. Yes, it's a serious document and yes, you have legal obligations . . . but, *Rule number four:* There are loopholes for every provision. Check any lease for an addition reading "Apartment is to be rented in 'as is' condition"; find out just what they mean by *as is*. If you prefer to rent on a monthly basis, your alternatives are sublets or residential hotels. There's less security for eviction recourse, but less responsibility, too. Your needs and preferences determine the type of apartment you're seeking. Safety should never be secondary. You won't save money on a cheap place with no front door lock in a dangerous neighborhood, if you're robbed. Check the front door, apartment locks, and window security. If they're inadequate, you have yet another expense. If you can afford a doorman building, do it. There is not only more safety, but service as well.

Rule number five: You pay for convenience in Manhattan, so you might as well have it. Your feet are your primary mode of transportation, so you don't want to trudge ten blocks every time you need groceries. Search out the nearest deli, laundry, and mass transit. You might sacrifice these conveniences for an ideal location within walking distance to work or school.

When shown the apartment, look at the upkeep of the building. The cleanliness and state of repair probably won't measure up to suburban standards, but you can get some idea of whether or not the super is dependable for future work. Find out if he lives in the building. After he has shown you the place, you may never see the super again. Inspect plumbing, electricity, appliances, and any other detail you can.

There are several methods to find apartments in New York City, but he who hesitates is homeless. There are brokers, referral services, newspaper ads, and roommate agencies. Choose the resource by your financial situation and *persevere*.

Rule number six: The best costs the most. A licensed real estate broker has the best listings, but rarely any bargains. Brokers require personal information in advance; you need to have job, bank, and character references. If you lack that stability, ask a well-established relative or close friend to cosign the application. The percentage-based fee (paid after you've happily signed a lease) amounts to about 1½ months rent. The initial cost is high, but brokers are reliable and eager for their commission; therefore they aim to please.

Referral services are *not* recognized by the Better Business Bureau and are notorious for luring advertisements for an apartment *exactly* like the one of your dreams. You pay a fixed fee to get your hands on the address of that apartment, and then discover that it was "just taken." But they *do* have places not-quite-as-nice-for-twice-the-price. We cannot generalize about all referral services, but be forewarned that many are ineffective. As with brokers, they require personal and financial data before giving any leads. *Rule number seven:* If it sounds too good to be true, it probably is.

Rule number eight: Wlkup flthru wbf a/c drm pkvu! Your first apartment-hunting effort should be to decipher the Sunday *New York Times* real estate section. This comprehensive listing puts the market into some perspective. There are few cheapies, but all sizes and areas are included. When you're serious about pursuing a *Times* ad, go to a newsstand on Thursday. You may pay the full price for this one portion of Sunday's paper, but your odds for apartment availability increase. *Rule number nine:* There'll always be someone—though not better or richer than you— that'll get there first.

The *Post* and *Daily News* listings are few, usually no-fee, and in the outer boroughs. Weekly papers offer some good ads, but beware of referral service listings. They also advertise roommate services and shares. Several publications are exclusively for apartment seekers. Purchased at larger newsstands, these are always worth a try. Determine an ad's source—broker, service, or owner—before responding to any ad.

Living with a roommate is the most practical way to rent in New York. Financially you may have no choice; emotionally it eases things in an occasionally lonely city. Some roommate services are not quite the rip-off as are other agencies, but some are. The fee is minimal, and personal guidelines are specified with each listing. Look into advertised shares. A person already living in an apartment can save you the costs of utility deposits and phone installation. A written agreement, although not customary, is recommended between roommates.

Friends and acquaintances are a vital source of leads. *Rule number ten:* Keep your eye on the apartment of any fiancée. Companies and colleges have either housing offices or posted ads. Banks, supermarkets, and other public places often have community bulletin boards to consult, too.

Determine your needs, tap every resource you can, and carefully evaluate the apartment. When you move in, bring a can of boric acid and a broom and brace yourself: you're about to become a New Yorker.

Gay Services

It's not easy to be gay in New York, but when you consider the plethora of services available to gays, it's not that difficult, either. There are clinics, counseling services, bookstores, roommate services. There are even doctors who'll try to analyze you back into heterosexuality, if you want (those, mercifully, are not listed here). For the gay in New York, these endeavors needn't be conducted *sotto voce* and in a trench coat any more. Gay services are available, known, and even listed in the phone book.

Chelsea Clinic, 303 9 Ave., 239-1700
This is not an exclusively gay clinic but a free clinic, operated by the Department of Health that serves a lot of gays. Repeat, free.

Gay Counseling, 61 Gramercy Park N., 475-0390
If you're broke, you don't have to worry about meeting with peer counselors here; the rates are based on how much you can and want to pay. Furthermore, the first visit is free. Nothing could be cheaper, except maybe the deep, dark secrets you'll spill.

Gay and Lesbian Community Services of New York Inc., 110 E. 23 St., 533-2619
You can walk in off the street to this organization, which offers employment, psychological and legal counseling, and consciousness raising, for no fee. There will be no discussion of Donna Summer's new album.

Gay Men's Health Project, 74 Grove St., 691-6969
This gay collective offers free testing for gonorrhea, syphilis, and Type B hepatitis, but doesn't treat (though

it can refer people to sympathetic physicians or clinics).
It's an invaluable service, and there's no appointment
necessary, Monday through Thursday 7:30 to 10 P.M.
Besides, it's also a place where you can catch up with all
your old "friends."

Gay Lifestyle Tours, 305 Broadway, 286-8989
This year, this agency only organized one gay tour—a
trip to the gay rodeo in Reno, Nevada. It may have been
the first time homosexuality met the cowboy tradition
since the Village People.

Gay Movers, Ltd., 808 Pacific St., Brooklyn,
731-4773
This moving service isn't exclusive to gays, but it is
sympathetic to them. The rates are $35/hour for two
men in a van, and $45/hour for three. And when have
men ever been that cheap lately?

Gay Roommate Service, 156 W. 74 St., 580-7696
For $35 you can register for a year and get a free listing
of gay people who are looking for gay roommates. Or
you can call and list your apartment for nothing and
start receiving the barrage of phone calls from
interested dwellers. The trick is to pick out the serious
folk from the pervs—unless you want the pervs.

Gay Sexual Freedom, 381 Fifth Ave., 683-6035
A membership-only club with members in all 50 states,
Gay Sexual Freedom plans activities like discussion
groups, parties, sports events, travel, and theater. It's all
an excuse to meet, greet, and be gay. If you have bad
luck in bars, you'll probably end up here.

Gay Switchboard, 110 E. 23 St., 777-1800
If there's any gay service not included on this list, or
any information lacking about what's on the list, the
Gay Switchboard has it. If they don't, it doesn't exist.
This free service keeps lists of clinics, counselors,
political organizations, and upcoming gay events, and it
even offers a crisis number (532-2400) available at all
times for major personal problems. It's rumored they
also list names and numbers scrawled on gay bar
bathroom walls.

Identity House, 544 Sixth Ave., 243-8181
If there's something (or someone) you want to get off
your chest, this is the place to go. Group discussion and
individual meetings are conducted with peer counselors

(that means they may have some social work
background, but probably not), and it's all by voluntary
contribution. Identity House will make referrals when
necessary.

National Gay Task Force, 80 Fifth Ave., 741-5800
One of the few major gay civil rights organizations (with
the demise of the Gay Activists Alliance New York
office), the NGTF tries to educate the public on gay
rights and to get legislature passed in favor of gay rights
and also acts as a Central Clearance for information on
gay events. It's an uphill struggle, but the NGTF fights
it valiantly.

Oscar Wilde Memorial Bookshop, 15 Christopher
St., 255-8097
"This is not a porno shop," the people here are quick to
point out. "It's a gay liberation bookshop." Anyone
who's not liberated can get their rocks off somewhere
else.

They Walk by Night

They're big, they're fast, they're smart. They're the
most vile pests you've seen since your younger siblings
moved out and, what's worse, they're in *your* apartment.
That's right. Whether you pay $200 or $2,000 a month
for the privilege of living here, and whether you see
them or not, they're there. To stay. Exterminators,
powders, and the wide array of commercial products
available will at best only control the number of roaches
you see. At worst, they are money thrown away.

What to do? The following lists of do's and dont's
may provide some help. But then again . . .

Five Ways to Get Rid of Roaches

1. See to it that an exterminator visits your building
at least once a month. If you're in a rent-stabilized
apartment, this is your legal *right*. If you're not
receiving this service, petition your landlord. Should he
fail to comply, file a complaint with the Conciliation
and Appeals Board (265-5920). You will win. Some folks
insist that only a privately engaged exterminator,
preferably offering at least a 3-month guarantee, will get

rid of roaches for a time, since the ones hired by the landlord are the cheapest.

2. For spot spraying, or between exterminator's visits, the most effective commercially available spray is Black Flag's "Special City Formula" in the blue can.

3. Roach traps do work, but consider before buying that you're trying to keep roaches *out* of your apartment. Traps *attract* roaches, some of which may decide not to "check in."

4. Cleanliness counts but is seldom sufficient. Before going to bed, wipe up all standing water in sinks and tub. Roaches need water more often than food. By the way, they can stay submerged for 45 minutes without drowning.

5. The industrious may want to close gaps between baseboard and floor with caulking, spackling paste, or any other suitable filler. Mosquito netting is cheap, and effectively seals vents in kitchen and bathroom if secured on all sides with duct tape or other adhesive.

Ten Ways *Not* to Get Rid of Roaches

1. MX Missile: Expensive, not a proven deterrent, may inconvenience neighbors.

2. The cast of *42nd St.:* Roaches won't want to "come and meet those dancing feet."

3. 45 revolver: Very satisfying, but requires clearance from your probation officer.

4. *The Best of Marie Osmond:* Will only drive roaches to the next apartment. Short memories will bring most of the survivors back in days.

5. *Australopithecus robustus:* Likely insectivore, but hard to find (Bloomingdale's already sold out at time of writing), difficult to conceal from Richard Leakey.

6. Richard Leakey: Bright, charming, an improbable choice, off looking for #5 anyway.

7. Holding roach by scruff of neck, tie rear legs to center pair. Pinion forelegs behind head with paper clip. You have just discovered the derivation of the term "roach clip." Congratulate yourself on this insight. Smile. The nail should be positioned just above the left ventricle, where it intersects the tibia and cerebellum.

Two hammer strokes recommended, "just to make sure."

8. Same as above, but use silver carpet tack for vampire or wereroaches.

9. Add tiny lamps, furniture, and wall-to-wall carpeting to your roach motels. Better still, stack 18 motels side by side, in vertical tiers of nine each, and be the proud landlord of New York's first roach condo. Raise the rent 200, 300 percent, whatever you like! Impoverished roaches will check out forever. The C.A.B. will never know.

10. Tape roaches to wall, approximately four feet from floor. With the aid of a strong friend, hold landlord horizontally, head pointed toward wall. Use as you would a battering ram. (Note: Bald landlords make better battering rams.)

Women's Services

Art

A.I.R., 63 Crosby St., 966-0799
A.I.R. is an all-woman cooperative gallery; members exhibit individually on a monthly rotational basis. The 20 or so members also put on a group show annually and occasionally sponsor an invitational exhibition, usually consisting of women's art from outside NYC and often from out of the country. Free lectures, usually on women's art, often accompany exhibitions, so call for current scheduling information.

Feminist Art Institute, 325 Spring St., 242-1343
In the spring of 1981, the institute sponsored a "political consciousness/political action" conference to rally support for all the women's organizations in the city. One outgrowth of the conference was a concerted effort by NYC women to unite in search of housing for women's groups. As the conference evidenced, the institute is heathily nonpartisan and committed to action as well as art. Along with exhibition space for women artists, the institute offers a two-year arts program, numerous courses and workshops on art practice and theory, and a lecture program that analyzes the role of women from a variety of political perspectives.

Women Make Movies, 100 Fifth Ave., Room 1208, 929-6477

Women's Interart Center, 549 W. 52 St., 246-1050

Keane Mason Gallery/Womanart, 50 W. 57 St., 757-4644

Women in the Arts Foundation, Inc., 325 Spring St., Room 328, 691-0988

Women's Experimental Theater of Women's Interart Center, 552 W. 53 St., 279-4200

Media

New York City offers a variety of women's, lesbian, and feminist publications. In the past few years small publications have begun to surface to accommodate the needs of the specific interests of different women; needs that continually require clarification for the advancement of feminism but seldom receive priority recognition because the battle for the basics is still on.

The following list includes straight and gay publications as well as publications aimed at special interest groups: Third World women, women in prison, etc. I refrain from elaborating on the political ideologies represented in the individual publications because they are often diverse and often changing, and just as often the names of the publications are self-explanatory. A lot of the freshest writing in feminism occurs within these small publications, and I'm proud to say, as a New York City feminist, it isn't mainstream—if you want that, buy *Ms.* Most of the women's publications are available at the women's bookstores, and most collectives accept submissions of women's writing.

Woman News, P.O. Box 220, Village Station, New York, NY 10014, 868-3330
One of the oldest feminist newspapers in the country, *Woman News* is probably the best single feminist publication in the city, if only because it is the most accessible to all women: not *too* straight, *too* gay, *too* white, etc. It regularly features an extensive two-page calendar of women's events happening around the city.

Azalea, a magazine by and for Third World lesbians, P.O. Box 200, Cooper Station, New York, NY 10003

Big Apple Dyke Newspaper (*B.A.D. News,*) 192 Spring St. #15, New York, NY 10012, 226-2821

Kitchen Table Press:
As of the deadline for the *Hip Pocket Guide*, the staff
of *Kitchen Table* had just migrated to NYC—it
promises to be a Third World lesbian publication.

13th Moon, Feminist Literary Journal, Drawer 4,
Inwood Station, New York, NY 10034, 569-7614

No More Cages, a prison newsletter for women by
Women Free Women in Prison, P.O. Box 90,
Brooklyn, NY 11215

Radio

WBAI (99.5 FM radio) 505 Eighth Ave., 279-0707
Womens Studies/Lesbian Hour

Programming info: published by WBAI in their folio,
next day's programming given each night at midnight,
events usually listed in *Woman News.*

Organizations

There are over 400 women's organizations in the city, all
dedicated to the advancement of social/political life as
we know it but expressing that general commitment in
different ways. Here are a few of the organizations.

Association of Libertarian Feminists, Workmen's
Circle Center, 369 Eighth Ave. (at 29 St.), 274-5059

Barnard College Women's Center, Barnard Hall,
117 St. and Broadway, 280-2067

Brooklyn Women's Martial Arts, 421 Fifth Ave.
(off 8 St.), Brooklyn, NY, 788-1775

CARASA (Committee for Abortion Rights and
Against Sterilization Abuse), 17 Murray St.,
New York, NY 10003, 267-8892

Chelsea Gay Association, 132 W. 24 St., New York,
NY 10011, 691-7950

Creative Women's Collective, 236 W. 27 St.,
12 floor, 924-0665

Dignity/NY Gay and Lesbian Catholics, Box 1554,
FDR Station, New York, NY 10150, 357-8788

DARE (Dykes Against Racism Everywhere),
P.O.B. 914 Stuyvesant Station, New York, NY 10009,
691-7150, ext. 6102

Dykes Opposed to Nuclear Technology (DONT),
Information: 477-4031

Gay Nurses Alliance, 44 St. Marks Pl., 875-3136

Gay Women's Alternative, Universalist Church,
Central Park West at 76 St., 532-2553

Hikin' Dykes, 799-2553

The Karate School for Women, 149 Bleecker St.,
982-4739

Lesbian Feminist Liberation, Women's Center,
243 W. 20 St., 691-5460

Lesbian Switchboard, 741-2610

National Council of Negro Women, Women's
Center, 198 Broadway, Suite 201, 964-8934

NYC Chapter/Feminist Writer's Guild,
P.O. Box 184, Village Station, New York, NY 10014

NY NOW, 84 Fifth Ave., 989-7230

NY Women Against Rape, Hotline: 777-4000; other
info: 477-0819

Non-Traditional Employment for Women,
80 Fifth Ave., Room 1603, 691-1860

Salsa Soul Sisters, Inc., 133 W. 4 St.

Women Against Pornography, 358 W. 57 St.,
307-5055

Women's Center, 243 W. 20 St., 741-9114

Women's Center of Brooklyn College, James Hall,
Bedford Ave. and Ave. H., Brooklyn, New York,
780-7777

Women in the Trades, 198 Forsyth St., Room 313,
674-3069

Women's Martial Arts Center, 16 W. 30 St., 685-4553

For Referrals of All Sorts

Women's Action Alliance, 370 Lexington Ave.,
New York, NY 10017, 532-8330

Lesbian Archives

(for historical and contemporary bio info, etc.)
Lesbian Herstory Archives, 93 St. and Broadway,
874-7232 (women only)

Bookstores

The women's bookstores in New York City specialize in books by and about women, offering valuable resource information about health and history, as well as contemporary magazines concerning women's issues, including feminist fiction, sci-fi, and children's literature. One of the most marvelous things about the city's women's stores is that they operate together, without an air of competitiveness. So if you go into La Papaya and they're out of Mary Wollstonecraft, they'll send you to Djuna Books—which, by the way, isn't named after Djuna Barnes, although I don't know why. You can also count on the employees at these stores to be more knowledgeable about anything in women's studies you're searching for than any librarian or regular bookseller will be.

Djuna Books, 154 W. 10 St., 242-3642

La Papaya Restaurant and Bookstore (formerly Women's Works), 331 Flatbush Ave., Park Slope, Brooklyn, 622-1926

Womanbooks, 201 W. 92 St., 873-4121

Health Services

While gynecological treatment is available at New York City neighborhood clinics, most women don't appreciate standing in the VD line—which is where gyne is located. And the city clinics, like most traditional male private practice, aren't structured sympathetically toward lesbians or straight women who would like progressive information about birth control. You can expect understanding treatment and progressive information at the following women-run clinics.

Feminist Health Works, 487-A Hudson St. near Christopher St., 929-7886

St. Marks Women's Health Collective, 44 St. Marks Pl., 228-7482

Chelsea Women's Health Team (at Chelsea Neighborhood Clinic), 303 Ninth Ave., 239-1700

Just in Case . . .

Here is a list of emergency telephone numbers in New York City ranging from 911 for a *serious* crisis, to Dial-a-Joke if you just need to hear a friendly voice. (Middle-of-the-night services, such as emergency food, are listed under "24-hour New York," p. 180.)

Emergencies

911—Ambulance, Fire, or Police Emergencies

Alcoholics Anonymous, 473-6200

Drug Abuse, 488-3954

This is the official drug hotline of the New York State Division of Substance Abuse Services. Counselors are available Monday through Friday, 9 A.M. to 5 P.M. An answering machine takes names and numbers after hours and on weekends and basically tells people to go to an emergency room if they're freaking out.

Fire (Manhattan only), 628-2900 or 911

Police (nonemergencies), call local precinct

Doctors' Emergency Service, 879-1000

Dentists' Emergency Service, 879-1000

Rape Help Line, 732-7706

Crime Victims' Hotline, 577-7777

Gas and Steam Leaks, 683-8830

Poison Control Center, 764-7667

Useful Services

AAA: Road Service, 695-8311

AAA: Highway Conditions, 594-0700

Better Business Bureau, 533-6200

Consumer Complaints, 577-0111

Moving Violations (Summons), 466-0700

Parking Violations, 598-0500

Towaway Information, 239-2533

Visitors to New York with cars must remember that parking regulations can vary from block to block, or from one side of the street to another. Read signs carefully to avoid towing or tickets.

Lost or Stolen Traveler's Checks

American Express, 248-4584

Citicorp, 980-9099

Thomas Cook, 921-3800

"Dial-It" Services

Big Apple Report, 976-2323

Dial-a-Joke, 976-3838

Horoscopes-by-Phone, 976-1000

Time, 976-1616

Weather, 976-1212

SPECIAL PLEASURES OF
NEW YORK LIFE

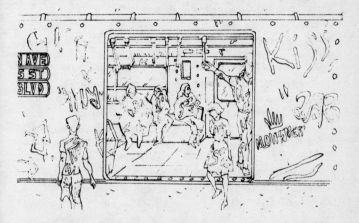

Arcades from Heaven

There are those who go to Times Square for dinner and
a play, and those who simply gawk at the procession of
hookers and hustlers that crowd one of the world's most
nefarious red-light districts. Me? I enjoy The Square for
its wealth of so-called "penny arcades." If you want to
have it out with a feisty pinball or video game, you'll
find dozens along the stretch on Broadway from 42 to
53 Sts.—New York's notorious arcade row.

It takes at least two bits nowadays to dislodge your
favorite game from its momentary stupor. And the
arcades have been swept by tides of modernization:
computers now run the show (they're all programmed),
and the designs (multilevel pinball, 3-D visuals) are
more intricate and outlandish than ever. But games will
be games, whether it's a Space Invader trespassing your
turf or some metallic duck with a fat bullseye egging
you on. In New York the locale's the thing.

Unlike the rest of Greater America, where game
rooms have become as essential a part of the suburban
mall as Baskin-Robbins and B. Dalton, the Apple's
arcades offer a distinct big-town ambience. Thankfully,
New York's sturdy, sometimes nostalgic, but ever-
flourishing arcade scene has survived. What follows is a
guide of where and where *not* to go.

Playland, 1580 Broadway (between 47 and 48 Sts.)
This is the only 24-hour arcade in town, which makes it
particularly perilous from midnight until dawn. During
the Space Invaders craze, Playland had more of these
machines—including several bootlegs that were first
introduced in Japan—than any other arcade around.
With ten lined up side by side, it had the effect of a
peaceable Zen exercise. Generally, this room has the
latest in pins and video, but there's one catch: the
games are not maintained well. For the occasional
player that's no real problem, but for regulars who
require optimum conditions in order to upgrade their
scores, it certainly is. Because of space limitations, most
older models are farmed out rather quickly. In fact, Air
Hockey is about as historical as Playland, one of New
York's oldest games emporiums, gets.

1485 Broadway (between 42 and 43 Sts.)
The closer to 42 St. you go, the funkier the
surroundings and the clientele become. But don't let
that stop you from checking this room out. Positively
the largest arcade (aside from the many in Coney
Island) in the city, it has plenty of space to stock just
about everything. For instance, whereas most arcades
have removed the Skee-Ball lanes for lack of room (and
also because they break down too often), this place still
has an abundance. Add up those tickets and win a
cotton candy goat for Sis. The owner has even preserved
the sacred coin booth on which the inscription reads
"Get your pennies here." The old-world flavor stops
there, however. Like most arcades, this one keeps apace
in the pins and video competition and also has several
of those sit-down racers for anyone who wishes to get
off his or her feet. Go, but be careful.

42 St. and Eighth Ave. Arcade
Be *extra* careful here. You've got your portable
Panasonic, the walk and the talk? Then this just may
be the spot for you. One flight down from the subway
entrance, this arcade has what could be called a
barbershop location. Unfortunately, the details go
downhill from there. This is the kind of place an out-of-
towner would naïvely stroll into. Whether he will make
it out all right is an entirely other story.

Fascination, 1597 Broadway (between 47 and 48 Sts.)
What once was a Times Square landmark, where all

types came to play this bingo-style dime game in which
bounding that green ball down the lane just right was
the trick, is no more. Last year, the owner was allowed
to junk the set of 50 (one for each state) terrifically
crafted oak game tables in favor of opening yet another
arcade. No one seemed to care or even notice. Did
Times Square really need another arcade—a bogus one,
at that? I think not and therefore, on principle, do not
recommend it.

1565 Amusements (Broadway and 46 St.)
People know this as the place that has the plastic fish
swimming around in the tub outside. Inside, the room is
small and I've found it to be especially unfriendly.
Don't bother.

Broadway Arcade (Broadway and 52 St.)
Probably the only arcade in town with a true clientele.
That's because once you go there you always seem to
find yourself going back. A pop and son run this place
and it shows. Games are everywhere and all are in
impeccable order. Since there's more than enough room,
they're constantly shuffling machines between what
appears to be first- and second-class sections. In front
are the most recent favorites; in back, off to the side,
last year's models. Skee-Ball meets Asteroids here.
Electronic baseball shakes gloves with its ancient
predecessor, the mechanical box with the wooden bat,
the silver balls, and an upper deck where indeed you
must slam a homerun. By far, the best-run arcade
around.

Below Times Square

Zoning regulations prevent more than four machines
from being in any establishment at one time. Hence, it
is nearly impossible to obtain an arcade license, unless
you already have one, as the Times Square operations
do. Because of these stringent laws, which date back to
the 1930s, there are only two other game rooms in
Manhattan to speak of. (Note: Several rooms have
recently popped up on the East Side, but they are
illegal and will come and go so quickly that it's not
worth mentioning their locations.)

Time-Out, Penn Station, Lower level
This is the city's only suburban-styled arcade. Pins and

video, gray walls, mirrors, tokens instead of quarters—
spare but very efficient. Here is where businessmen go
after a hard day's work; pin-stripers knocking away at
the pins. It gets *mobbed* after a sports event or concert
empties out of Madison Square Garden, directly above
the station. A busy spot that's as good as gold.

Chinatown Fair, 8 Mott St. (near the Bowery)
One of Chinatown's attractions beyond Peking duck,
ribs, chow mein, et al. Best known for the chicken in
the Skinner box that greets you as you walk in. It has
been rumored for some time that the owner is training a
chimp to deal poker. Games, games, games, even though
the room is too small. A haven for the livelier Soho
types.

Games People Play

Some people swap wives, others swap stories. But for a
select group of New Yorkers, the goal is to swap chess
pieces, pairs of dice, backgammon discs, and cards in
four suits. Every afternoon and far into the night,
crowds gather around game tables and roll dice or move
their pieces. Sometimes they play for stakes (there are
thousands of "after-hours" clubs for this), but usually
they play for the game—to win, perchance to dream of
victory in tournaments and regional championships.
They play backgammon. Billiards. Chess. Checkers.
Cards. Or unusual games like go, a 3,000-year-old game
from the Orient. The clubs where they play range in
style from West Side seedy to East Side swank. If
you're looking for something different to do on a
Saturday night—or any night—one of the game clubs
listed below might be just the thing. For high
entertainment at low prices, they can't be beat.

The Game Room, 2130 Broadway (at 75 St.), 24
hours, 595-0923
The Game Room is the funkiest place to play a game.
Patrons range from princes to punks, all bent on
playing to win, no matter how long it takes. "We have
tickets that go two days' long," says co-owner Jerry
Bernstein. "Some backgammon games last thirty to
forty hours." Even if you have only one hour, the Game

Room is worth a visit: the atmosphere is lively. This is the site of championship matches in chess, Othello, and Scrabble; there are also numerous computer games and chess aids. The Game Room has a full bar (open nightly to 4 A.M.), and offers cheeses, yogurt, pastries, and quiches. Other refreshments are available from a 24-hour restaurant next door. Rates: $1.50/hour to play (special rates for juniors), rates drop after the third hour. Major credit cards accepted on amounts over $5.

Julian Billiard Academy, 138 E. 14 St. (between Third and Fourth Aves.), 9 P.M. to 3 A.M., 7 days, 475-9338

Julian's is the oldest and best known of New York's pool halls. Rudolph Wanderone, a.k.a. Minnesota Fats, has played here. So do an incredible assortment of New Yorkers. Students, actors, businessmen, and bums can be seen at the 29 tables (24 pocket pool, 5 billiards). According to Ronnie Julian, the owner, pool is enjoying a resurgence as a family sport. "The day of the hustler is passing," he says. "It's coming back with families and for women." This pool hall has been owned by the Julian family since 1933 and has existed at the present site (next door to the Palladium) for more than 65 years. The hall was recently refurbished, with new tables, cues, and lights. Refreshments are available, and there is locker space for customers to store their cues. Hourly rates: $3 for one player, $4 for two or three, $5 for four.

Magic Cue Billiards, 1483 Broadway (at 43 St.), 9 P.M. to 3 A.M., 7 days, 391-1298

Vincent Sbarbati, owner of Magic Cue, has a business card on which is printed a pool cue, a billiard ball, and a top hat. It is intended to show that he wants Magic Cue to be the most elegant pool hall in town. With wall-to-wall carpeting, a game room, locker space to store cues, and other amenities, Magic Cue recaptures the image of billiards as a sport for gentlemen. Most of the customers are well dressed and well mannered. A sign reminds players: "No profanities, please." Opened in 1980, Magic Cue is also the city's largest pool hall, with 27 pocket pool tables, 7 billiard tables, and 3 snooker tables. Sbarbati plans to hold tournaments, including one for women. Free instruction is available. Hourly rates: $3 for one player, $4 for two or three, $5 for four.

Chess Mart, Inc., 240 Sullivan St. (at W. 3 St.), 12n to 12m, 7 days, 473-9564

Ionel Ronn, owner of the Chess Mart, is a chess master who believes in the power of music. To play here is to enjoy not only the game but strains of Mozart, Bach, and Beethoven as well. "Music affects the players," Ronn said. "It soothes them." In addition to music, it is worth noting that if you are from out of town, way out of town, Ronn speaks English, Hebrew, French, German, Italian, Rumanian, and "some Russian." So you could drop in to play an international game of chess, checkers, backgammon, or go. Refreshments include coffee, hot chocolate, soup, and cider. Rates: 50 cents an hour, 60 cents an hour for clock chess. Note: Chess lessons available.

The Mayfair Club, 220 E. 57 St., 1 P.M. to 2 A.M., 7 days, 593-2182

Class will tell, and at the Mayfair Club, it shouts. The playing rooms are spacious and well appointed; the patrons are upwardly mobile. The main games are backgammon, bridge, chess, and occasionally gin and the Hungarian card game klaberjass. The club is run by noted bridge expert Alvin Roth, who boasts that, regardless of the game, "our average players are superior" to any other. Certainly they play for higher stakes; although no money changes hands at tables, members say it is customary to play for stakes, with accounts kept at the main desk. The club has the best facilities of any listed here, including a lounge, full kitchen service during dinner hours, Sunday brunches, and a "midnight supper" each Friday. Why not? As Roth says, "For many people, this is a second home." On weeknights, you can order a steak dinner for about $14, and the Sunday brunch is free to all ("good will," says one member; another calls it a "welcome mat"). Rates: membership fees range from $50 to $200 a year, but visitors are welcome free and can play all night for about $6.

Village Chess Shop, 230 Thompson St. (near W. 3 St.), 12n to 12m, 7 days, 475-9580

Here is a Bohemian locale. Amid hundreds of chessboards stacked in this little shop are 12 tables, around which an incredible array of people are playing chess and backgammon. The atmosphere is comfy and studious, with players deeply involved in their games.

Most are "regulars," although a few chess masters are known to pop in; a single player can come down and find a playing partner within a few minutes. Refreshments include tea, coffee, cider, and cake. Rates: 50 cents an hour, 60 cents an hour for clock chess.

Zen Go Club, 10 E. 52 St., 5 P.M. to 10:30 P.M. weekdays; 12n to 8 P.M. weekends, 355-8733 eves., 582-4622

Go is an Oriental game, similar in some respects to checkers and chess, played on a board with a 19 × 19 grid. The Zen Go Club—or Manhattan Go Club, as it is sometimes known—is the only official go club in New York. You enter through the Dosanko (Japanese) Restaurant, adjacent to the Olympic Tower. Inside, there are 13 tables on which to play, and free instruction is available every Tuesday night. According to club president, Masao Takave, the game is very popular with professionals (doctors, lawyers, technicians, and the like). Refreshments are available from the restaurant. Rates: visitors are welcome, there is a $2 fee. Annual membership is $16. Note: Don't show off karate chops; most of the membership is as American as apple pie.

Annual New York

New York City is a real melting pot; every nationality and creed has a representation. Therefore, there are more holidays. Block associations on many streets organize for annual celebrations, usually bordering on summer (Memorial and Labor Days are popular times). A street festival can be a large party or a full-blown cultural holiday. The nationalistic ceremonies have been in existence for many years, but as politics change, speeches or counterdemonstrations sometimes can occur. The best references to annual events in New York are the Parks Department, Special Events (360-8196), which offers monthly listings; and the Convention and Visitors Bureau (397-8200), which provides a quarterly calendar of events.

January

Not much is happening, as everyone is recuperating from the December holidays. January offers after-

Christmas sales and white sales at some stores. The opera, ballet, and symphony are regrouping for the second half of their seasons.

February

Chinese New Year is a colorful pageant in Chinatown. Firecracker-phobes beware! For the exact date call the Chinese Community Center (267-5780).

March

March begins with the Bock Beer Festival at Lüchow's (1533 Broadway, at 51 St.). German beer, food, and music; reservations required. On the 17th, every New Yorker wears green and has an excuse for being off the wagon. The enthusiastic St. Patrick's Day parade runs from 44 St. to 96 St. on Fifth Ave.

March or April

The religious holidays of Easter and Passover may fall in either month. Easter activities are held in Central Park for children. "In your Easter bonnet . . ." anyone-can-participate parade (as long as some kind of hat is worn) on Fifth Ave. from 42 St. to 59 St. Greek Orthodox Easter (usually two weeks after the Julian date) should be experienced at least once; three of the city's cathedrals are Greek Cathedral, 319 E. 74 St.; St. Nicholas, 15 E. 97 St.; St. Vladimir's, 334 E. 14 St. Greek Independence Day is also held on the Sunday nearest March 25, celebrated with a Fifth Ave. parade and other festivities (Greek Consulate: 988-5500). The circus comes to Madison Square Garden around this time.

April

April is cherry blossom time at the Brooklyn Botanical Gardens. The second week, baseball season opens at Yankee Stadium, in the Bronx (293-6000), and at Shea Stadium (Mets), in Queens (672-3000).

May

The first Sunday in May is Spanish-American Day. The parade on Fifth Ave. stretches from 26 St. to 70 St. The

week surrounding May 15 is the May Wine Festival at
Lüchow's—a German celebration complete with oom-
pah band. May 17 is Norwegian Constitution Day; a
parade is held in Brooklyn (for information call
238-1100). Memorial Day, a legal holiday, is the Monday
nearest to the 30th. U.S. Veterans pay homage with
marches in all boroughs. In Manhattan, the route
follows Riverside Drive from 72 St. to the Soldiers and
Sailors monument at 90 St. From the end of May
through June, the Washington Square Art Show is
exhibited, on weekends and holidays, from noon until
sundown. The show features everything from *kitsch*
crafts to serious stuff. It's located at Washington Square
and spills onto the streets to the north and south. This
is the time when the regular music season, as well as the
academic year, comes to a close, but the street fairs and
festivals are just getting warmed up. Every street fair
can't be listed, because, at one time or another,
practically *every* street has one. Mile-long stretches of
each avenue shut down to vehicular traffic on different
summer weekends. These fairs, sponsored by local
retailers, feature all kinds of food, merchandise, and
entertainment.

June

From June 5 to 15 is the feast of St. Anthony. Centering
on Sullivan St., near Houston St., it is the first of the
summer's Italian festivals. The feast features carnival-
like rides, booths and a wide variety of Italian foods.
June 6 marks Swedish Flag Day, a parade, dancing and
singing in national costume (for exact location, contact
the consulate: 751-9500). June 12 is Rose Day at the
Bronx Botanical Gardens; every inch of the place is
blooming now. The Day of San Juan Bautista, patron
saint of San Juan, Puerto Rico, is celebrated on the
Sunday nearest to June 24.The third or fourth Sunday
of June is the Irish *Feis,* a large Irish culture fair
presented in the Bronx or Brooklyn. The summer
cultural season begins: the Mostly Mozart Festival at
Lincoln Center, Newport and New York Jazz Festivals.
Special free events are held in Central Park. These
include Shakespeare-in-the-Park and outdoor
performances by the Metropolitan Opera Company and
the New York Philharmonic.

July

July is another good month for sales. The 4th of July, a legal holiday, is celebrated throughout the city. During the day there is usually a harbor show visible from Battery Park. After dark, Macy's puts on a spectacular fireworks display, easily seen along the Hudson River between 72 and 125 Sts. July 14 is Bastille Day; inquire at the French Consulate (535-0100) for planned festivities. The Puerto Rican Commonwealth has its anniversary on July 25. For information about those Central Park activities, call 260-3000.

August

St. Stephen of Hungary's Day, August 20, is the date Hungarian Catholics lead a parade that ends at St. Patrick's Cathedral. The end of the month, through September, is the second half of the Washington Square ("world's largest") Art Show.

September

The first Monday of the month, a Labor Day parade on Fifth Avenue is probable. 1981 marked the first one in 13 years, but it'd been annually held prior to that time. Later on the same day is the West Indies parade—a colorful ethnic pageant on Seventh Ave. between 111 St. and 142 St. September 15–16, the Mexican New Yorkers celebrate their Independence Day (Consulate: 689-0456). The football season opens in the middle of the month. On E. 7 St., between Second and Third Aves., the Ukrainian population of New York holds its annual festival. For the exact date of this unusual event, contact the Ukrainian Congress, 228-6840. The week surrounding September 19 is the Feast of San Gennaro, the granddaddy of the southern Italian street fairs. Located on Mulberry St. between Canal and Houston, the festa offers more pizza, calzoni, zeppole, and sausages than you've ever seen—lots of games, Italian entertainment, and souvenirs. The Jewish high holidays of Yom Kippur and Rosh Hashonah occur during September. The third Saturday is the Steuben Day Parade for German New Yorkers, up Fifth Ave. to 86 St. The regular music season opens toward the end of September or beginning of October.

October

On October 5, or the nearest Sunday, is the Pulaski Day
parade, from 26 to 52 Sts. on Fifth Ave. Floats, bands,
and traditional peasant costumes of the Polish people
are featured. October 10 (Ten-Ten Day) is the
anniversary of the Chinese Republic's establishment. A
small-scale version of Chinese New Year is celebrated
on Mott St. in Chinatown. Columbus Day is the Italian
equivalent of St. Patty's Day. Just as every New Yorker
is Irish in March, this day they're all Italian. The
parade is on Fifth Ave. between the 40s and 80s. The
basketball and hockey seasons begin (Madison Square
Garden: 564-4400) around now.

November

November 11 is Veterans (Armistice) Day; a Fifth Ave.
parade and memorial services are held. Thanksgiving—
the annual Macy's parade is perhaps the most famous of
New York parades. Known for its gigantic balloon
figures, floats, celebrities, and entertainment of all
types, it runs from Central Park West and 77 St., down
Broadway to Macy's at 34 St.

December

December is ALL holiday. The dazzling display
windows and interiors of Fifth Ave. stores are decorated
to the hilt. New Year's Eve, everywhere you look there's
a party—dining, dancing, and drinking. The annual
New York tradition, as broadcast on national television,
is to watch the illuminated ball, or apple, atop the One
Times Square building descend at midnight. But Times
Square is not recommended for the crowd-wary.

New York's Ugliest Buildings

Most New Yorkers have a personal list of buildings that
work badly from the inside: flimsy construction and
soundproofing, inadequate light and ventilation, slow
elevators, wasteful layout, or just plain unpleasant
rooms. This is a list of buildings that work badly from
the *outside* . . . buildings that either damage the public
environment or fail to improve it when there existed a

special opportunity to do so. Who is to blame? It may
be legal restrictions, hard-bitten clients, unscrupulous
contractors, political haggling, or just poor designs. But
wherever the fault lies, the negative results remain, and
the city suffers accordingly.

(Buildings are listed from uptown to downtown. All
are in Manhattan.)

Harlem State Office Building (125 St. near Lenox
Ave.)
This patronizing intruder from Albany pays little
attention to the scale and quality of Harlem and 125 St.
Should central Harlem's tallest building really be a
monument to state bureaucracy? There was an
unequaled opportunity to create a low-scale community
and civic center, but authoritarian attitudes prevailed.

Columbia University Law School (116 St. and
Amsterdam Ave.)
An air-conditioner on a stone pedestal, the Law School
finds its only "expression" in a gigantic, oppressive
piece of sculpture glued to its front—if it can indeed be
said to *have* a front. But the unforgivable feature is a
graceless bridge across Amsterdam Ave., which elevates
the law students to a concrete French garden while
consigning almost everyone else to gaseous gloom on the
sidewalk underneath.

Mt. Sinai Hospital (Fifth Ave. and 100 St.)
No other building on the perimeter of Central Park is so
unforgiving in form, so immodest in scale, so
unsympathetic in color, or so indifferent to its own local
and metropolitan impact. An illiterate wrestler at a
dress ball.

Nevada Tower Apartments (Broadway at 70 St.)
The diagonal meanderings of Broadway often create
difficult triangular sites that nonetheless have great
dramatic potential, as can be seen in the famous
Flatiron Building (Broadway at 23 St.) or Times
Square. At Broadway and 72 St., where the Ansonia and
the Central Savings Bank have already demonstrated
happy and ingenious solutions to the problem, the
Nevada Tower apartment building is a landmark of
mediocrity in architectural and urban design. A great
opportunity was apparently not even noticed.

New York Cultural Center (Columbus Circle)
The potential was enormous: a chance to terminate 59

St. visually, to give shape to Columbus Circle, and to
honor an important corner of Central Park. The result?
A characterless, almost willfully unimaginative solution
that just won't go away.

Pennsylvania Plaza/Madison Square Garden
(32 to 34 Sts. between Seventh and Eighth Aves.)
The demolition of the old Penn Station in 1963 was the
injury and this replacement the added insult. It respects
neither the pedestrian, nor the life of the street, nor the
surrounding buildings, nor the symbolic importance of a
railroad terminal. Apparently, it was built with
automobiles and rentable square feet as exclusive
concerns, and its concrete environment is perhaps the
most uninviting of any public space in the city.

**St. Vincent's Hospital—O'Toole Medical Services
Bldg.** (Seventh Ave. and 12 St.)
A case of eccentric architectural expression winning out
over sensitive adjustment to a sensitive intersection.
The little triangular park and surrounding buildings
might have formed an attractive nucleus between the
Village and the West Village, but this white shellfish
repels all efforts to civilize the space.

New York University Towers (LaGuardia Place)
Whatever the merits of the concrete frame structures
themselves—the choice of classic modern urbanism—
"The Tower in the Park" falls heavily on the Village,
whose special character and scale were rather
spectacularly ignored. The "park" is more a barrier to
Soho than a binder, and gives Houston St. a certain
freeway scale not unlike the city of Houston.

World Trade Center (Church St.)
It's not the towers or the fact that there are two, but
rather the way they meet the ground. The creation of a
raised treeless plaza represents a kind of grandiose,
formalistic urbanism, completely unsympathetic with
existing patterns of urban activity. The plaza seems
intended primarily for military parades. Climatically it
is a disaster, being unshaded in the summer and
windswept in the winter, when it must be closed anyway
because of icicles falling from the towers.

The enclosed shopping mall, which *does* make sense
in New York's climate, is inferior to any number of
similar arcades both here in the city (Rockefeller
Center, Citicorp Center) and around the world. It is

inferior in terms of natural light (which remains unenjoyed in the plaza above), materials and design, and connections to the existing street pattern. The Trade Center is overscaled, heavy-handed, and isolated and is already causing problems for the development of adjacent areas.

Zoning ripoffs (throughout the city): A class-action entry for those buildings that, under the revised zoning laws, received extra allowable floors in exchange for providing public amenities, mainly parks and plazas. Many builders legitimately complied, adding to the city's inventory of well-designed and well-used public spaces. Others, however, paid the public back with crooked dividends: "parks" on the north where little sun will fall and few plants grow; "plazas" containing little more than some fancy paving, a begrudging bench or two, and some potted shrubs. Another ploy is the "indoor park," hidden from public view and general usage. Two prestigious offenders: the Galleria (57 St., between Park and Lexington), whose doormen treat the nearly unmarked park like private property, and Fifth Ave.'s Olympic Tower, whose management had the audacity to lease out their public space to an expensive *café/pâtisserie,* giving the passerby the impression he must pay to sit in a park for which, in effect, he has already paid.

Famous Murder Sites

New Yorkers take a strange pleasure in the city's crime rate. Not that anyone enjoys getting mugged, robbed, raped, or any of the other things that can happen to a person in any major American city, but a majority of New Yorkers take pride in their very survival—in their continuing ability to live in a city that many fear uninhabitable.

There is also some kind of superstition that goes on when a place is passed where something awful occurred. The Brown Building, on Washington Place (right off the Square), now serves as an NYU office building. But it has a past, as the notorious Asch building, where the famous Triangle Fire took place and over a hundred young women were incinerated or leaped to their deaths in 1911. Here are some other ghost-ridden spots, where killers have lurked.

1. **Gramercy Park**—the park itself, not the neighborhood that surrounds it—was the site where *Fitzhugh Coyle Goldsborough* shot and killed popular novelist *David Graham Phillips.* Convinced that Phillips had based a book on his socialite sister, Goldsborough shot the novelist several times and then blew his own brains out in the center of the park around noon on January 23, 1911. Phillips died a few days later.

2. A literary murder of a different stamp occurred on January 1, 1973, at **253 W. 72 St.** It was here that a young schoolteacher named *Katherine Cleary* was murdered by a man she had picked up in a bar only hours earlier. The story later became the background for a book—and later a film—entitled *Looking for Mr. Goodbar.* Cleary was murdered in a studio apartment on the seventh floor of this one-time hotel turned apartment house.

3. *Malcolm X*, charismatic black leader of the sixties, was slain at **Harlem's Audubon Ballroom** (at 166 St. and Broadway) on February 21, 1965, by several of his onetime followers who had become disenchanted with his philosophy.

4. At **814 Fifth Ave.** (near 62 St.) stood the house where financier and swindler *Serge Rubinstein* was found strangled on January 27, 1955. An apartment house now occupies the spot.

5. Riding the subway home one evening, a sharp-eyed salesman spotted fugitive bank robber Willie (the Actor) Sutton. When he reached his stop, salesman *Arnold Schuster* followed the criminal and had him arrested. An instant hero, the publicity was to cost Schuster his life. A few days later, on March 8, 1952, Schuster was shot and killed as he walked home, collapsing in front of **913 45 St.** in the Borough Park Section of Brooklyn. The attack was a mystery until 1963, when Joe Valachi revealed that Schuster had been ordered killed by Albert Anastasia, so-called "Lord High Executioner" of Murder Inc. The reason? Anastasia "hated squealers."

6. *Anastasia* himself was dead by the time his savagery was revealed. On October 25, 1957, he entered

the **New York Sheraton Barber Shop** (Seventh Ave. and 55 St.) for a shave. A team of men, headed by Joey "Crazy Joe" Gallo, entered and shot him several times in front of the horrified barber and other customers. Few mourned.

7. *Gallo* himself was rubbed out in a spectacular blaze of gunfire at 5 A.M., April 5, 1972. He had gone downtown to Little Italy to eat with his family, knowing he was on enemy turf but hoping the lateness of the hour would protect him. It was a fatal miscalculation, and his new wife and sister saw the gunmen enter **Umberto's Clam House** (corner of Mulberry and Hester Sts.), shoot Gallo several times, and then race off. Gallo chased the killers to the street, and collapsed and died in the intersection.

8. Another gangland rubout took about 10 years to be fully effective. Mafia boss *Joe Columbo* was shot at an Italian-American unity rally at **Columbus Circle** (59 St. and Broadway, beneath the statue of Columbus) on June 28, 1971, and remained in a coma for years before dying recently.

9. One of New York's most guilt-provoking scandals was the needless death of *Kitty Genovese*. Walking home from the subway late one night (March 13, 1964), she was attacked by a Winston Moseley, a drifter with a lengthy assault record. Over 30 people heard her screams for help as Moseley stabbed her, left for a few minutes, and then came back to finish her off. Nobody did anything—witnesses claimed they thought it was a lovers' quarrel, or just didn't want to get involved. By the time somebody called the police, Genovese was dead. New Yorkers had a hard time living this one down (**82-62 Austin St., Kew Gardens, Queens**).

10. Finally, painfully, there is the **Dakota** apartment house (1 W. 72 St.), where *John Lennon* was killed on December 8, 1980. There is much more to the building than just this nightmare, but remember that it is a very private residence.

Plazas and Parks

If you crave loads of amusement in a natural setting, Central Park has zoos, 5 ballfields, 2 museums, a

bandshell, several restaurants, a skating rink, a bird
sanctuary, a theater, pony rides, boat rides, 15
playgrounds, and 800 acres of crowd.

But if you just want to sit down for a moment and
reassemble your sangfroid, get to know the city's vest-
pocket plazas and parks. There are dozens of them
tucked away here and there, and while not all are green
and quiet, most offer doses of that treasured local
commodity: calm. Try the parks first:

Greenacre Park (behind a sculptured gate on the
north side of E. 51 St. between Second and Third
Aves.)
The best small park in the city, no bigger than a candy
store. Has a 25-foot waterfall that masks traffic noise,
comfortable chairs, banks of low flowers and trees, and
a babbling brook.

Paley Park (53 St. just east of Fifth Ave.)
Much like Greenacre, but rather jammed at lunchtime.

Tudor City
This huge housing project on a hill at the easternmost
end of 42 St. contains two safe, serene little parks.
They're private property, but go ahead . . . nobody
minds.

Gramercy Park
Also private, but the E. 21 St. gate (at Lexington Ave.)
is sometimes open during the summer.

Stuyvesant Square Park (at Second Ave. and E. 17
St.)
Lush, green, and very quiet most of the day, and has an
air of country living even Central Park can't match.

Further downtown, **City Hall Park** (between
Broadway and Park Row) and **Bowling Green** (at the
foot of Broadway), are a respite from the financial and
government district humdrum (but avoid them at
lunchtime unless you enjoy crowds and evangelists'
harangues).

Plazas aren't to everyone's taste. They're bare, hard,
and often ugly. But they are usually a boon to the
footsore pedestrian, and the ones listed below are
probably the most pleasant paved areas in the city:

Grand Army Plaza (Fifth Ave. and Central Park
So.)

Corning Glass reflecting pool (Fifth Ave. at 56 St.)

Olympic Tower's indoor garden (Fifth Ave. at 51 St.)

Channel Gardens at Rockefeller Center (Fifth Ave. between 49 and 50 Sts.)
Has benches, often overcrowded.

Time Life Building's America Plaza (Sixth Avenue between W 50 and 51 Sts.)

St. Bartholomew's courtyard (Park Ave. at 51 St.)

Seagram Building (Park Ave. at 52 St.)

The Galleria (57 St. just east of Park Ave.)
An indoor arcade, but you apparently must pay to sit down (see "New York's Ugliest Buildings," page 223).

Citicorp Center (Lexington Ave. and 53 St.)—spectacular.

Police Plaza (behind the Municipal Building at Chambers and Lafayette Sts.).

The City Politic

Cynical observers have often remarked that Americans actually live in a one-party state, where the only difference between Democrats and Republicans is their party name. These cynics suggest that both parties should merge, to form a new, more honest political organization: the DemoReps. Or the RepubliDems. But voters in New York City have many alternatives from the far right to the old-communist left. The following is a brief summary of some of the inhabitants in the city's bizarre political menagerie:

Citizens Party (Left)
This is the brainchild of Professor Barry Commoner, the environmentalist. It bills itself as the "egalitarian, majoritarian" party, and runs on a socialist-style plank. While many of its positions would seem well intentioned, the party's obsession with semantics and bylaws interferes with the meat-and-potatoes of political reality—such as winning elections.

The Communist Party (Left)
Yes, they really do exist. And they actually run candidates in most city and state elections. However,

the Communists often seem to be a tired party of worn-out leftists and FBI agents (it was once revealed that a quarter of the membership rolls consisted of paid government informants). Nevertheless, if you feel like one of the downtrodden masses, why not vote for them? You have nothing to lose but your chains, as Marx once said. One drawback: No one remembers a Communist candidate actually winning.

The Conservative Party (Right)
They are just what they say they are. The Conservatives are strongest in the outer boroughs, where some elections see candidates running on strange multiparty lines (there is a Conservative-Republican-Democratic-Liberal councilman).

The Democratic Party (Center)
New York is a Democratic town, so this is the party to join if you want to be correct, or if you want to do business with the city. Democrats run everything from the lowest community board to the mayor's office. The party embraces the best and the worst elements of political life.

DSOC (Left)
The Democratic Socialist Organizing Committee, popularly known as DSOC, sprang up within the Democratic party in the late sixties as a response to the venality of some party politicians, practices, and policies. While it runs no candidates on its own, it represents the far-left wing of the party in power, and often has the most exciting conventions (other leftist groups love to disrupt their meetings, because they feel DSOC members have compromised with the bourgeoisie . . . or something like that).

Free Libertarian Party (No Rating)
Although many argue that this party is merely a political gadfly (as is the Libertarian party mentioned later), its stands for freedom of speech and action are sometimes courageous. If Puritans were Communists, their descendants might be Free Libertarians.

The Liberal Party (Center Left)
This party often holds the key to power in the city and in the state. Wits say the Liberals exist so that disgusted Democrats will have an honorable alternative. The number of Liberals in appointive office far exceeds

the number of elected Liberal officeholders, because the
party has been so successful in working out political
"deals." The highest party member in elective office,
Councilman Henry Stern, is a witty and wily politician,
whose stands on issues can be courageous (supporting
gay rights) or eccentric (reforming hot dog vendors).

Libertarian Party (No Rating)
In a nutshell, this party stands for the abolition of
government regulations of all kinds, while strongly
supporting the freedoms in the Bill of Rights
(particularly free speech). Its platform attracts many
liberal-to-right intellectuals who, if more desperate and
daring, would be outright anarchists. Its antiregulation
stands have assured that party coffers overflow.

New Alliance Party (Left)
One of the best-organized parties in the city, with its
power base in the South Bronx. It is tainted with
corruption (rumor has it some member labor unions use
the party workers to help enforce labor peace on
construction jobs). Nevertheless, the party may play a
key role in city politics in coming years, having
supported many of the successful minority candidates
for political office.

New York First Party (Right)
This is the creation of a weekly newspaper publisher.
Sources say it was formed so the publisher's wife could
run for office when the major parties rejected her. The
things lovers do! Citizen Kane, where are you?

The Republican Party (Center-Right)
The last Republican mayor, John Lindsay, left the party
during his first term and became a Democrat. This is
the party of perennial "outs." Their strength is in the
outer boroughs; also, they wield some city power
through their influence on state budget allocations
(rural New York is very Republican).

The Right-to-Life Party (Right)
A classic single-issue party, most of whose candidates
run on other party lines as well (mostly Republican and
Conservative).

The Socialist Workers Party (Left)
They draw a young, lively membership and publish a
regular newspaper. Although no candidate has won

elective office, you'll find the party represented at all sorts of conventions and meetings, wherever left-leaning folks congregate.

Spartacist League (Left)
These are the radicals (their name derives from the German league of the same name, formed right after World War I). They are the left wing of the left. And they can be nasty, interrupting the meetings of groups they feel have "compromised" the left with more bourgeois political elements.

The Tax Payers Party (Right)
This is another single-issue party, drawing support from Archie Bunker-type homeowners out in Queens and Brooklyn. Unlike the party of the same name in New Jersey, the New York party has no power because its leaders haven't learned how to deal with other parties, so it remains an absurd political footnote in election returns.

The U.S. Labor Party (Twilight Zone)
The party of Lyndon LaRouche. Who knows what it now stands for? In 1980, LaRouche tried to run for the Democratic presidential nomination. He lost. The party newspaper is full of LaRouche's rantings and ravings. The party thrives on paranoia, and members are a little like the zombies of kinky religious sects. Although some information in the newspaper is interesting, the basic gist of the reporting is that the Queen of England secretly rules the world, in a diabolical alliance with Soviet leaders and American industrialist pawns.

Unity Party (Left)
This party was formed to support the mayoral candidacy of Democrat Frank Barbaro in 1981. It may survive because it has attracted a number of voters turned off by the compromised positions of the Democrats and Liberals.

Yippies (Left)
The Yippies are the joyful left, a holdover from the sixties, with a touch of paranoia. They have one of the best political newspapers (the *Yipster Times* has been proven correct time and again, after establishment types denied its hair-raising investigative reports). They also give the best fund-raising parties in town. Slum chic.

City Sports

If you're a jock, or at least want to know where you can
stay fit, the city has a number of public and private
sports facilities. They range from the free to the very
(and I mean very) expensive. The natives might be city
slickers, but they are very keen on staying fit, in
addition to being fanatical fans of local sports teams.
But enough chitchat. If you enjoy life "pour le sport"
and sportingly, consider the following:

Indoor Sports (General)

For gymnastics, swimming, martial arts, and much,
much more, try the YMCA (either the McBurney
branch, at 215 W. 23 St., or the Vanderbilt branch, at
224 E. 47 St.), or the YM/YWHA (1395 Lexington Ave.,
at 92 St. The New York Athletic Club (180 Central
Park So.) has everything you could imagine, but it's
private. Very private. In addition, there are
neighborhood sports facilities that can be contacted
through local block associations, the Parks Department
(see next entry), or the Police Athletic League.

Outdoor Sports (General)

Although many private establishments are mentioned in
the following entries, the city's Parks Department
maintains a dazzling array of free or low-cost facilities.
Contact the Recreation Office at 397–3110.

Archery and Marksmanship

The YMCA and YM/YWHA organizations offer
archery; several police organizations have shooting
ranges.

Baseball

If fans aren't too tired from cheering or booing the
Yanks and the Mets, there are a number of concrete
playing fields in high school and junior high school
playgrounds. But the best diamonds are in Central
Park, north of 90 St. Every spring and through the
summer, the fields are in heavy use. If you're lucky, you

may see TV, radio, and other celebrities play, as the
city's cultural institutions love to form baseball teams to
show how "grass roots" they are.

Basketball

See the "Indoor sports" entry. Also, parks as listed in
"Handball" entry. Some others: playground at First
Ave. and 66 St., playground at Second Ave. and 20 St.,
schoolyard of the Robert Wagner Junior High School
(220 E. 76 St.).

Bicycling

Although more people ride than ever before, motorists
are rude, and the city seems to have tried to kill the fad
through its indifference. There are several bicyclist's
organizations (the YMCA or YM/YWHA may provide
contacts; also try the American Youth Hostel
Association). Best general riding is along the East and
West Drives in Central Park lunch hours, weekdays.
Never go there on a weekend: It's a madhouse of
runners, bikers, and skateboard freaks.

Bocce Ball

There are several bocce ball courts around town,
particularly in old Italian neighborhoods. Try those in
Roosevelt Parkway (between Canal and Houston Sts. on
the Lower East Side), or others at Second Ave. and
Houston St.

Cricket and Lacrosse

They're about as popular as lawn bowling and croquet.
Not very. Some games are played in Central Park and
Riverside Park.

Croquet and Lawn Bowling

These two aren't very popular, perhaps because they are
so nonviolent, but there is a pleasant court in Central
Park.

Football, Soccer, and Rugby

There are a number of men's, coed, and women's soccer teams, particularly in the Yorkville section (East 80s). The various clubs play in Central Park in good weather, or in various sports clubs (including some "Y" branches). Rugby and soccer teams also use the playing field on Randalls Island (reachable via 125 St.).

Golf

While there are a few miniature ranges around town, the nearest regulation course is in Van Cortlandt Park in the Bronx.

Handball

Most public parks with playgrounds have a wall for handball, tennis practice, or squash. Some definites: Central Park (go north of the 90 St. Reservoir), John Jay Park (77 or 78 Sts., east of York Ave.), Tompkins Square Park (8 St. and Avenue A; beware, it's dangerous), and Hamilton Fish or East River Park (Houston St. at Avenue C or at Franklin D. Roosevelt Drive).

Horse Riding

There are bridle paths in Central Park, but several stretches are full of treacherous gullies and potholes. Just like city streets. However, there is a decent track in Van Cortlandt Park in the Bronx.

Racquet, Squash, and Tennis

These sports are for both social climbers and serious fitness buffs, and clubs cater to one or the other group as a rule. The Wall Street Racquet Club (Wall St. and East River), the Gramercy Tennis and Racquetball Club (708 Sixth Ave., near 23 St.), and the Village Courts (110 University Pl.) are decent facilities, all encased in a distinctive balloon-like green-and-white fabric. The Wall Street club is built on a pier over the water. For squash, you might try the New York Health and Racquet Club (20 E. 50 St.), or Town Squash (151 E. 86 St.). For lower rates, you might look into the "Y," or, in good weather, the city's own courts in Central Park and

elsewhere. Finally, if you're a student, Columbia and
Fordham universities and several other schools maintain
terrific gymnasiums and clay courts.

Roller Skating/Ice Skating

There are numerous roller discos, but for people who
enjoy outdoor sports, there are several rinks. The three
most notable are the Wollman Rink in Central Park,
the Rockefeller Center Rink (Rockefeller Plaza between
49 and 50 Sts., and the Lasker Rink, at the northeast
corner of Central Park, 110 St. and Lenox Ave.

Running

The New York City Marathon, whose course runs
through all five boroughs, is held every October and
draws a million viewers as well as several thousand
participants. But for us normal folks, the best outdoor
running is found at several sites: East River Promenade
(63 to 81 Sts.), the perimeter of Washington Square
Park (Fifth Ave. and Waverly Pl.), Gramercy Park's
perimeter (21 St. at Lexington Ave.), the unused portion
of the West Side Elevated Highway (between Chambers
and Gansevoort Sts.), and Central Park (around the
Reservoir, enter at 90 St. and Fifth Ave.).

Skiing/Sledding

Believe it or not, a number of mature city slickers turn
into playful children at the sight of the first snowfall
that yields enough snow to make a snowball. They use
the "slopes" of Central Park and the hilly areas north of
Columbia University to sleigh and ski.

Street Theater Venues

Mayor LaGuardia may have banned the organ-grinders
long ago, but free sidewalk entertainment provided by
the colorful, the highly talented, and the marginally
sane continues to be a big part of the scenery here. You
can catch some kind of act any time of day in most
parts of the city, but discovering the street theater
cream, like spotting prime real estate, is still largely a
matter of knowing where to look.

Right now, most of the cream rises in **Washington Square Park** (at Fifth Ave. and Waverly Pl.) in the summer. Tricky skaters cavort to soul and salsa under Garibaldi's statue in the middle of the park, while under the arch, a wizened old musician plays sentimental standards (interspersed with political diatribes during election years) on a full-sized, felt-bedecked upright piano he hauls to the park every day by hand. There are card readers, palmists, astrologers, radical theater troupes, a conceptual-artist-*cum*-juggler who does rapid two-ball passes to science fiction sound effects, and a macho fire-eater who performs in full firefighter's regalia. Musicians include folk, rock, jazz, flamenco, and free-form solo guitarists (electric and/or acoustic), string quartets doing Bach-to-Bartók, one or two new-wave and heavy metal garage bands, and one crowd-pleasing rock quartet, who perform nothing but utterly uncanny live reproductions of Beatles favorites. And then there is the infrequent rehearsal by the NYU Drill Team (attractive young women with fiberglass rifles), the Sunday painters, etc. All of this doesn't go on all at once, but on any sunny weekend, it will sure seem like it.

Parts of this circus—often the best parts—can be seen in and around **Sheridan Square** (at Seventh Ave. and West Washington Pl.) and **Jefferson Market.** For other dependable venues, head uptown to:

Time-Life plaza, at Sixth Ave. and 50 St.
String groups and full-strength brass bands during the day; hotshot skaters by night. Other artists of various brands collect throughout nearby Rockefeller Center.

Donnell Library, entrance on 53 St., between Fifth and Sixth Aves.
Quality classics for everything from lone cello to eight voices.

Main Branch Library Steps, at Fifth Ave. and 41 St.
Mimes, comedians, and folk musicians.

Metropolitan Museum steps, at Fifth Ave. and E. 82 St.
A lady with a heavenly marimba, wandering bagpipe players, and a rotating group of what are probably the finest mimes in the city—all weekend regulars.

Citicorp Center plaza, Lexington Ave. and E. 53 St.

The friendly corporate giant sponsors semiregular series of free concerts by quality groups here.

Hallmark Gallery entrance, Fifth Ave. near W. 56 St.
The one reliable spot to find sidewalk magicians. Some are so good that it's tough to navigate this side of the street.

Bethesda Fountain in Central Park
Another version of Washington Square's three-ring extravaganza, usually dominated on weekends by legions of steel drum, timbale, conga drum, and other percussion players. Other good spots in the park include the West Drive from 72 St. to Columbus Circle (daredevil skaters), the Bandshell (a miscellany), and Grand Army Plaza (more mimes).

Grand Central Station/Pershing Square, right under the bridge where Park Ave. meets 42 St.
There is a Dixieland band every weekday.

Subway Graffiti

Rumor has it that the first scrawled magic marker signature in New York's subways was left by a character known as "Taki 183," back in 1969. True or not, New York subways are perhaps the most graffiti-laden public vehicles in the world. There are subway gangs that cover entire cars with emblems, forms, and scenery. Some are virtually works of art, involving preliminary sketches and precision execution. Unfortunately, these works of art draw frowns from city officials, who spend thousands of dollars to have the decorated cars scrubbed with paint remover, which leaves them looking uglier than ever. However, the subway artist is a quick-study specialist, as it were, and you should have no difficulty finding examples on almost any train you take.

The best places to see the graffiti are trains that run on the older IRT and BMT lines: the Lexington Ave. line (the 4, 5, or 6 trains), and the Broadway/Seventh Ave. lines (the 1, 2, 3, N, and RR trains). For some reason, the newer equipment on the Sixth Ave. and Eighth Ave. lines (the A, B, D, E, and F trains) does not receive as much attention. There are exceptions—I once rode in a new F train car in which every inch of wall and seat space was covered with initials and nicknames. One curious note: Except for the gangs that paint entire cars, most graffiti artists avoid the windows and lights.

There is another type of graffiti that can be seen in the train stations themselves. Perhaps because the city has reduced subway service in the past few years, making people wait longer for trains, there is more time to scrawl thoughts and obscenities on the station walls. New Yorker's of all types get involved. The billboards in most subway stations are turned into registers of social mood; the profound and the profane appear side by side. Naturally, the authors prefer ads that have white space, or pretty men and women (the things New Yorkers would have them say and do!?!). Often, such graffiti become a bizarre dialogue, in which the participants neither know nor see one another. Sample dialogue: "Kill animals and let them rot." "Love animals, don't eat them." "Plants are living things, too!" "Don't eat, die now." Some comments are political: "Fight gun control, support defense. If we spend more money on arms, companies get big contracts and hire more workers and the economy improves and . . . AARGGHHH! They got me." Still other comments are conceptual: One person travels around leaving elaborate genealogies of royal houses, to which others add. Part of the lineage of the kings of France thus went: "Lothair I; Lothair of 'Lotharingia' Lorraine; Luther, Father of the Reformation; Lex Luthor, Superman's Enemy."

The best places to spot such graffiti are, again, on the city's older subway lines, and local stations are better than express stations as a rule. On the Lexington Ave. line, see the work at Astor Pl. (uptown), 23 St., and 77 St. On the Seventh Ave. line, check out Sheridan Square (uptown), 23 St., and Columbus Circle. On the Broadway line, try 8 St. Also worth noting: the passageway connecting Times Square stations with the Port Authority building. Happy hunting!

Ten Important Things to Know About Hailing Taxicabs

1. Carry lots of cash, in small, easy-to-change bills and coins, any tolls and expenses that might be incurred

on your journey, and 15 to 20 percent extra for tips.
("The shorter the trip, the higher the tip.")

2. Try to look pretty damn respectable and normal,
particularly if going anyplace that is not the airport,
Manhattan below 96 St., or near where the cabbie drops
off his cab.

3. Only those cabs with the numbers lit up (on roof)
are available. Note the "off-duty" lights on either side
of the number.

4. Hold your arm up as high as possible when hailing
and do not try to put more than four people in a
standard cab, five in a Checker, especially if everyone is
going someplace different.

5. Look for a corner other than the one the rest of
the city has gathered at to hold the hourly Cab Hailing
Competition for your spot. The blocks in between the
avenues can sometimes be cab mines.

6. If it is raining, if possible (and it may well be if
you have followed Point No. 1) quiet any raging lusts or
hungers at a nearby hotel or restaurant until the rain
has stopped. (See HOTELS and RESTAURANTS.)

7. If it is Rush Hour, see Point No. 5.

8. Even if it is only from your map, have a very
specific idea about where you want to go and how you
want to get there and do not let the cabbie deviate from
the course you have prescribed *at the beginning of the
trip*.

9. Be as cordial and nondescript as you are able and
politely decline any offers of a "scenic" route, extra
services for extra money—*anything* not stated on the
list of services and fees that *must* be visible in the
passenger area.

10. Do not comment in any way upon the cabbie's
appearance, taste in music, use of illicit or controlled
substances, or refusal to do what cabbies are required
by law to do (take anyone anywhere within the five
boroughs by the most direct route for the posted fee
schedule), if you are in a hurry. Take down the cabbie's
medallion and hack numbers and comment to a
representative of Jay Turoff and the Taxi and
Limousine Commission if anything is amiss. The
complaints number at the Taxi and Limousine

Commission is 825-0420. For Lost and Found, dial 825-0416.

11. Refrain from making loud noises, love, or bombs while in the cab and *never* tell a cabbie he reminds you of Harry Chapin.

BRIDGE AND TUNNEL

One and Three-Quarters Cheers for the Bronx

Nowadays, the Bronx is best known for its southern portion, a slum so pockmarked by physical deterioration that it is often compared with Western European landscapes after World War II. Like Harlem ("Cotton Comes to . . ."), the South Bronx has been glorified by at least one major motion picture (*Fort Apache, The Bronx*) and deservedly so. For visitors, there is virtually no other attraction in America just like it: One will find the skeletons of burnt-out buildings and an eerie quiet. But while the South Bronx is unequivocally our most startling evidence of urban decay, it is not all there is to know about the Bronx.

For example, did you know the Bronx is the only part of New York City that is on the mainland of the United States? Or that it was originally part of Westchester until New York County (Manhattan) annexed it in 1898? Sure, you've heard about the "Bronx cheer" and are well informed enough to recognize the names Yankee Stadium and Robert Klein (who was born near Gun Hill Road) and maybe an English professor told you about Edgar Allan Poe composing two of his more celebrated poems, "Annabel Lee" and "Ulalume," while residing in his cottage in what is now called Poe Park (just north of Fordham Road).

The Bronx was purchased by the West India Trading Company in 1639 and then settled by a Dane named Jonas Bronck, and it is he to whom the Bronx owes its name. Bronck owned quite an estate, and as the story goes, curious neighbors would constantly be peering through the high wrought-iron gates for glimpses of him and his well-manicured wealth. Thus was born the phrase, "Let's go over to the Bronck's." When names were being suggested for the borough, "the Bronx" was the overwhelming favorite.

During the centuries that ensued, the Bronx grew from a collection of pastoral farming villages inhabited mostly by Dutch and Germans to a prodigious metropolis of its own. The Italians, Irish, and Jews who arrived in the early 1900s, followed by Southern blacks and Puerto Ricans, carved the Bronx into its characteristic neighborhoods; highways, parks, and boulevards (such as the Grand Concourse—from 138 to 205 Sts.) were constructed; and in 1923 Yankee Stadium, probably America's finest outdoor sporting arena of its kind, was christened. It should be noted that over the last 58 years no other baseball team has evoked more love and hate among fans than the always feared and controversial Bronx Bombers.

Back then there were three sections in the Bronx: West, Middle, and East. No South Bronx (which incidentally Yankee Stadium sits in the middle of). Only in the last two decades has that address become an all-too-familiar one.

How to Get There

CC, D, 1 to 6 trains. Express buses from Madison Ave. Cross-Bronx Expressway from New Jersey or New England. Major Deegan Expressway from Queens, Brooklyn, and Manhattan. FDR/Harlem River Drive across any number of bridges. From Westchester, the New York Thruway and Hutchinson River Parkway.

What to Do

Go to the Zoo, Stadium, Botanical Gardens, Poe Cottage, Woodlawn Cemetery, Co-Op City, Lehman College, Van Cortlandt Park, Pelham Bay Park, City

Island, Orchard Beach, or Tony's Pizzeria for a Sicilian slice and Italian ice on Bedford Park Boulevard.

Brooklyn

Nobody laughs at you any more if you live in Brooklyn. The jokes about the fractured dialect, the gangs, the Bums, and the D trains are forgotten fads. Now people want to know how you secured a floor-through apartment for under $500, or why co-ops are affordable on tree-lined blocks, or how you turned that abandoned, gutted hole of a building into a brownstone. Geography may determine history, but in New York City 1980s real estate shapes attitudes and lives.

The pain of certain losses is subsiding. The late 1950s and early 1960s saw the exodus of Brooklyn's beloved institutions. First the *Brooklyn Eagle,* whose ancestry included native son Walt Whitman, was shuttered. Then, the rallying cry of "Ya, bum, ya" was silenced when the Dodgers traded Flatbush Ave. and Ebbets Field for Chavez Ravine, Los Angeles, and millions of dollars for the O'Malley coffers. The legendary Brooklyn Fox of Flatbush Ave. bolted its door; no more screaming teenagers would ever screech out the name of their reigning idol. And the identity of Brooklyn seemed to fade!

Replacing these losses has been renewed pride. At one time, when cities were unfashionable, neighborhoods deteriorated. Now in the eighties, neighborhoods are thriving. Urban pioneers and homesteaders are supplanting the transient and disenfranchised. While the studio apartment symbolizes the single life of the Manhattanite, in Brooklyn the stoops signify family life, socializing on the block, and a common meeting ground for late-night chats.

Brooklyn's 2,600,000 people, who could compose the nation's fourth largest city, or for that matter, the twenty-fourth largest state, now live in sectors with distinguished names like Cobble Hill, Boerum Hill, Kensington, and Clinton Hill. Community papers abound: the *Brooklyn Paper,* the *Home Reporter* of Park Slope and Bay Ridge, the *King Courier,* the *Phoenix,* the *Brooklyn Spectator,* and the *Brooklyn Heights Press* feed local news to its inhabitants.

Nor has Brooklyn lost all its history. Nothing compares to the sight of the Brooklyn Bridge at sunset. The silver wires in its harp-like shape and the swoop of the cables give the bridge its lyrical quality. The bridge is not just a crossing to Manhattan; it stands as a symbol of man's deepest creative impulses and enduring achievements.

Beneath the Brooklyn Bridge, the River Café, a restaurant anchored in the East River, uses its glass windows to reveal panoramic vistas of the lights of the Manhattan skyline. While the elite swarm here for dinner, anyone can stride to the bar and order a glass of wine, to see that wondrous view.

The honky-tonk atmosphere of Coney Island borders on tacky at times, but the Cyclone descends faster than a bullet, and the ferris wheels and merry-go-rounds still delight children of all ages. The yellow and green Nathan's sign, true American folk-art, emblazons Surf Avenue at night. The nickel tab for Nathan's franks may have vanished several years ago, but the franks remain in their grilled wonder.

In Brighton Beach, where many young people journey twice a year to visit grandparents, the Brighton Beach Baths continues to flourish. For the aficionados of the ancient New York City game of handball, played with a blackball, not a Spaldeen, thank you, Brighton Beach is the place to be. Modernists play paddleball to the glares of their handball brethren.

Bar-goers, don't forget to visit Bay Ridge, the bar capital of the world. I dare anyone to drink a draft beer at each bar from 65 St. to 96 St. on Fourth Ave. and walk a tightrope. Earthy bars like Hobnail's Pub, sophisticated bars like Greenhouse and Skaffle's, English bars like Pippin's, disco bars like Mustard Seed, folksy bars like Beard's, neighborhood bars like Manar's, singles bars like Griswold's all stay packed with secretaries, office workers, lawyers, and TV repairmen.

What happened to the left-wing, progressive, marching liberals of the sixties? Many are living in Park Slope, as close to an integrated, mixed-class community as one will find. On Sundays, Park Slopers eschew the *de rigueur* brunch on Manhattan's Columbus Ave., preferring the authentic $1.50 scrambled eggs and home fries of the Purity Coffee Shop. Walking up President

Street or Carroll Street, mothers and fathers wheel their babies in strollers to Prospect Park, looking tranquil and self-satisfied.

Brooklyn is not without its problems. East New York, in certain sections, is as burnt-out as the South Bronx, and no president even makes promises there. The "A" train zips along through Brooklyn to Queens and Manhattan, but often the blasting radios and the marijuana smoke make traveling difficult at best.

Conflicts and troubles have not caused Brooklyn to lose its sense of humor. Any place that provided the birthplace for Woody Allen, Jackie Gleason, Danny Kaye, Phil Silvers, Buddy Hackett, Mickey Rooney, and Abe Burrows can't forget to smile. People walk the streets with T-shirts that say "Brooklyn," plain and simple, or another one that declares "This is no dress rehearsal; this is my life."

In 1969, native and Park Slope dweller Pete Hamill said "Brooklyn has become the sane alternative: a part of New York City where you can live a decent urban life without going broke." Those words seem prophetic today.

The renaissance of Brooklyn is ongoing. Brooklynites dream of an even better world in the future: outdoor cafés lining Atlantic Ave., brownstones booming out of the rubble of East New York, and a third New York City baseball team, housed in Brooklyn, that one day will beat the traitorous Los Angeles team in the World Series. When it happens, the conquering Brooklynites can have a ticker tape parade, and the entire city will line the sidewalks on the 11-mile stretch of Flatbush Ave., from Junior's to Kings Plaza.

"Queents"

A 10-exit blur on the Long Island Expressway, an arrival at Kennedy International Airport, a departure from LaGuardia . . . Except for its two airports and east/west highways, this borough of nearly 2 million residents is the most ignored of the city's outer four by visitors to this sprawling mega-metropolis. And can you really blame them? We don't have the famous East River promenade and historic brownstone districts of Brooklyn, the ferry ride or spectacular bridge to Staten

Island, or even the attraction of this country's most notorious urban disaster area—the South Bronx.

Let's face it, when struggling young cosmopolites relocate to this city, you never hear them say: "Wow, I hope I can find an apartment in Queens!" They would rather starve in a Manhattan tenement or settle on Atlantic Ave. in downtown Brooklyn than sport a Queens address. Unlike Brooklyn, our nouveau-chic neighbor to the south, Queens cannot claim to be even the next-best place to live.

Okay, so Queens is not Manhattan or Brooklyn. It's true that by comparison our local theater and arts are parochial, night spots lukewarm, and architecture less than distinctive. Given that much of Queens was developed after World War II, it's not surprising that the borough has the equivalent architectural excitement of a Holiday Inn. But since most of us didn't move here for the night life or the architecture, you won't find many complaints. We're in Queens because of the neighborhoods, the affordable living space, the free parking, and the trees. And whatever we don't have here can be found within an hour for the price of a subway ride. Besides, if Queens were anything like Manhattan, who could afford to live here?

For half the cost and twice the space of a Manhattan studio apartment on the far East Side, you can find (if you look hard) a spacious one-bedroom apartment in Kew Gardens, Queens, an enclave in central Queens with broad tree-lined streets, turn-of-the-century homes, and pre–World War II apartment houses. So what if Manhattan's a subway ride away, and my friends from Manhattan never visit? At least I don't have to keep my piano in the bathtub—and my bathtub isn't in the middle of my kitchen.

Although Queens is first and foremost a place to live, there is more to this borough than one might guess. Try as we might, it's impossible to forget that we do have two of the busiest airports in the country. This is one of the few places you will find homebuyers inquiring about airport traffic patterns. Flushing Meadow Park is the former site of both the 1939 and 1964 World's Fairs. Today Flushing Meadow hosts the recently relocated U.S. Tennis Open (held here each fall), and the New York Mets, who try to play baseball at Shea Stadium (take the #7 subway train to Willets Point, Flushing, and follow the signs). Our other large park, Forest Park, boasts one of the largest natural stands of oak trees in New York City (a favorite with local residents is a Sunday stroll along Forest Park Drive from Metropolitan Ave. to Woodhaven Blvd.). We even have our own department stores and a huge glitzy indoor shopping center in Rego Park—called, appropriately, the Queens Center.

Much of Queens is really best seen from the air, but a couple of neighborhoods and local landmarks are worth a visit, and can be accomplished in half a day. But before you leave the familiar grid of Manhattan Island for the unplanned confusion called Queens (much of the borough consists of what were once separate villages, which were swallowed up as the city grew), be sure to have a subway map and a detailed street map of Queens. Also, you might want to practice the correct pronunciation of Queens: "Queents."

With your maps in hand and your feet in a comfortable pair of shoes, you'll be ready to board the "E" or "F" train (to Jamaica) for the ride into what many Manhattanites consider frontier country. If you do happen to get lost, and want to find your way back to Manhattan, just ask someone how to get back to the City. Don't worry, they won't direct you to San Francisco.

Forest Hills ("E" or "F" train to Continental Avenue)

Home of the West Side Tennis Club (members only), former site of the U.S Open, Forest Hills (really two communities—Forest Hills, and the very exclusive Forest Hills Gardens) is by no means representative of the rest of the borough, but no less representative than Fifth Ave. is of Manhattan. Exit the subway on the south side of Queens Blvd. at Continental Ave. Walk down Continental Ave. to Austin St. and you'll be at the crossroads of the "East Side" shopping district of Queens. Best visited on a Saturday, this bustling, four-block stretch of shops offers everything from designer jeans (lots of designer jeans) to gourmet foods and trendy cafés. Don't be surprised by the foreign languages: Russian, German, and Hebrew. In the 1930s and 40s many Jewish refugees settled in Forest Hills (and its neighbor to the east, Kew Gardens), and recent waves of immigrants from Russia and Israel have added to the already international flavor of the community.

After a survey of the shops along Austin St., head back to Continental Avenue and continue one block past McDonald's (even in Forest Hills), under the Long Island Railroad overpass, and you'll find yourself in Station Square, across from the old Forest Hills Inn. No, this is not England, just a good 20th-century fabrication of an English suburb complete with winding tree-lined streets, cast-iron street lamps, and red-tiled roofed row houses and homes. Forest Hills Gardens, a private community, was laid out after World War I as an urban suburb. And while the city has grown up around it, the community has remained physically unchanged for most of the last 50 years. In a city famous for tearing itself down every few years this picturesque, American Tudor style neighborhood stands out as a monument to survival.

Kew Gardens

You can walk from Forest Hills through Forest Hills Gardens to Park Lane (the beginning of Forest Park), or you can take the "E" or "F" train to Union Turnpike, Kew Gardens.

Kew Gardens, just after the turn of the century, was a resort community complete with lakes, hotels, and vacation homes. The lakes and hotels are now gone, but Kew Gardens (considered the Upper West Side of Queens and now the civic center of the borough) is still one of the most beautiful neighborhoods in Queens, with many old homes, tree-lined side streets, and six-story pre-World War II apartment buildings.

Exit the subway on the south side of Queens Boulevard and make your way over to Lefferts Blvd. Local residents refer to the section of Lefferts between Austin St. and Metropolitan Ave. as the Village. While the Village is no longer the main shopping street of the neighborhood, you will still find an interesting mix of stores, including a Jewish bakery, Mimi's Candy Shop, The Homestead Gourmet Shop (don't miss the cherry/cheese strudel) at 81-45 Lefferts, and several not too expensive antique stores. The local Italian restaurant/pizzeria on Lefferts (just look for the building with the

artificial stone siding) serves the best lasagna this side
of the 59th Street Bridge. And what Village would be
complete without its very own gay disco, Flavors (just
off Lefferts Blvd. at 120-31 83 Ave.—strictly gay).

Following an afternoon in Kew Gardens and Forest
Hills, you can catch a $2 first-run movie at the
Cinemart Theater at 106-03 Metropolitan Ave. (between
Ascan and Continental Aves. in Forest Hills—by bus
from Kew Gardens, or a five-minute cab from Queens
Blvd. and Continental Ave.). But best of all, after the
movie you can cross the street and step into the most
famous local landmark of all, Eddie's Sweet Shop, at
105-29 Metropolitan Ave. (520-8514). Eddie's is an old
(not old-fashioned, but really old) ice-cream parlor,
complete with tiled floors, mahogany-paneled walls,
marble counter, and tin ceiling. The ice cream is
homemade (eat your heart out, Häagen Dazs), as is the
whipped cream, which is kept in the see-through
refrigerator piled high in a huge bowl. Not too long ago,
the ice cream at Eddie's was rated as number 1 in New
York City, which brought a flood of Manhattanites from
the Upper East Side. Fortunately, after a few weeks of
traveling the subway, the Manhattan crowd gave up,
returning Eddie's to its local regulars. Besides ice cream,
Eddie's serves cappuccino and espresso. If you're on a
diet—stay away.

The other evening at Eddie's, while sipping
cappuccino, one of my recently transplanted
Manhattan-born friends sat across from me extolling
the virtues of Brooklyn life in comparison with the
provincial backwaters of Queens. So as not to dampen
his enthusiasm, I didn't mention that over 30 years ago
my parents (then young cosmopolites themselves) left a
rapidly deteriorating and provincial Brooklyn for one of
the city's newer suburbs—Kew Gardens, Queens.
Queens will never be another Manhattan or for that
matter another Brooklyn, but one day, "Queents" will
be Queens, and then I can say that I knew it when—and
I'm in no hurry.

Staten Island

It's safe to guess that 75 percent of Manhattan residents
have never set foot on Staten Island itself, but most

have ridden the famous ferry over to the dock, changed ferries, and returned to Manhattan.

But Staten Island is New York's fifth borough, and very much a part of the city. It's a combination of rural, suburban, industrial, and small-town urban elements. Wildlife refuges, 5,000 acres of parks, and many working farms contrast with brand-new condos and shopping malls. There is heavy industry on Staten Island—even a town named Linoleumville!—as well as chemicals, shipping, and manufacturing.

It's safe to guess that many Staten Islanders never leave *their* borough either. Because Staten Island has somehow managed to avoid real urbanization, it contains some of New York City's safest neighborhoods. The population is generally middle-class—very poor and very rich neighborhoods exist, but not in the same extremes as one finds in other boroughs.

Staten Island is rich in history. Within only a few miles, the visitor can see a colonial Dutch farm; a little red schoolhouse dating from 1695; and two Civil War forts. Grand Victorian homes—complete with gables, wooden porches, and stained glass—dominate some of the older residential areas of the Island.

There are recreational facilities galore—for swimming, boating, golf, picnicking; there's even a zoo. Thorough sight-seeing is best done by car. But Staten Island has the cleanest, most modern trains in the MTA system (although they do not connect with the other boroughs), as well as good bus routes. Staten Island is accessible from Manhattan via the Staten Island Ferry or via bus over the Verrazano Narrows Bridge, from Brooklyn. The ferry ride is worth the 25 cents for the view of the harbor, the Statue of Liberty, and the lower Manhattan skyline.

INDEX